MW00612433

Word, Like Fire

Carter G. Woodson Institute Series

Deborah E. McDowell, Editor

University of Virginia Press

Charlottesville and London

VALERIE C. COOPER

Word, Like Fire

Maria Stewart,
the Bible,
and the Rights of
African Americans

University of Virginia Press
© 2011 Valerie C. Cooper
All rights reserved
Printed in the United States of America on acid-free paper
First published 2011

1   3   5   7   9   8   6   4   2

Library of Congress Cataloging-in-Publication Data

Cooper, Valerie C., 1961–
Word, like fire : Maria Stewart, the Bible, and the rights
of African Americans / Valerie C. Cooper.
p.   cm. — (Carter G. Woodson Institute series)
Includes bibliographical references (p.   ) and index.
ISBN 978-0-8139-3188-3 (cloth : alk. paper)
ISBN 978-0-8139-3207-1 (e-book)
1. Stewart, Maria W., 1803–1879. I. Title.
BX6455.S76C66 2011
230.089'96073—dc22
2011014240

For Catherine, Gertrude,
James Jr., James Sr., Maurice,
and all who have
gone on before

Is not my *word like* as a *fire?*
saith the LORD; and like a
hammer that breaketh
the rock in pieces?
—Jeremiah 23:29

Contents

Acknowledgments

Therefore, since we are surrounded by so great a cloud of witnesses, . . .
let us run with perseverance the race that is set before us.
—Hebrews 12:1 (Revised Standard Version)

Oh, how great is the cloud of witnesses to this project, and—in the marathon to bring this work from idea to book—how often was their perseverance tested! I wish to thank the many who have participated in bringing these pages to life by their encouragement, their patience, their hard work, and their diligence. To my many mentors at Howard University School of Divinity (HUSD), and to those at Harvard Divinity School (HDS), who modeled the scholarly course to which I aspire, I can only try to express my great gratitude. I must make special mention of Alice Ogden Bellis, Kelly Brown Douglas, Cain Hope Felder, William Fox, Michael Willett Newheart, Gene Rice, and Cheryl Sanders, who encouraged me to pursue doctoral studies while I was their student at HUSD, and who continue to encourage me today. HDS professor Allen Callahan and Abraham Smith, who, at the time, was down the road at Boston University, provided me with new ways of looking at the intersections between the disciplines of New Testament studies and African American studies. Joycelyn Moody, while a women's studies fellow at HDS, opened my eyes to the richness of the spiritual narratives of African American women as history, as theology, and as literature. Mark Noll, as visiting professor of evangelicalism at HDS, filled in the spaces between the history and the theology of that great movement. To Allen Callahan, Harvey Cox, Evelyn Brooks Higginbotham, Karen King, Albert Raboteau, and Cornel West, who advised me in the conception of this project as a dissertation, and to François Bovon, Karen King, and Laurie Maffly-Kipp, who saw this project through to its successful defense, I can never fully express the debt of gratitude I owe. They are mentors, they are friends, and they are men and women of the most excellent scholarship.

When all I had requested was a quiet place to write, Bill Leonard, then dean of the Wake Forest Divinity School, graciously provided me with much more: an academic home for the final stages of dissertation writing. I am grateful to the Louisville Institute for providing funding for that year of writing at the Wake Forest Divinity School. When subsequently invited to join the Department of Religious Studies at the University of Virginia, I was warmly welcomed into a close and collegial cadre of scholars, many of whom have advised me as my dissertation was transformed into a book manuscript. This institutional and personal support is very much appreciated.

I am grateful to those who read all or part of this manuscript in any of its various incarnations; it has benefited from the insights of Kevin Hart, Stanley Hauerwas, Paul Jones, Chuck Mathewes, A. G. Miller, Peter Ochs, Vanessa Ochs, Heather Warren, and Vincent Wimbush. Brian Blount, then the newly installed president of Union Presbyterian Seminary, generously shared his time and wisdom by advising me on the process of revising and securing a publisher for my manuscript, as did Edward J. Blum, Randall Jelks, David Kyuman Kim, Charles Marsh, and Corey Walker. Conversations with students from my "African Americans and the Bible" seminar and the Scripture, Interpretation, and Practice (SIP) graduate program at the University of Virginia have also sharpened this text. I single out SIP graduate students Ben Maton and Kelly Figueroa-Ray for particular commendation: their thoughtful engagement with my work was invaluable to me.

I cannot begin to express my gratitude adequately for the invaluable work of the Carter G. Woodson Institute for African-American and African Studies at the University of Virginia. Woodson Series Editor Deborah E. McDowell has been friend and advocate, as has Cynthia Hoehler-Fatton, Associate Director of the Woodson Institute. I am honored to become part of its august history and legacy through the inclusion of this volume in the Carter G. Woodson Institute series at the University of Virginia Press. I must also acknowledge the hard work of the staff at the University of Virginia Press, including Richard Holway and Mark Mones, as well as freelance manuscript editor George Roupe; this text has benefited from their close and careful readings. Each of these men and women provided the sort of support that cannot be underestimated: they believed in me and in this project.

Colleagues and friends Susan Abraham, Greg Goering, Bennie Wade Green, Tom Greggs, Claudia Highbaugh, Ann McClenahan, Laura Muench-Nasrallah, Vance Ross, Jalane Schmidt, and Elaine Swartzentruber provided thoughtful readings of the text, timely encouragement, or, equally important, chocolate. They joined their thoughts and prayers to those of friends and family too numerous to mention here, except to admit that I simply could not have approached this finish line without their support.

Most particularly, I must thank my parents, James and Charlene Cooper, who foresaw this day for me before I could even begin to imagine it for myself. To this great cloud of witnesses, including all those ancestors in whose name I run and upon whose shoulders I am carried although they themselves were barred from this race, I give great thanks with a joy that, even as I write these words, overflows.

Sources and Resources

Although Maria Stewart's *Productions of Mrs. Maria W. Stewart* has appeared in several publications, either in part or as a whole corpus, I have chosen the Oxford University Press edition, in the collection *Spiritual Narratives,* as my main resource for her writings. The 1988 Oxford edition reproduces the 1835 *Productions* in the original typeface, emphases, punctuation, and pagination and contains the five speeches Stewart produced between 1831 and 1833, as well as several interstitial religious meditations. It is this version that I regard as the best and most accurate representation of Stewart's writing. (Although there are sometimes questions regarding the authenticity of the author's voice in some women's spiritual narratives from the nineteenth century, the lack of significant changes to Stewart's essays and speeches between the 1835 edition and her self-funded 1879 edition suggests to me quite strongly that both editions reflect Stewart accurately.)

The biblical texts that Stewart quotes were taken from the King James Version of the Bible, and I used a King James Bible to identify them.

Introduction

*W*HAT IF YOU DID the work of a theologian and no one noticed? Maria Stewart may have had one of the most unrecognized and underappreciated African American theological voices of the nineteenth century. She is believed by many to have been the first American woman of any race to have given a political speech before an audience of both men and women[1] and to have left copies of her remarks to posterity. Although these speeches are political in nature, they are also deeply theological and use the Bible extensively to buttress Stewart's arguments on behalf of blacks' and women's rights and empowerment. Understanding Stewart's theology deepens and enriches one's understanding of her political thought.

A black woman who was born free in Hartford, Connecticut, in 1803, Maria Stewart produced and delivered a series of five speeches in Boston and New York between 1831 and 1833. Collected with additional meditations on religious themes, these speeches were published in 1835 as *Productions of Mrs. Maria W. Stewart* and again in 1879—the year of Stewart's

---

1. In *Black Abolitionists,* Quarles calls Stewart "the first native-born American woman to speak in public and leave extant texts of her addresses." Benjamin Quarles, *Black Abolitionists* (New York: Oxford University, 1969), 7. Later writers note Stewart's address of a "promiscuous audience," or one composed of both men and women. See, for example, Marilyn Richardson, ed. *Maria W. Stewart, America's First Black Woman Political Writer: Essays and Speeches,* Blacks in the Diaspora (Bloomington: Indiana University Press, 1987), 69; and Charles I. Nero, "'Oh, What I Must Tell This World!' Oratory and Public Address of African-American Women," in *Black Women in America,* ed. Kim Marie Vaz (Thousand Oaks, CA: Sage, 1994), 263.

death—as *Meditations from the Pen of Mrs. Maria W. Stewart.* Stewart predates the better-known abolitionists and women's rights advocates Frederick Douglass and Sojourner Truth in that her public speaking career began before theirs.[2]

Unfortunately, relatively little is known of Stewart's life beyond the few facts that she is willing to disclose in her writings and that can be gleaned from extant public records.[3] She tells us little about herself in *Productions of Mrs. Maria W. Stewart.* She discloses a little more in *Meditations from the Pen of Mrs. Maria W. Stewart,* which includes letters of commendation of Stewart from others, as well as somewhat autobiographical comments from Stewart herself entitled "Sufferings during the War." Of the period between the delivery of her last speech in Boston in 1833 and the events narrated in "Sufferings during the War," which begin in the 1850s, we know almost nothing, except that Stewart spent part of this time teaching in New York and Baltimore before finally settling in Washington, DC. We have no pictures of her, although she was said to have been a beautiful woman.[4] Indeed, Stewart herself seems intent upon obscuring the details of her own life story except for those that solidify her credentials as a Christian woman of good character. Rather than speak about herself, Stewart quotes the Bible again and again.

As a protégée of the radical black abolitionist David Walker, Stewart picks up and extends Walker's themes of African American exceptionalism, the belief that God has a special relationship with and concern for black people. A free black, Walker is best known for his book *David Walker's*

2. Richardson, *Maria W. Stewart,* xiv.

3. Chief among the historians who have reported what is known about Stewart is Marilyn Richardson, whose biography, *Maria W. Stewart, America's First Black Woman Political Writer,* remains the most expansive examination of Stewart's life and includes copies of her speeches as well. *Spiritual Narratives,* which is part of a series edited by Henry Louis Gates Jr., reprints all five of Mrs. Stewart's speeches and her religious meditations in facsimile and includes Stewart's speeches along with the autobiographies of black women preachers Jarena Lee, Julia A. J. Foote, and Virginia W. Broughton. *Spiritual Narratives,* Schomburg Library of Nineteenth-Century Black Women Writers (New York: Oxford University Press, 1988). William L. Andrews includes one of Stewart's speeches in *Classic African American Women's Narratives.* "Maria W. Stewart, Religion and the Pure Principles of Morality, the Sure Foundation on Which We Must Build," in *Classic African American Women's Narratives,* ed. William L. Andrews (Oxford: Oxford University Press, 2003), 3–15.

4. Richardson, *Maria W. Stewart,* 3.

Appeal to the Coloured Citizens of the World, which uses the Bible to inveigh passionately against the slave regime. While Walker prophesied God's coming judgment upon America for its sins in enslaving Africans, Stewart resisted advocating violence. Instead, she put her own spin upon the idea of African American exceptionalism, pairing it with strong arguments for female empowerment and African American economic advancement and social uplift. In her articulations of African American exceptionalism and the need for independent black economic and political power, Stewart's work foreshadowed and even anticipated some of the Black Nationalist thought[5] that would be further developed in the twentieth century by men like Marcus Garvey.

Stewart is a theologian in the sense that as she is using and interpreting scripture, she is wrestling with theodicy, the central issue of theology. Theodicy's question, "why do bad things happen in the world, especially if God is both good and powerful?" is answered by Stewart through her speeches.[6] In her addresses, Stewart lashes out at the sinfulness of the slavocracy and at the complacency of blacks who labor under its yoke rather than resisting it actively. Further, she paints a picture of the God of ultimate justice who is about to set this horribly unbalanced social order aright by meting out a much-deserved, swiftly coming judgment upon slavery and slaveholder alike. Stewart's thesis—that bad things are happening to African Americans because the slavocracy is sinful, because some blacks are complacent, and because God's hand of judgment is, for the moment, still—is part of her broader prophetic understanding that God would, both soon and suddenly, intervene in history to right the wrongs being committed against black slaves and, by extension, against all black people.

5. Just as Stewart's theological thought has been underappreciated, so has her Black Nationalist rhetoric. While noting "the scant reference to Stewart in histories of black nationalism," Lora Romero calls Stewart's work a Black Nationalist rhetoric aimed at producing racial unity. For Romero, "Stewart's remarkable but underanalyzed polemics against slavery and racism" remain almost forgotten in terms of their Black Nationalist content. Lora Romero, *Home Fronts: Domesticity and Its Critics in the Antebellum United States*, New Americanists (Durham, NC: Duke University Press, 1997), 55, 53.

6. "Stewart wrestled with the perennial conundrum of a supposedly just and merciful God's ostensible willingness to tolerate the continued and undeserved suffering of the innocent." Richardson, *Maria W. Stewart*, 15.

Reading Stewart by Reading
Stewart's Use of the Bible

Although her work has been widely categorized as political speech, it also rings with evangelical religious fervor because it is liberally sprinkled with biblical references. The Bible is the text most often quoted in Stewart's speeches. Although she tells us very little about her education, she freely admits, "During the years of childhood and youth [the Bible] was the book that I mostly studied; and now, while my hands are toiling for their daily sustenance, my heart is most generally meditating upon its divine truths."[7] When Stewart inserts biblical verses into her writing, they are not just stylistic flourishes; they are the heart and soul of her message.[8] Stewart's words cannot be fully understood if divorced from the Bible verses with which they are entangled.

Modern binaries of sacred versus secular (or even church versus state) are not relevant to Stewart, who acknowledges no such divisions in her writing. Indeed, her religious message underscores and intermeshes with her political rhetoric in powerful ways; her use of scripture unlocks hidden layers of meaning that are inaccessible unless one understands her political message in the light of her theology and biblical usage. Stewart stands in a long line of men and women who have spoken with the voice of scripture, quoting biblical passages as a means of appropriating the Bible's authority while telling their own stories.

The excellent scholarship that has preceded my own work has sought to understand Stewart within the confines of particular disciplinary concerns, seeing her work either as primarily political[9] or as primarily reli-

7. Maria W. Stewart, "Productions of Mrs. Maria W. Stewart, Presented to the First African Baptist Church and Society in the City of Boston," in *Spiritual Narratives*, 24.

8. I substantiate this point in chapter 1.

9. Some historians evaluate Stewart's public activism in the broader context of her work with David Walker or for the abolition of slavery. Peter P. Hinks, *To Awaken My Afflicted Brethren: David Walker and the Problem of Antebellum Slave Resistance* (University Park: Pennsylvania State University Press, 1997); Quarles, *Black Abolitionists*. Others classify Stewart's speeches as part of a broader genre of protest literature. Patrick Rael, *Black Identity and Black Protest in the Antebellum North*, John Hope Franklin Series in African American History and Culture (Chapel Hill: University of North Carolina Press, 2002); Richard Newman, Patrick Rael, and Phillip Lapsansky, eds.,

gious.[10] To my knowledge, no one has yet attempted to analyze Stewart's political thought by means of her religious content. Using an interdisciplinary approach that combines the insights of previous scholarship on Stewart with attention to those of biblical scholarship, my work attempts to bridge the chasm between analyses of Stewart's biblical appropriation and of her political speech.

Most often, Maria Stewart's use of the Bible throws additional light on her political arguments. Through her choices of scripture, Stewart elaborates a well-developed theology, underscores her own passions or ambivalences, and outlines a plan of black and female empowerment that is both political and pragmatic. Her command of the Bible is masterful, her recall of biblical text is encyclopedic, and in nearly every case, Stewart applies scripture in such a way that her political or pragmatic program is amplified.

I am not trying to write a historical or literary analysis of Stewart's work,

---

Pamphlets of Protest: An Anthology of Early African-American Protest Literature, 1790– 1860 (New York: Routledge, 2001); Timothy Patrick McCarthy and John Campbell McMillian, eds., *The Radical Reader: A Documentary History of the American Radical Tradition* (New York: New Press, 2003); Manning Marable and Leith Mullings, eds., *Let Nobody Turn Us Around: Voices of Resistance, Reform, and Renewal: An African American Anthology* (Lanham, MD: Rowman and Littlefield, 2000). Some scholars have identified Stewart's work as feminist thought. Beverly Guy-Sheftall, ed., *Words of Fire: An Anthology of African-American Feminist Thought* (New York: New Press, 1995, distributed by W. W. Norton). As mentioned previously, Stewart's work has also been evaluated as part of the broader corpus of Black Nationalism. Romero, *Home Fronts*, 52–69. See also Rael, *Black Identity and Black Protest.*

10. Despite the fact that she includes so many biblical quotations in her writings and speeches, relatively few scholars have been attentive to the theological content of Stewart's work. However, two are worth noting here. Chanta Heywood has classified Stewart as one of the "Prophesying Daughters," pioneering black women preachers whose messages were delivered at a time when women were rarely authorized to preach by Christian institutions and organizations in the United States. Chanta M. Haywood, *Prophesying Daughters: Black Women Preachers and the Word, 1823–1913* (Columbia: University of Missouri Press, 2003). Joycelyn Moody, who has studied the rhetoric of several religiously motivated nineteenth-century African American women writers, including Stewart, finds in her writing a sophisticated intermingling of religious forms (such as the prophetic lament) in the exhortations of a woman Moody calls a "protofeminist" writing a "theology of survival." Joycelyn Moody, *Sentimental Confessions: Spiritual Narratives of Nineteenth-Century African American Women* (Athens: University of Georgia Press, 2001), 26–50.

since such scholarship has already been ably undertaken, but to provide a biblical analysis of her work. Indeed, I am deeply indebted, in particular, to Marilyn Richardson's excellent history of Stewart's life and public career.[11] Because Richardson has already documented much of what is currently known of Stewart's life, I am freed to pursue other avenues of analysis. In this, I turn to the insights of biblical scholarship for the tools to understand Stewart's work.[12] Although this methodology may be foreign to some, its results ultimately complement previous scholarship on Stewart by outlining the ways that her theological and political programs intertwine and undergird one another.

My choice of this methodology was somewhat serendipitous. In graduate school I was enrolled in a course on African American women's spiri-

11. Richardson, *Maria W. Stewart.*

12. The recent works of several scholars suggest that analysis of biblical usage can illuminate political and cultural conflict and change. *The Talking Book: African Americans and the Bible,* by Allen Dwight Callahan (New Haven, CT: Yale University Press, 2006), represents a relatively new area of inquiry for biblical scholars, who more typically focus their attention on the period, millennia ago, when the Bible was being written and canonized. Callahan joins other biblical scholars who have shifted their focus from antiquity to the more recent past and have chosen to examine contemporary communities of interpretation and the meaning they make of scripture. Among the classically trained New Testament scholars who, like Callahan, are reshaping biblical scholarship are Vincent Wimbush, Brian Blount, Demetrius K. Williams, and Cain Hope Felder. Using the tools of biblical scholarship, each of these men has written or edited books that consider the biblical hermeneutics of black communities and the effects such hermeneutics have upon religious and cultural formation in these communities. Their explorations of blacks' use of the Bible are also interdisciplinary and draw upon the scholarship of historians, literary scholars, and others, bringing these disciplines into conversation with that of biblical scholarship. See, for example, Vincent L. Wimbush and Rosamond C. Rodman, *African Americans and the Bible: Sacred Texts and Social Textures* (New York: Continuum, 2000); and Vincent L. Wimbush, *Theorizing Scriptures: New Critical Orientations to a Cultural Phenomenon, Signifying (on) Scriptures* (New Brunswick, NJ: Rutgers University Press, 2008). Professor Wimbush has since opened the Institute for Signifying Scriptures at the Claremont Graduate University in Claremont, California. The institute "facilitates research on the work we make scriptures do for us." http://www.signifyingscriptures.org/. See also Brian K. Blount, *Cultural Interpretation: Reorienting New Testament Criticism* (Minneapolis: Fortress, 1995); Blount, *Can I Get a Witness? Reading Revelation through African American Culture,* 1st ed. (Louisville, KY: Westminster John Knox, 2005); Blount, *Go Preach! Mark's Kingdom Message and the Black Church Today,* The Bible and Liberation (Maryknoll, NY: Orbis Books, 1998); Blount, *Then the Whisper Put*

tual narratives—including Stewart's speeches—at the same time that I was taking a Greek exegetical class on the Gospel of Luke.[13] As I read one of Stewart's speeches, I happened to note that she alluded to the parable of Lazarus and the rich man, which is found only in the Gospel of Luke. I don't believe that I would have made that discovery had I not also been reading Luke for the exegesis class. Reading Stewart through her allusion to Luke opened new possibilities of interpretation for me. I began to wonder: how might understanding Stewart's use of the Bible help us to understand Stewart? Given that Stewart tells us so very little about herself, might examining her hermeneutics be another means of learning about her? Curious, I began to document Stewart's biblical allusions in the hopes of finding more such examples. The ultimate result of this search is the text you have before you.

A Rosetta Stone

In "Reading Darkness, Reading Scripture," New Testament professor Vincent L. Wimbush argues persuasively for the urgent need for more scholarship on African American biblical use and interpretation. Specifically, Wimbush points to the importance of elaborating African American hermeneutics because of its essential role in "the phenomenology of social-cultural formation."[14] Wimbush goes on to argue that understand-

---

on Flesh: New Testament Ethics in an African American Context (Nashville: Abingdon Press, 2001); and Blount et al., eds., *True to Our Native Land: An African American New Testament Commentary* (Minneapolis: Fortress, 2007). See also Demetrius K. Williams, *An End to This Strife: The Politics of Gender in African American Churches* (Minneapolis: Fortress, 2004); and Cain Hope Felder, *Stony the Road We Trod: African American Biblical Interpretation* (Minneapolis: Fortress, 1991); and Felder, *Troubling Biblical Waters: Race, Class, and Family,* Bishop Henry McNeal Turner Studies in North American Black Religion, vol. 3 (Maryknoll, NY: Orbis Books, 1991). Dr. Felder is the founder of the Biblical Institute for Social Change at the Howard University School of Divinity in Washington, DC, an educational resource "committed to restor[ing] the psychological, social, and spiritual development of persons of African descent given the biblical and theological distortions that historically have prevailed in the Christian tradition."

13. Joycelyn Moody taught the course on African American women's spiritual narratives; François Bovon taught the exegetical course on the Gospel of Luke.

14. Vincent L. Wimbush, "Reading Darkness, Reading Scriptures" (unpublished paper, African Americans and the Bible Conference, Union Theological Seminary, New York City, April 8 1999), 17.

ing the uses of sacred text in the formation of African American identity is crucial because of its importance to the understanding not only of black identity but also of scripture. Noting the ongoing centrality of the Bible to black life, he asks:

> What are people doing when they create and continue to define themselves by, address each other through and on the basis of, sacred texts? What psychosocial dynamics are in place when such things happen? What sociopolitical dynamics? What status and gender-specific dynamics? Toward what psychosocial, sociopolitical good and/or ill do these dynamics play? Until these and other such questions are addressed in the context of academic programs in Bible it seems to me that no truly critical breakthroughs can be experienced. By this I mean breakthroughs not only in biblical studies, not merely in religious and theological studies, but in the study of social and cultural formation in general. The phenomenon of the sacred text is so tightly interwoven, so deeply imbedded, within so many aspects of the collective worlds represented here that I dare say no truly critical breakthrough is possible apart from addressing it.[15]

That is, Wimbush sees the Bible as a touchstone for understanding much of black history, literature, religion, and culture. Indeed, for him it is the Rosetta stone: it is the key to translating and decoding the deeper meanings of African American life in particular as well as the deeper meanings of scripture in general.

Answering Wimbush's call "to pursue the academic study of the Bible . . . with the focus not upon the study of texts but upon the study of society and culture and the ways in which 'texts' function within them,"[16] this book charts Maria Stewart's use of scripture and the ways in which biblical texts function in her speeches. Delving deeply into the corpus of one thinker in one historical moment, I am treating the Bible as deeply implicated in, and ultimately inseparable from, Stewart's political thought, with the expectation that such in-depth analysis of Stewart's hermeneutics will yield insights into the meaning of scripture and insights into Stewart as well.

15. Ibid., 18–19.
16. Wimbush and Rodman, *African Americans and the Bible,* xiii.

Black (Women) Preachers

The genre of the slave narrative has been well studied. However, Maria Stewart was born free. Her works (along with those of other free African American women preachers like Jarena Lee, Julia Foote, and Virginia W. Broughton)[17] comprise a separate category of nineteenth-century black women's writing from that of the slave narrative in that they address the condition of antebellum African American women from the vantage point of freedom.[18] These women's writings are unapologetically theological in nature and heavily influenced by evangelical theology. Such materials' religious content has been less well studied until recently.

Maria Stewart identified her messages as "speeches," not sermons. Nevertheless, her words ring with evangelical fervor and images of redemption and of judgment. She begins and ends her speaking career with her testimony: the story of her own personal experience of salvation, and even of vocation or calling to the work she has undertaken. If anything, her words straddle the line between secular and sacred address, frequently blurring the borders.[19] The only difference between Stewart's speeches and, say, the sermons of itinerant preachers Jarena Lee or Julia Foote is their context, not their content. Lee and Foote preached in churches and in homes; Stewart spoke in lecture halls. Nevertheless, their message was often very much the same.

17. Jarena Lee, "Religious Experience and Journal of Mrs. Jarena Lee, Giving an Account of Her Call to Preach the Gospel," in *Spiritual Narratives*, 1–97; Julia A. J. Foote, "A Brand Plucked from the Fire: An Autobiographical Sketch by Mrs. Julia A. J. Foote," in *Spiritual Narratives*, 1–124; Virginia W. Broughton, "Twenty Year's Experience of a Missionary," in *Spiritual Narratives*, 1–140.

18. See, for example, Adrienne M. Israel, *Amanda Berry Smith: From Washerwoman to Evangelist*, Studies in Evangelicalism, no. 16 (Lanham, MD: Scarecrow, 1998); and Elizabeth Keckley, *Behind the Scenes* (New York: G. W. Carleton, 1868).

19. At times, I compare Stewart to women like Sojourner Truth, who spoke primarily in secular contexts. At other times, I compare Stewart to women like Jarena Lee, Julia Foote, and other early female preachers, whose messages were clearly intended as sacred. Because Stewart's speeches contain similarities to both types of public address, I think it appropriate to draw comparisons to both types of public speaking. Because Stewart called what she was doing making "speeches," I also use that terminology. Whatever we call them, there is often little difference between a speech by Stewart and a sermon by anyone else.

What differentiates political or civic speech from preaching? In Maria Stewart's case, there is very little difference, as she freely uses the Bible to frame political arguments. Stewart made no claim to be a preacher, and she eschewed the pulpit, choosing instead to give her public speeches from lecterns far removed from any sanctuary. Perhaps she did so to avoid contemporary controversies around a woman's right to serve as a preacher. Nevertheless, the text she most often quotes is the Bible. It is in this use of scripture that Stewart most resembles a preacher despite her choice of venue.

What does it mean to preach? In its most basic sense, to preach is to proclaim the Gospel; it is to tell the story of God's redemptive activity in the world; it is to speak words from God to God's people. Who is a preacher? Here the definition is less clear because such identification has become ensnared in gender politics and church polity. Women have been preaching the Gospel ever since Mary Magdalene was sent by Jesus to proclaim to the rest of the disciples that the tomb was empty.[20] Nevertheless, even today, some churches and denominations deny women the title of "preacher," preferring instead to call their actions "testifying," "witnessing," or even "prophesying." To be called a preacher is to lay claim to the ecclesial authority to speak for God, and it is precisely that authority that has been denied women in some places and at some times.

Although Maria Stewart never claimed to be a preacher, that is what I call her. It seems to me that, given the clearly theological content of her messages, she was doing the work of the preacher—irrespective of the nature of the venue in which her messages were delivered. If, as I suggest, Stewart was doing the work of a preacher, then it is appropriate to consider her words alongside those of other black evangelical preachers of her time—women like Jarena Lee and Julia Foote.[21] If we take seriously Stewart's work as a preacher, we can then more easily address her theology, putting it alongside that of contemporaneous preachers like Lee and Foote.

As French philosopher Paul Ricoeur explains, it is the choice of text that defines *preaching*. Ricoeur writes, "You preach on canonical texts, but

20. The Greek word *apostolos*, meaning "one who is sent," is the term from which the English word "apostle" is derived. Since Mary Magdalene was literally "sent" by Jesus, she was an apostle to the rest of the disciples—who were later to be called apostles. See John 20:14–18. (Elsewhere in the Gospels, it is an angel who sends Mary Magdalene to the other disciples. See Matthew 28:5–8.)

21. I discuss this in more detail in chapter 3.

not on profane. . . . Preaching is the permanent reinterpretation of the text that is regarded as grounding the community."[22] The community referred to here is the church, the gathering of believers. According to Ricoeur's definition, Stewart, in using the Bible—a document that defines the church—engaged in the act of preaching. For only among believers is the Bible sacred, or even authoritative. Using the Bible as extensively as she did, Stewart was doing the work of a preacher, gathering a community of believers who would be convinced to act by her use of their defining text. In this respect, she was also doing the work of a theologian, making meaning of the biblical text by her interpretation of it.

Traditional scholarship has tended to underestimate and devalue the sustaining contributions of black women to cultural and theological development in this country in two ways: it has relied heavily in its examinations on text and on clergy, both of which have tended to privilege the contributions of men, who have historically had freer access to education and to ordination. If the title of theologian were only to be awarded to those who had received formal theological education or who had been ordained, many important religious thinkers, both male and female, would have to have been excluded from the category.[23] Black theology and black religion have been shaped significantly by rich vernacular traditions of black culture; to discount these influences would result in undervaluing black women's roles in shaping such traditions. Studies that fail to recognize that ordained preachers were not the only people doing theological reflection risk ignoring the significant roles of the laity and, particularly, lay women, in black churches and theological communities.

This is important in the case of Maria Stewart, because neither was she

22. Paul Ricoeur and Mark I. Wallace, *Figuring the Sacred: Religion, Narrative, and Imagination* (Minneapolis: Fortress, 1995), 70.

23. Although it does not include Stewart, Christiana de Groot and Marion Ann Taylor's *Recovering Nineteenth-Century Women Interpreters of the Bible* (Atlanta: Society of Biblical Literature, 2007) is an example of a text that continues the developing trend of identifying sources of theological thought and biblical hermeneutics outside of the ranks of the formally theologically trained or of the ordained clergy. Similarly, Eileen Razzaria Elrod's *Piety and Dissent: Race, Gender, and Biblical Rhetoric in Early American Autobiography* (Amherst: University of Massachusetts Press, 2008) omits Stewart but nevertheless makes the case for expanding the category of biblical hermeneutics to include considerations of nontraditional sources like slave narratives and religious autobiographies, such as the one composed by Jarena Lee.

ordained nor did she claim any clerical privilege; nevertheless, her works contain significant theological content. Stewart is doing the work of a preacher in her proclamation of scripture; she is also doing the work of a theologian in her interpretation of the same. Even in black churches where women were strictly prohibited from officially sanctioned ordination, women still exercised significant and powerful leadership roles in those same churches and in the black community at large.[24] That we are still discussing Stewart today, and that many of her words seem so prescient, attest to the enduring significance of her relatively small corpus.

Fortunately, a new generation of scholars is crafting new tools and methodologies that take seriously nontraditional sources like oral tradition as recorded in the spirituals[25] or folk culture as described in music and fiction.[26] In so doing, they are opening scholarship to new ways of thinking about the roles of laity in black religious formation and about the ways that religious formation takes place beyond the academy, and even outside church walls, in the broader cultural marketplace. This is particularly significant in the case of a woman like Stewart, for whom documentation about her religious training and affiliation is, at best, sparse.[27]

24. See, for example, Evelyn Brooks Higginbotham, *Righteous Discontent: The Women's Movement in the Black Baptist Church, 1880–1920* (Cambridge, MA: Harvard University Press, 1993); Judith Weisenfeld and Richard Newman, eds., *This Far by Faith: Readings in African-American Women's Religious Biography* (New York: Routledge, 1996); and Cheryl Townsend Gilkes, *If It Wasn't for the Women—: Black Women's Experience and Womanist Culture in Church and Community* (Maryknoll, NY: Orbis Books, 2001).

25. See, for example, Cheryl Townsend Gilkes, "'Go and Tell Mary and Martha': The Spirituals, Biblical Options for Women, and Cultural Tensions in the African American Religious Experience," *Social Compass* 43, no. 4 (1996): 536–81; and James H. Cone, *The Spirituals and the Blues: An Interpretation* (Maryknoll, NY: Orbis Books, 1991).

26. See, for example, Abraham Smith, "Toni Morrison's *Song of Solomon:* The Blues and the Bible," in *The Recovery of Black Presence: An Interdisciplinary Exploration: Essays in Honor of Dr. Charles B. Copher,* ed. Randall C. Bailey and Jacquelyn Grant (Nashville: Abingdon, 1995), 107–15; and Lawrence W. Levine, *Black Culture and Black Consciousness* (New York: Oxford University Press, 1977).

27. There are indications from the time when she lived in Washington, DC, after the Civil War, that Stewart was an Episcopalian and perhaps even a member of St. Mary's Parish, now located in the Foggy Bottom region of the city. However, records pertaining to the earlier portion of her life, and particularly the time she spent in Boston, are more difficult to come by. I have not found records pertaining to her religious training

Evangelical (Women) Preachers

Evangelical is a multivalent term, and it is important to distinguish what in particular is meant by classifying women like Maria Stewart as evangelical. The term itself is derived from *evangel*, or "good news," and served as a specialized designation for the four canonical Gospels of the New Testament: Matthew, Mark, Luke, and John. Later, it came to describe those churches and groups descended from the Protestant Reformation and Martin Luther's break with Roman Catholicism. It has come to have an even more specialized meaning in the United States, where it has been influenced by the Great Awakening and other particularly American phenomena.

In the United States, the term *evangelical* describes those Christians who emphasize (1) a spiritual rebirth or "born again" experience of salvation, (2) the authority of the Bible and a fairly literal reading of the biblical text, (3) personal piety, and (4) a commitment to missions, or evangelism.[28] Evangelicals today span the spectrum from fundamentalists to Pentecos-

---

during this earlier period beyond her own reference to a "Sabbath School" in which she was educated. One small hint of that earlier church affiliation is the fact that the 1835 edition of her speeches was "Presented to the First African Baptist Church and Society of the City of Boston" (Stewart, "Productions of Maria Stewart"). However, this is, at best, slender evidence. According to Marilyn Richardson, the pastor of the African Baptist Church, Rev. Thomas Paul, performed Stewart's marriage, which at least suggests that Stewart had some ties to the church. Richardson, *Maria W. Stewart*, 3.

28. My definition of *evangelical* is based upon that in Mark A. Noll, *The Rise of Evangelicalism: The Age of Edwards, Whitefield, and the Wesleys*, A History of Evangelicalism, vol. 1 (Downers Grove, IL: InterVarsity, 2003), 15–21. Noll credits D. W. Bebbington with having originated his version of this definition. See D. W. Bebbington, *Evangelicalism in Modern Britain: A History from the 1730s to the 1980s* (London: Unwin Hyman, 1989), 1–17. Historian Randall Balmer, while delineating the contours of evangelicalism slightly differently, nonetheless concurs with Noll on the basic outline of American evangelicalism. While Balmer omits item 4 from his definition, he notes that the spread of the charismatic movement into Roman Catholicism means that evangelicals can also be found there. Like Noll, Balmer also emphasizes the centrality of the Bible to the origins of evangelicalism, noting that "historically, the term often refers to the theology of the Protestant Reformation in the sixteenth century, when Martin Luther 'rediscovered the gospel' after its eclipse in the scholastic theology of the Middle Ages." Today, however, Balmer says that evangelicalism is "quintessentially American" and born of the absence of a state church, which has produced a kind of "free market of religion" in the United States. Randall Herbert Balmer, *Mine Eyes Have Seen the Glory: A Journey into the Evangelical Subculture in America* (New York: Oxford University Press, 1993), xiii–xvi, 280.

tals and can be found in holiness camp meetings, charismatic Bible studies, and parachurch organizations like Campus Crusade for Christ or the Full Gospel Businessmen's Fellowship. Important aspects of Evangelical theology in the life and thought of Maria Stewart are a fairly literal interpretive approach to scripture, the use of the Bible as an authoritative source central to much of her argument against the oppression of blacks and of women, the centrality of her salvation experience as authorization for ministry, and her evangelistic zeal in getting her messages out into the free market of religious ideas that was nineteenth-century America.[29]

Stewart's words echo with the cadences of the King James Bible in an explicit appeal not only to the authority of literacy[30] but also to the authority of scripture as personal legitimation. She invokes not only specific texts and verses but also biblical imagery and ideas. Often, the texts she quotes are easily identified, but occasionally they are more obscure and difficult to discern. Many of her allusions are to the Hebrew Bible: the Psalms and Proverbs seem to be her particular favorites. With one text in particular, Psalms 68:31, Stewart attempts to reclaim Africa from the denigrations of the modern West.[31] By speaking in the manner of the King James Bible, by quoting it frequently, by likening her experiences to those of the ancient Israelites, and, in essence, by speaking with the Bible's voice, Stewart appears to inhabit the texts and wrap herself in the mantle of the Bible's authority. In this, Stewart internalized the Bible in a significant and transformative way.

Scripture as Script

According to a study by Mary McClintock Fulkerson, twentieth-century Pentecostal women's testimonies frequently followed specific patterns mirroring the outlines of biblical narratives that describe the call to ministry of familiar characters like Joshua or Gideon.[32] By rephrasing the events of their own lives using ideas from Bible stories that were well known to

29. Stewart delivered her speeches but also had them published twice as a means of spreading her message to a wider audience.

30. The importance of literacy as legitimation is explored in chapter 2.

31. See chapter 4 for a discussion of Stewart's interpretation of Psalms 68:31, the so-called Ethiopian prophecy.

32. Mary McClintock Fulkerson, "Joyful Speaking for God: Pentecostal Women's Performances," in *Changing the Subject: Women's Discourses and Feminist Theology* (Minneapolis: Fortress, 1994), 239–98.

the listening congregation, the women in effect took on the authority of those scriptures. In so doing, these women demonstrated two qualities that are very highly prized in evangelical circles, where the Bible is the central source of theological reflection: first, they showed that they have not only memorized scripture but internalized it in some significant way, and second, they demonstrated that their salvation and lived experiences lined up with that same scripture. They appropriated the authority of scripture by demonstrating that they knew it and are obedient to it—indeed, they argued that they have the right to wield the Bible in their preaching specifically because they are under its authority. These women appropriate the authority of scripture by applying it to their own lives.

Although Maria Stewart was not a Pentecostal,[33] she shared several characteristics with the Pentecostal women in Fulkerson's study: like those women, Maria Stewart approached the Bible with a deeply evangelical sense of its significance. (It is clear from her frequent use of scripture that Stewart believes it wields a weighty authority.) And like many Pentecostal women, Stewart must justify her groundbreaking public career to those who would oppose it on biblical grounds.

For the Pentecostal women in Fulkerson's study, the use of scripture is "performative." These women not only explicate Bible verses but do so in a manner demonstrated by their demeanor, and even their gestures, that make them seem imbued with the power of those verses and that of the Holy Spirit. The authority of these women's testimonies is born of the fact that "[their] stories are constructed out of traditions of the Pentecostal community, even as they are creative versions of these traditions."[34] The women's stories are legitimated in the minds of their listeners because they ring with the cadences of scripture even as they also echo chords common to the life of the entire community—chords forged of shared culture, experience, history, and a love of the Bible.

When these Pentecostal women "tell of their calls [to ministry], they highlight the ideas that legitimate their ministry."[35] They answer those

33. Although I have previously noted my inability to document Stewart's early religious formation, it is quite easy to say that she was not a Pentecostal simply because it would be an anachronism at best. Most scholars date the origin of the modern Pentecostal movement to the turn of the twentieth century, which was well after Stewart's death.

34. Fulkerson, "Joyful Speaking for God," 261.

35. Ibid., 263.

critics who would argue that it is inappropriate for women to serve as ministers or preachers (because of scriptural prohibitions against women's public speaking or other activities that might cause them to have "authority over men")[36] by appealing to a higher authority: God. It is important for these women to demonstrate that they do not seek public ministry out of any desire for power, influence, or self-aggrandizement; rather, they emphasize that it is God's will, not their own, that motivates them. They balance, on the one hand, their self-identification as meek and submissive women, with undertaking bold and audacious public careers on the other, and it is in their submission to God, and their boldness in God's service, that they seek validation of their vocations. Their actions are thus not to be understood as grandstanding or tradition-breaking; rather, they argue, they are only being obedient to God as every generation of humanity has been called to be. As one Pentecostal woman explains, "I wouldn't have chosen this as my profession had it not been for God. . . . God just sorta pushed me into this."[37]

The implications of this line of reasoning are clear: the women are saying, "Don't blame me for this ground- and tradition-breaking public ministry. I'm just being obedient to God. This was all God's idea! How could I be a good Christian and resist this calling?" Then, with every invocation of a Bible story documenting the call of an unlikely, unwilling, or seemingly unworthy candidate, like Gideon, Deborah, or Jonah, the women demonstrate that their own callings, though seemingly unlikely, are nonetheless not without biblical parallels.

Early in her public career, Maria Stewart explains the obvious source for much of her inspiration when she writes, "I have borrowed much of my

36. Today, as in Stewart's time, there are those who would argue against allowing women to hold any leadership positions in religious life unless they are limited to leadership over other women only. While these attitudes still persist today in some quarters, they were far more common in Stewart's day and are often built around texts such as 1 Timothy 2:12, "But I suffer not a woman to teach, nor to usurp authority over the man, but to be in silence," and 1 Corinthians 14:34–35, "Let your women keep silence in the churches: for it is not permitted unto them to speak; but they are commanded to be under obedience, as also saith the law. And if they will learn any thing, let them ask their husbands at home: for it is a shame for women to speak in the church." I address the response of Stewart and her contemporaries to critiques based upon gender in chapter 3.

37. Quoted in Fulkerson, "Joyful Speaking for God," 265.

language from the holy Bible."[38] What is true of the Pentecostal women just discussed is also true of Maria Stewart: they all seek legitimation through their use of scripture. That is, by internalizing scripture and appropriating the Bible as though it were their own voice, these women refute what might seem to be scriptural prohibitions against their activities by demonstrating their obedience to the scripture. Stewart, in fact, speaks a kind of "Bible-ese": she has so shaped her ideas in scriptural-sounding words and phrases that it is sometimes difficult to tell where the Bible ends and where Stewart begins. Again and again, the words that Stewart chooses to speak are the words of the Bible. It has become her mother tongue.

In this process of legitimation and internalization, Stewart's use of scripture is quite interesting, and her writing is as courageous and insistent as she was. She is able to speak quite boldly, while paradoxically protesting her own meekness and insignificance, because of her implicit claim that the words are not hers but God's. At times the allusions to specific biblical texts or to biblical imagery flow one upon the other in quick succession in her prose. Because Stewart is so facile with the Bible, her selection of specific texts is telling, as are the choices she makes in arranging these allusions. Stewart's fluid use of scripture functions to legitimate her in the minds of her listeners.

It is also important to note that Stewart's use of scripture is performative. Hermeneutics is like the performance of a play where script, performer, audience, and stage are inextricably linked. Two levels of interpretation are taking place for the benefit of the audience. These two levels result in "double mimesis [as] the writer represents and the actor represents."[39] In order to interpret the performance accurately, the audience must understand both the author's meaning and the actor's interpretation and performance of that meaning. The "truthfulness" of the performance is found in the unity of the text of the play and the content of the performance. In the most truthful performances, the actor "disappears entirely in the recognition of what he is representing."[40]

Continuing the metaphor of scripture as script, one could liken interpreting the Bible to performing a play by Shakespeare or one of Beethoven's

38. Stewart, "Productions of Maria Stewart," 24.

39. Hans-Georg Gadamer, *Truth and Method*, trans. Joel Weinsheimer and Donald G. Marshall (New York: Continuum, 1996), 117.

40. Ibid., 114.

musical compositions.[41] The performer must begin with a familiarity with the work involved; it is the text that defines the outward limits of any good performance. (One must remain true to the work being performed because the work is the structure upon which the resulting performance must hang.) Nevertheless, performing the work requires that the performer provide the emphases and ultimately even embody the work. Through performance, through demeanor and gesture, the performer becomes the embodiment of that which she performs.

For those who consider the Bible to be the word of God, to perform the biblical text is to participate with God in bringing the truth of that text into being in the world. For those for whom the Bible is authoritative, its performance is ultimately also transformative because the text itself is transformative for those who hear and believe.[42] Here, mimesis and poesis join: when the scripture is the script, the performer mediates meaning to her audience through her own body. In this way, Stewart links the performative and the prophetic as she quotes (or inhabits) scripture before her audiences.

Stewart and the Pentecostal women of Fulkerson's study are evangelicals with a shared sense of the authority of scripture. A careful comparison of their appropriation of scripture points to a commonality that is characteristic of evangelicals: by filling their written and spoken words with biblical imagery, phrases, and whole verses, Stewart (in the nineteenth century) and her Pentecostal sisters (in the twentieth century and presumably into the present) appropriate the authority of those same scriptures even as they demonstrate their expansive knowledge of them. By this appropriation, the evangelical woman is able to speak quite boldly. The words, after all, are not hers: they are the weighty words of scripture, which other evangelicals will recognize and value. It is the authority of scripture that opens the door to each woman's further ministry.

Maria Stewart used the Bible to refute racism and sexism and to construct a kind of proto-womanist theology and self-understanding that served as a powerful tool to carve a niche for herself and other women who

---

41. Nicholas Lash, *Theology on the Way to Emmaus* (London: SCM Press, 1986), 42.

42. "We talk of 'holy' scripture, and for good reason. And yet it is not, in fact, the script that is 'holy,' but the people: the company who perform the script." Ibid.

followed in a hostile time and contested public space. She quoted scripture as a means of countering racism and sexism, of explaining her emergence into the public sphere, and of constructing a positive self-understanding in the face of the double jeopardy she endured as an African American and as a woman. She did not internalize the pejorative and limiting hermeneutics arrayed against her by others,[43] nor did she accept second-class citizenship as her lot; instead, she pioneered a tradition of African American women's biblical interpretation that was sophisticated and subtle and that insisted upon her equality before God and humanity. Understanding and decoding Stewart's use of the Bible is central to translating her theology, her ideology, and her prophetic vision for the people she called the "sons and daughters of Africa" in ways that reading her works simply as a political program for racial advancement might miss.

As she read the biblical text, Maria Stewart contended that the Bible spoke to her and of her, and she employed a hermeneutic that privileged as its interpretive key her identity as an African American and as a woman. In imagery and ideology, Stewart recast African Americans not as slaves and servants but as "People of the Promise": as African peoples, she reasons, they enjoy a special relationship to God. By appropriating scripture,

43. We cannot forget that during Stewart's lifetime, the Bible was used extensively to defend slavery and patriarchy. See, for example, Sylvester A. Johnson, *The Myth of Ham in Nineteenth-Century American Christianity: Race, Heathens, and the People of God* (New York: Palgrave Macmillan, 2004); and Stacy Davis, *This Strange Story: Jewish and Christian Interpretation of the Curse of Canaan from Antiquity to 1865* (Lanham, MD: University Press of America, 2008). Both of these texts document interpretations of Genesis 9, the so-called curse of Ham, which the slavocracy used to argue that blacks were cursed by God to be slaves forever. For broader historical overviews of this theological development from a historical vantage point, see Charles Irons, *The Origins of Proslavery Christianity: White and Black Evangelicals in Colonial and Antebellum Virginia* (Chapel Hill: University of North Carolina Press, 2008). Mark Noll's *The Civil War as a Theological Crisis* (Chapel Hill: University of North Carolina Press, 2006) tracks the competing claims of pro- and antislavery forces in the antebellum United States by documenting and comparing the two camps' use of the Bible to build their arguments. Clearly, the Civil War was a political crisis for the nation; what Noll highlights is the extent to which the issues of the crisis also fueled, and were fueled by, theological and cultural battles in pulpits and seminaries across the country. As Noll explores each side's certainty that it had the right interpretation of scripture, one begins to see how passions aroused by a theological crisis were further enflamed by a political one.

Stewart also appropriated the authority of the Bible at a time in American history—following the Great Awakening's revival of evangelical fervor—when the Bible wielded extraordinary cultural authority. Her rich and frequent choices of scriptural references—the texts she used and those she ignored—are also of critical importance here. In a way, their uses form a kind of canon of texts within the Bible; it is this canon I will consider to discern the contours of Stewart's theological world and concerns.

The Bible as a Complex Cultural and Historical Force

Contemporary readers sometimes "need to be reminded how central the Bible has been to the development of national life."[44] Nevertheless, the Bible is also, for some, a troublesome text, which has been used to argue for slavery and against women's rights. Yet it is a text to which Maria Stewart returned again and again.

In order to quote the biblical text so extensively, Maria Stewart must hold two ideas in tension: that the Bible is an authoritative source for her, even as she subverts, undermines, or reinterprets biblical texts with which she disagrees, such as those others interpret to mandate blacks in slavery or women in submission to men. However, Stewart is not alone in maintaining such a tension in her work. Swimming against the stream of contemporary feminist theologians who consider themselves "post-Christian," Elisabeth Schüssler Fiorenza disagrees with those who would discard the Bible as hopelessly sexist and patriarchal when she writes that "Western feminists cannot afford to deny our biblical heritage if we do not want to strengthen the powers of oppression that deprive people of their own history and contribute to the reality of constructions of androcentric texts."[45]

While Schüssler Fiorenza owns that the Bible is a central facet of Western history, and certainly Western women's history, she nonetheless acknowledges the difficulties that certain interpretations of certain biblical

44. Nathan O. Hatch and Mark A. Noll, introduction to *The Bible in America: Essays in Cultural History*, ed. Hatch and Noll (New York: Oxford University Press, 1982), 5.

45. Elisabeth Schüssler Fiorenza, *Bread Not Stone: The Challenge of Feminist Biblical Interpretation*, 10th anniversary ed. (Boston: Beacon, 1995), 84.

texts have caused for those same women, and for others, as when it has been used to uphold the silencing of women or the legitimacy of slavery. Ignoring the Bible is not an option, as it would only result in strengthening the authority of androcentric and white supremacist interpretations of biblical texts. Instead of ignoring troubling texts, Schüssler Fiorenza proposes the use of a canon outside of the canon, one that considers women's lives as authoritative sources of hermeneutical and theological reflection, thereby allowing her to bring women's voices into dialogue with the biblical texts she considers problematic. As abolitionists discovered in the battle against slavery, Schüssler Fiorenza affirms that the Bible is too central a text to Western culture to be abandoned by feminist theory, despite the presence of *Haustafeln*[46]—texts like Ephesians 5:21–6:9[47]—which have been used to justify the subordination of women and slaves. Rather than discard the Bible as irretrievably patriarchal, as her postbiblical feminist colleagues have done, Schüssler Fiorenza seeks to construct a hermeneutical lens that would privilege both women's experiences and certain aspects of the biblical narrative that they would find liberating.

Some would argue that Schüssler Fiorenza (and Stewart, for that matter) faced a Herculean task in her efforts to reframe the Bible, with its often-quoted *Haustafeln*, or codes of submission, as a tool of liberation. To the contrary, however, a closer examination of the ways African Ameri-

---

46. *Haustafeln* are household codes of subordination found in the New Testament that refer generally to women, slaves, and children and describes their proper roles as being subordinate to those in authority over them: for wives, this would be their husbands; for children, their parents; and for slaves, their masters. The texts have been used historically to set up hierarchies of patriarchal social order. See, for example, Clarice J. Martin, "The *Haustafeln* (Household Codes) in African American Biblical Interpretation: 'Free Slaves' and 'Subordinate Women,'" in Felder, *Stony the Road We Trod*, 206–31.

47. Ephesians 5:22–24, 33: "Wives, be subject to your husbands as you are to the Lord. For the husband is the head of the wife just as Christ is the head of the church, the body of which he is the Savior. Just as the church is subject to Christ, so also wives ought to be, in everything, to their husbands . . . and a wife should respect her husband" (New Revised Standard Version). Ephesians 6:5–7: "Slaves, obey your earthly masters with fear and trembling, in singleness of heart, as you obey Christ; not only while being watched, and in order to please them, but as slaves of Christ, doing the will of God from the heart. Render service with enthusiasm, as to the Lord and not to men and women." (New Revised Standard Version).

cans have understood the Bible highlights its use as just such a tool to privilege their voices and experiences. In the hands of black exegetes, the Bible became, at times, a hammer to shatter oppression, a lamp to shed the light of hope, and a wedge to undermine the very foundations of racism and sexism. Using a hermeneutical lens similar to that which Schüssler Fiorenza would advocate for later generations of readers, Maria Stewart and other black women highlighted texts that undermined their opponents' supposed authority over them or that reinforced their own claims to human dignity and divine favor, while rhetorically minimizing or ignoring those texts that seemed to do otherwise. Rather than discard the Bible as irretrievable, Stewart used it to refute her opponents.

"African-American women spoke from a doubly disadvantaged location" as a consequence of their race and gender. As a result, one finds in their hermeneutic response a "critical interplay between 'spiritual' experience and the authorizing interpretation of scripture lead[ing] to an implicit privileging of sociopolitical experience."[48] In a subtle strategy to retrieve the biblical text for use in arguments in favor of black uplift and empowerment, African American women like Stewart used their lives and history as the prism through which scripture was refracted and subsequently evaluated. In this volume, I examine the critical interplay between spiritual experience and authorizing interpretation of scripture that characterizes Stewart's speeches.

Jazz

In analyzing African American women's history, it is not enough to consider questions of gender alone, as has been the weakness of some traditional feminist inquiry; rather, it is also essential to examine the ways in which race complicates issues of gender. Unlike traditional models of scholarship, which, like classical music, tend to emphasize a single musical idea or theme (such as the lives of white women), examining the complicated history of race and gender requires a scholarly approach more like jazz, where "the various voices in a piece of music may go their own ways but still be

---

48. Elisabeth Schüssler Fiorenza, "Transforming the Legacy of the Woman's Bible," in *Searching the Scriptures*, vol. 1, *A Feminist Introduction*, ed. Elisabeth Schüssler Fiorenza, Shelly Matthews, and Ann Graham Brock (New York: Crossroad, 1993–94), 7.

held together by their relationship to each other."[49] Just as jazz musicians have greater freedom and flexibility to interpret themes musically, so scholars should acknowledge that the significant issues of the lives of women of color are sometimes resoundingly different than those of white women. For example, while American women have shared concerns about issues like equity and fair pay in the workplace or the availability of quality child care, white women and women of color are often at odds over those concerns and have tended to see them from extremely different perspectives. Women of color who were already in the workplace, often out of economic necessity, have historically provided the domestic services as maids and nannies that allowed white women to move into the workplace. Therefore, when women of color struggled for equity and fair pay in the workplace, that workplace was often in the homes of white women. As a result, any potentially shared concerns the women faced were disproportionately influenced by race.[50]

The emergence of "womanist" as a category of inquiry and study separate and distinct from "feminist" points to the concern of many scholars that gender analysis alone is insufficient without taking into consideration the significant and complicating effects of race.[51] Scholars need to "expose the role of race as metalanguage by calling attention to its powerful, all-encompassing effect in the construction and representation of other social and power relationships, namely, gender, class, and sexuality."[52] Race functions as metalanguage through which other identifiers, such as gender, tend to be interpreted. Race becomes the master modifier, significantly changing the meaning of all other identifiers, such as those of gender or class. Together, race and gender have worked to produce a kind of double jeopardy for black women, but they also produce the possibility of multiple levels of discourse in their writings.

49. Levine, *Black Culture and Black Consciousness*, 133, as cited in Elsa Barkley Brown, "'What Has Happened Here': The Politics of Difference in Women's History and Feminist Politics," in *"We Specialize in the Wholly Impossible": A Reader in Black Women's History*, ed. Darlene Clark Hine, Wilma King, and Linda Reed (Brooklyn, NY: Carlson, 1995), 41.

50. Brown, "'What Has Happened Here.'"

51. Ibid., 39–56.

52. Evelyn Brooks Higginbotham, "African-American Women's History and the Metalanguage of Race," in *"We Specialize in the Wholly Impossible": A Reader in Black Women's History*, ed. Darlene Clark Hine, Wilma King, and Linda Reed (Brooklyn, NY: Carlson Publishing, 1995), 3–4.

Tongues and Interpretation

Beginning with W. E. B. Du Bois's conception of African Americans' "double-consciousness,"[53] many expositors have described the multiple levels of discourse inherent in the lives of African Americans and discernible in their literature. Building on Bakhtin's "double-voiced discourse," Henry Louis Gates Jr. points to the particular way in which this functions in African Americans' appropriation of the Bible, noting that "making the white text speak with a black voice is the initial mode of inscription of the metaphor of the double-voiced."[54] For Gates's purposes, discourse moves between the white text—the Bible—and black orality, or between literature and vernacular, and so on. However, while I am unwilling to concede the Bible as a "white text" as Gates has, and although much of Gates's work focuses on the discourses of black men, it is nevertheless important to unpack the ways in which some African American exegetes understood the Bible to speak with a uniquely black voice and particularly with a black woman's voice.

Mae Gwendolyn Henderson examines the complexity and diversity of dialogue in black women's writing as a function of black women's gendered and racial identities and relations of otherness.[55] Henderson appropriates the biblical metaphor of "speaking in tongues" as an image representing the intricate interplay of self and other, known and unknown, and familiar and unfamiliar speech that characterizes the narratives of black women.

53. This phrase is by now familiar to many, because it has been so often cited and incorporated into the work of other scholars who have built upon Du Bois's brilliant and classic characterization of the black experience in America. The original passage is so beautiful, so poetic, and so true that it bears repeating here: "It is a peculiar sensation, this double-consciousness, this sense of always looking at one's self through the eyes of others, of measuring one's soul by the tape of a world that looks on in amused contempt and pity. One ever feels his two-ness,—an American, a Negro: two souls, two thoughts, two unreconciled strivings; two warring ideals in one dark body, whose dogged strength alone keeps it from being torn asunder." W. E. B. Du Bois, *The Souls of Black Folk*, 1st Vintage Books/Library of America ed. (New York: Vintage Books/Library of America, 1986), 364–65.

54. Henry Louis Gates, "The Trope of the Talking Book," in *The Signifying Monkey: A Theory of Afro-American Literary Criticism* (New York: Oxford University Press, 1988), 131.

55. Mae G. Henderson, "Speaking in Tongues: Dialogics, Dialectics, and the Black Woman Writer's Literary Tradition," in *Changing Our Own Words: Essays on Criticism, Theory, and Writing by Black Women*, ed. Cheryl A. Wall (New Brunswick, NJ: Rutgers University Press, 1989), 16–37.

First and foremost, Henderson's intent seems to be to shatter the privilege that one mode of discourse exercises at the expense of other modes and to open the way for more complex understandings of the formulation and meaning of black women's writings in particular. Not only do black women need to be understood on many levels, but their observations of and by others also need to be heard in ways that honor that complexity. For Henderson, a black woman's race and gender produce alternating categories of otherness that inform her writing: she expresses a "dialogic of differences" from white men in her gender and race, white women in her race, and black men in her gender, even as she demonstrates a "dialectic of identity" in "those aspects of self shared with others."[56] Seeing a danger in the failure of others to comprehend this complex inner dialogue of black women, Henderson warns against the reification of black women as objects both inscribed with the words of others and read or interpreted through others' words and experiences.

Henderson ties together such disparate levels and types of discourse by invoking the biblical image of speaking in tongues as a metaphor for the dialogue of black women in the wider world. In the Bible, tongues-speech is the mystical and miraculous experience of humans speaking in the languages of other nations, but also speaking in languages spoken only in heaven and known only to God. The words appear as glossolalia[57]—as languages known only by God—and also as heteroglossia,[58] as the many

56. Ibid., 16–37.

57. Glossolalia, speaking in *unknown* tongues, is speaking in languages that are not the spoken languages of earth but are known only to God. (God may, on special occasions, give people the ability to interpret these languages, but in general, they are incomprehensible to human ears.) Such language is described at length in 1 Corinthians 14, where the Apostle Paul admits that while he speaks in tongues more than anyone (verse 18), such speech is not comprehensible to his rational mind (verse 19). Glossolalia, in this context, represents speech that is not comprehensible on earth. Nevertheless, it is regarded as efficacious in prayer and worship because its mystical content links the believer directly to God. See for example 1 Corinthians 14:4–19, where the Corinthian correspondent encourages the congregants to seek interpretation for their speech in *unknown* tongues—glossolalia—so that others will be able to understand them. This example seems to suggest that such tongues do not consist of languages known or ordinarily spoken on Earth.

58. This term describes the ecstatic experience of speaking in a known human language that one has not otherwise learned. Henderson notes the Pentecost experience as described in Acts 2:1–13 as a description of such. In Acts 2, pilgrims from through-

languages of many earthly nations and peoples. Consequently, for Henderson, the multilayered dialogue of black women's writing represents a type of glossolalia—a secret, ecstatic discourse that needs to be interpreted to others outside of that experience—and also, sometimes even simultaneously, represents a kind of heteroglossia, a universal language that needs no interpretation because it is a mother tongue that speaks comprehensibly to the entire world. In this Du Boisian double consciousness, black women's writings simultaneously can function as babble, scattering hegemony, even as they also operate as prophetic praise, gathering and unifying believers.

While Henderson's understanding of black women's discourse as heteroglossia conforms to Hans-Georg Gadamer's ideas of the universality of human experience (so that although the speaker uses her own language, she is understood by others in theirs), her use of glossolalia (in a sense that is complementary to Bakhtin's descriptions of "inner speech" that takes place in the psyche) complicates the matter. Henderson suggests that there is a deeper discourse, most clearly understood only by those who stand in the same relation to power, or the same subset of tradition, as the speaker stands; this is, for the black woman, glossolalia. Henderson writes that it would be a mistake for those who stand outside of a black woman's experience to believe that they can interpret the words as they would their own language. Those who prejudge meaning solely in a Gadamerian sense of universality would be mistaken in their interpretations. Despite some shared conditions of life and even elements of culture, there will always be areas where the conflicting truth claims of tradition, culture, worldview, and relationship to power will obscure understanding if not confronted.

For several reasons, Henderson's application of the metaphor of tongues provides a useful heuristic for evaluating black women's nineteenth-century biblical appropriation and hermeneutics. The word *tongues* itself helps to foreground the particular oral nature of much of Stewart's use of the Bible. In her hands it was not chiefly a literary text to be read quietly but rather a sourcebook for preaching, proclamation, and even conversation. As Vin-

---

out the Jewish Diaspora are able to understand Jesus's disciples as though the disciples spoke the pilgrims' native languages. Indeed, in a reversal of the confusion wrought at the Tower of Babel, God miraculously unifies pilgrims and disciples, as the disciples' speech is suddenly comprehensible to the pilgrims' ears. This event is literally *heteroglossic*: the disciples are able to speak the languages of others (*hetero* meaning other, *glossia* meaning language). It is even *xenoglossic*: the disciples are able to speak the languages of strangers (*xeno*, meaning stranger, *glossia* meaning language).

cent Wimbush notes, African Americans "continue to define themselves by, address each other through and on the basis of, sacred texts."[59] That is, they continue in the twenty-first century as they did in the nineteenth to use language rich in biblical imagery and allusions.

Further, *tongues* implies not only words, but whole languages, and in this sense, *tongues* also suggests the symbolic and semantic worlds in which words are embedded. If we understand black women's writing as a kind of tongues-speech, as Henderson recommends, we must recognize the possibility that the words rest in new and unexpected semiotic and grammatical frameworks. I would locate some of these frameworks in the lives and histories of the black women themselves and in meanings they drew from the biblical text. That is, the words and works are glossolalia to the wider, listening world, specifically because their meaning is drawn from the lives of black women, and yet they are heteroglossia in that those words are sometimes made comprehensible to others who have not lived or shared them.

Finally, the metaphor of tongues is useful because it suggests that, at times, the work of an interpreter is necessary. If black women's words are sometimes incomprehensible to others who have not lived the life of a black woman, then such words will need to be translated to be understood by others. The Corinthian correspondent notes in 1 Corinthians 14 that even the glossolalic can be translated to others. Thus the present volume aspires—by means of the Bible as Rosetta stone—to make Stewart's words and her deeper meanings intelligible to all.

The metaphor of tongues is therefore useful on several levels. First of all, it suggests orality, a central characteristic of much of Stewart's work. Second, to argue that black women speak in tongues, as Henderson does, is to suggest the urgent need for an interpreter who will decode that which is glossolalia to those outside of the community of black women. More important, it demonstrates the centrality of the lives of black women to their speech event, and as a consequence, to their hermeneutical lenses.

Lift Every Voice

Despite the preponderance of extant spiritual narratives and religious testimonies and treatises written by black women during the nineteenth and

59. Wimbush, "Reading Darkness, Reading Scriptures," 18–19.

early twentieth centuries, to date surprisingly little scholarly attention has been given to their theological or biblical content.[60] Part of the problem here may lie in the organization and division of the scholarly guild. Those trained in literary criticism or history sometimes feel ill-equipped to deal with materials like Stewart's speeches, containing as they do so many biblical references and so much theology. And until recently the emphasis in biblical scholarship has been on more ancient manuscripts and those that are more helpful in reconstructing the theology and praxis of the early church.

Historical-critical method served as the standard approach of biblical scholarship for the better part of the twentieth century. A product of post-Enlightenment European fascination with science, historical criticism was originally touted as a scrupulously objective approach to the study of the Bible. However, historical-critical method itself has come under increasing criticism within the academy. The charge has been led, in the main, by scholars who contend that although historical criticism proclaimed its objectivity, it was in fact the production of a very particular historical and cultural moment—in Europe and in the West. The centrality of historical-critical method pertained until the 1970s, when it began to be critiqued and displaced by other methods such as literary and cultural criticism. This traditional scholarship has been replaced by "men and women, readers and critics . . . from all corners of the world and all configurations of social location in the world . . . [who began] to read and interpret the biblical texts out of their own contexts, addressing not only one another but also the world at large."[61]

Scholars began to question the claim that historical criticism was an objective method or that the exegesis it produced was objective. Indeed, the very possibility of scholarly objectivity has come under attack in the light of postmodern and other analyses. Certainly, decades of the practice of historical criticism within the academy had produced results that were hardly objective and tended to privilege the concerns of its predominantly white, male scholars. Some critics have noted that by emphasizing text over tradition, historical-critical biblical scholarship served to lock the true meaning

60. Moody, *Sentimental Confessions*, ix–xiv.
61. Fernando F. Segovia, "'And They Began to Speak in Other Tongues': Competing Modes of Discourse in Contemporary Biblical Criticism," in *Reading from This Place*, ed. Fernando F. Segovia and Mary Ann Tolbert (Minneapolis: Fortress, 1995), 5–6.

of the text in the past, with perhaps irretrievable authorial intent, rather than allowing it to flourish within contemporary hermeneutical circles. It elevated the meaning to be found in the texts' Greco-Roman[62] or Judeo-Palestinian origins, thereby assuring jobs into perpetuity for generations of historians, classicists, and philologists who most frequently sprang from the ranks of literate elites. It tended to be "preoccupied with the notion that a text has one legitimate meaning,"[63] which allowed some readings (such as those produced in the guild) to be valued as orthodox and others (such as those produced elsewhere, including the church, and certainly, in the wider community) to be discarded as heterodox or at best suspect.

Training in traditional biblical scholarship has sometimes tended to muzzle African Americans with a method that fit them very badly while invalidating other approaches to the discipline.[64] By inscribing a Euro-centric method of reading and understanding the Bible, historical-critical method stood in opposition to many of the ways that hermeneutics was traditionally practiced in the black community. In contrast to the claims of objectivity made by some historical-critical scholars, African American biblical interpreters frequently admit that theirs is an unashamedly rela-tional enterprise. It acknowledges its roots in black Christian tradition and in African American history and life. Further, it uses that history as the prism through which scripture must pass in order to be interpreted.

African American hermeneutics tends to emphasize authorial intent as divine intent, seeing scripture as the living declaration of an ever-living God, not the moribund word of archeological artifact. Because black ex-egetes understand God to be a liberator, they read the text through that expectation of liberation. This permits them the license to construct a

62. Gay Byron criticizes the disproportionate concern with Rome, which she views as a consequence of the ethnocentric concerns of whites in the academic study of the Bible: "As an African American biblical critic, I am concerned with this imbalanced preoccupation with the Roman Empire, especially in light of the fact that Rome was only one of the four great kingdoms of the ancient world, alongside Persia, China, and Axum." Gay L. Byron, "Ancient Ethiopia and the New Testament: Ethnic (Con)Texts and Racialized (Sub)Texts," in *They Were All Together in One Place? Toward Minor-ity Biblical Criticism*, ed. Randall C. Bailey, Tat-siong Benny Liew, and Fernando F. Segovia (Atlanta: Society of Biblical Literature, 2009), 161.

63. William H. Myers, "The Hermeneutical Dilemma of the African American Biblical Student," in Felder, *Stony the Road We Trod*, 46.

64. Ibid., 41–42.

kind of canon within the canon, which highlights passages like the Exodus story and its message of freedom from slavery.

In his book *Troubling Biblical Waters*, black biblical scholar Cain Hope Felder undertakes to "'trouble' . . . the placid waters of Eurocentric historiography, exegesis, and hermeneutics on questions of race, class, and family."[65] In other words, Felder sees the Bible as a text of liberation whose message is often shackled by the prejudices inherent in Eurocentric interpretation. Seeking to recover the Bible's positive image of blacks, Felder likens his task to "what the French philosopher Michel Foucault called 'the insurrection of subjugated knowledges.'"[66]

Felder makes the point that the Bible, from the earliest shaping of the text from oral traditions to the final redaction and selection of the canonical process, reflects the point of view of the victors: those whose battles are won are those whose tales are told. In the same way, he suggests, for many years scriptural interpretation bore the polemical skew of the dominant cultures that produced them; the voices of others were not heard in them. However, new and glossolalic voices are emerging in biblical interpretation. For example, black, feminist, and womanist writers are reevaluating the scriptures to redefine race and gender roles and preconceptions and to uncover the themes of liberation such as Felder describes in *Troubling Biblical Waters*.

Mystery writer Agatha Christie once wrote, "Nobody seems to go through the agony of the victim."[67] Black, feminist, and womanist writers bring the voice of the victim (rather than the victor) to the dialogue to the extent that they reflect concerns from the underside of society that are too infrequently represented in texts produced by society's elites. They participate in the "insurrection of subjugated knowledges" as they bring to light those elements of the biblical narrative that are alien to the dominant culture because they are part of the agony of the victim—that which only another victim of exclusion or silencing could recognize or understand. Seeing from another perspective, and often using new tools of analysis, these new interpreters are producing new understandings of the meaning of biblical texts and new applications of these texts for modern situations.

65. Felder, *Troubling Biblical Waters*, xiv.
66. Ibid.
67. As quoted in J. Cheryl Exum, "Murder They Wrote: Ideology and the Manipulation of Female Presence in Biblical Narrative," *USQR* 43(1989): 19–39.

They are making the biblical text accessible not just for victors but for subjugated peoples as well.

I have likened hermeneutics to a lens in that it provides a paradigm through which one may read and interpret the biblical narrative. Now I'd like to suggest another metaphor for the work of hermeneutics: a mirror. James 1:22–25[68] links listening to the Bible (or "Word") and seeing oneself in a mirror, suggesting that truly hearing scripture results in a kind of intense self-understanding. You see yourself as you truly are by the light the Bible reflects upon you. Similarly, African American hermeneutics links self-awareness and interpreting scripture in a way that suggests that the mirror is ultimately indispensable to the interpretive act. The interpretation cannot and should not be divorced from the person of the interpreter—from that individual's history, race, gender, and social location. It cannot, and it should not, strive to be "objective" but instead should intentionally reflect the individual's experiences and concerns.[69] It is the mirror of self-knowledge that forms a surface to hold and reflect the interpretive image. African American hermeneutics routinely reject any approach that sees "through a glass, darkly."[70] That is, African American hermeneutics would reject any approach that, while claiming its own objectivity, fails to see that it has cast its own reflection in its interpretation.

"One of the persistent paradoxes of African-American religious experience is the resistance of black Christians to the results of historical-critical methods and the centrality of the Bible to black faith," writes James H. Evans.[71] Black exegetes regularly harmonize scripture, interpreting one verse in the light of others and making of the Bible a unified whole where historical-critical biblical scholarship would prefer to see historically and

68. James 1:22–25: "But be doers of the word, and not merely hearers who deceive themselves. For if any are hearers of the word and not doers, they are like those who look at themselves in a mirror; for they look at themselves and, on going away, immediately forget what they were like. But those who look into the perfect law, the law of liberty, and persevere, being not hearers who forget but doers who act—they will be blessed in their doing" (New Revised Standard Version).

69. It is my contention that biblical hermeneutics always does reflect the individual's experiences and concerns. I only wish that we would be honest about that rather than claiming an objectivity that is not possible in human beings.

70. 1 Corinthians 13:12 (King James Version).

71. James H. Evans, *We Have Been Believers: An African-American Systematic Theology* (Minneapolis: Fortress, 1992), 45.

literarily disparate and disconnected parts. Part of this strategy of harmonization functions rhetorically to disarm texts that black exegetes find objectionable, such as those used to argue for slavery. By interpreting the *Haustafeln* in light of examples from the life of Jesus or Bible verses like Galatians 3:28,[72] for example, African Americans found ways to detoxify such codes of subordination.[73] By ignoring this tendency to harmonize scripture, one also misses the important rhetorical function of that harmonization.

While black churches would agree with Western scholarship in their shared intention to seek truth, they would prefer the route of the believer to that of the skeptic. The deeply evangelical theology of many black churches tends to produce Bible readers who take church tradition and oral tradition very seriously, including their own oral traditions of interpretation in sermon and song. Indeed, another indication of the importance of these oral traditions is the call-and-response that routinely accompanies sermons in African American churches, forming a kind of contemporaneous oral commentary upon the sermon and on the entire worship experience. These same black churches are filled with Bible readers who would never seriously question the divinely inspired character of scripture, nor would they hesitate to use words like "inerrant" or "infallible" when describing it, although what is meant by those terms might ultimately be debated.

Other elements of current biblical scholarship make it a tough sell in the black community. For example, Rudolph Bultmann's quest to demythologize the New Testament, in order to bring it in line with the post-Enlightenment West's quest to elevate rationality, would find little resonance in churches where the congregants have had to battle the post-

72. This is a text often regarded as a declaration of radical human equality across lines of class, nationality, and gender. Galatians 3:28: "There is no longer Jew or Greek, there is no longer slave or free, there is no longer male and female; for all of you are one in Christ Jesus" (New Revised Standard Version).

73. Reading troublesome texts through those that emphasize equality and liberation (by harmonizing scriptures across whole books or even whole testaments) is one method black exegetes have used to deemphasize texts that might be interpreted to limit gender or racial equality. As such, harmonizing scripture fulfills an important function unrecognized in historical-critical methods, which see each book and testament as the product of particular times and locations, unable to be reconciled or studied together. See, for example, Renita J. Weems, "Reading Her Way through the Struggle: African American Women and the Bible," in Felder, *Stony the Road We Trod*, 55–77; and Martin, "The *Haustafeln*," 206–31.

Enlightenment West in its fascination with absurd and arbitrary racial hierarchies masquerading as rational and impartial science.[74] It was precisely to the emotive immediacy of worship, and to personal identification with the mythos of the text and the person of Jesus, that African Americans repaired when wounded and excluded by a modernity that purported to be objective but was merely racist. African Americans have had too much trouble with the absurdity and tragicomic nature of modernity to embrace it as enthusiastically as the rest of the West has done.[75]

Interpersonal Interpretation

Drawing on M. A. K. Halliday's work in sociolinguistics, Brian Blount suggests that a limitation of normative biblical scholarship as currently practiced in the academy is that only the textual (or grammatical) and ideational (or conceptual) aspects of the biblical text are considered. He would advocate adding a third plane of evaluation for the work of hermeneutics: the interpersonal. The interpersonal aspect of linguistics takes

74. Cain Hope Felder argues that categories of race based upon skin color and "theories that claim to provide a 'scientific' basis for white racism" are "peculiar post-Enlightenment by-products of modern civilization." Cain Hope Felder, "Race, Racism, and the Biblical Narratives," in Felder, *Stony the Road We Trod*, 128. More recently, the Human Genome Project has questioned the validity of complexion- or characteristic-based racial designations. Rather, race as we understand it is a social/ historical construction much more than it is a genetic reality. Moreover, evolutionary findings suggesting that modern humans all descend from African ancestors make racial prejudices against people of African descent particularly ridiculous from a genetic standpoint. Natalie Angier, "Do Races Differ? Not Really, Genes Show," *New York Times*, August 22 2000; Angier, "Race No More Than Skin Deep, DNA Indicates," *Cleveland Plain Dealer*, August 22, 2000; J. M. Ledgard, "We Are All African Now," *Intelligent Life*, Summer 2009, 66–71.

75. Cornel West identifies the roots of racism in the Enlightenment's elevation of the West as superior to the rest of the world and in its tendency to see others through its own "normative gaze"—analysis that sees Western standards of intellect, culture, and beauty as normative, and, therefore, the rest of the world as deficient. Blacks' encounters with this normative gaze, and the consequences of the powerful and painful racism it spawned, have been tragicomic in their arbitrary nature. In many ways, black cultural life is the consequence of communal attempts (from the extremes of nihilism to the life affirming) to survive in the face of racism's powerful, potentially deforming pressures. Cornel West, *Prophesy Deliverance! An Afro-American Revolutionary Christianity*, 1st ed. (Philadelphia: Westminster, 1982), 27–44, 47–65.

into account the hearer's social location and the context of the speech event. According to Halliday, "text, as a written speech event . . . does not have a single, closed meaning, but a 'meaning potential'"[76] that is discovered only when the context of the speech event and the social location of the hearer are evaluated.

The Bible is the central text of Western cultural, literary, and even political development. Throughout history, it has demonstrated its power to shape communities, to fuel social movements, and to inspire individuals and groups to feats of tremendous bravery or sacrifice. The Bible has also been appropriated to validate slavery, racism, and gender oppression throughout history. Biblical hermeneutics is not just the act of making meaning of a text; it is also the act of channeling that text's amazing power to indict, to inspire, to chastise, or to create within the communities that consider the text authoritative. Blount argues that rather than being "scientific," "accurate," or "neutral," traditional methods of historical-critical and literary analysis are "sociologically and linguistically restrictive, and, therefore, ideological"[77] because they exclude the marginal members of society. Making his case that "generations of Western scholarship have . . . discourage[d] social and political interpretation,"[78] of the New Testament, Blount demonstrates that the hermeneutical paradigms of scholars like Bultmann are not the universal projects they were purported to be but are contextualized by the scholar's own historical and cultural situation.[79]

For Blount, consideration of the interpersonal aspects of hermeneutics serves as a corrective for interpretive schema in which "the dominant culture too often presents only its interpretations as 'correct' or 'scientific.'"[80] His work outlines the sociolinguistic mechanism by which the interpreter's cultural context influences the hermeneutical enterprise. He recommends a means by which interpretation from the center of society and from its margins can be kept from veering off into unrecognizable and irreconcilable extremes. He would hold all hermeneutics to the standards of Halliday's linguistic triad: they must be true to the textual and ideational aspects of the biblical text, thereby satisfying historical-critical and literary

76. M. A. K. Halliday, as quoted in Blount, *Cultural Interpretation*, 15.

77. Blount, *Cultural Interpretation*, 3.

78. Ibid., 5.

79. See, for example, ibid., 34–36, for a critique of the limitations of Bultmann's project of demythologizing the New Testament.

80. Blount, *Cultural Interpretation*, 16.

methods of biblical scholarship, but they must also be true to the interpersonal aspects of the interpretive community, as liberationists require.

For it is from its particularity, from its roots in African American experience, that black biblical interpretation draws its life. Vincent Wimbush asks, "What might happen if . . . African American experience . . . were the starting and focal point for reading, for interpretation? What if the reading of and thinking about the Bible . . . were problematized and read through and in connection with African American experience?"[81]

Indeed. What if? What if we posit that black people read the Bible as though they were authoritative sources within themselves and within their communities? What if we acknowledge that finding a different meaning in the Bible than the majority culture did (particularly on issues like slavery) had a survival advantage for black people? What if we suggest that black people interpreted the Bible without significant recourse to what others in biblical studies or hermeneutics were doing in their respective, but separate, worlds? What if we simply admit that too often, Western scholarship and the unknown bards of black biblical interpretation set about distinctively different tasks, in distinctively different ways? What if we admit that when it comes to biblical interpretation, blacks and whites, men and women, believers and nonbelievers, sometimes speak different languages, requiring an act of translation and interpretation to be mutually understood?

African American hermeneutics has moved from a first generation of scholars like Charles Copher, whose work centered on the identification of Africans in the biblical narrative, to a second generation of scholars like Brian Blount, Allen Callahan, Cain Hope Felder, and Vincent Wimbush. Blount, Callahan, Felder, and Wimbush represent the second generation of African American biblical scholarship in that, armed with the tools of historical-critical method, they are able to mount a credible critique of the scholarly suppositions of the (predominantly white) academy in ways that their less well-trained forebears of the nineteenth century, like Maria Stewart or Jarena Lee, were unable to do. Blount, Callahan, Felder, and Wimbush all combine elements of historical-critical method with considerations of the history of interpretation and reception of the biblical texts in question. They regard not only the ancient communities of the Bible but also contemporary communities of faith as important resources. That

81. Wimbush, "Reading Darkness, Reading Scriptures", 9–10.

is, they bring their exegeses into dialogue with contemporary faith communities and thereby highlight the interpersonal aspects of the hermeneutic enterprise. In so doing, they take seriously the impact of their texts, and the history of reception of those texts, upon specific contemporary communities.

Doers of the Word

In some ways, African American hermeneutics sees the Bible as a mirror, in that in the Bible, at times African Americans see themselves as if in a mirror. Actually, it would be more accurate to say that African American hermeneutics brings a heavy load of black life to every engagement with the biblical narrative. The social locations, experiences, and concerns of black people are all inseparable from what African American exegetes are able to make of that which they have read in the Bible. Although itself the product of particular times, particular regions, and particular social and theological concerns, the Bible nonetheless also contains, for many readers and interpreters, material very relevant to their own times, places, and concerns.

It would be difficult to overestimate the centrality of the Bible to African American social, literary, and cultural formation. Almost from the beginning of their sojourn in America, black people made the Bible their particular possession. Inspired by the text that seemed to embody all that the slavocracy sought to deny them—not just literacy or humanity, but divine right—blacks sang, sermonized, troped and embellished upon the biblical narrative, weaving their way into and out of it, returning to it again and again. They saw themselves in the Bible: they saw parallels to their own lives and to the oppression they endured. They were the Israelites, struggling under Pharaoh's lash. The Negro spiritual could ask, "Were you there when they crucified my Lord?"[82] of the moment of Jesus's crucifixion on Calvary, fully expecting that the hearers would draw enough from their own well of alienation, disappointment, and loss to inscribe themselves imaginatively into the passion narrative. The unknown African Americans who composed the spiritual could ask, "Were you there?" because, as theologian James Cone notes, "they found themselves by his side."[83]

82. "Were You There?" in *Songs of Zion*, ed. J. Jefferson Cleveland and Verolga Nix (Nashville: Abingdon, 1981), 126.
83. Cone, *The Spirituals and the Blues*, 49.

Some would argue that it is precisely from the disadvantaged in society, from "the man with his back against the wall,"[84] that the truest biblical interpretations may emerge. Because Jesus's own origins were with the disadvantaged of his society, and because his people were suffering under Roman oppression, it is essential "to inquire into the content of [Jesus's] teaching with reference to the disinherited and the underprivileged."[85] It may very well be that here African American hermeneutics and historical-critical biblical scholarship converge: considering the history of black people may help us better examine the life of Jesus and contextualize him as a member of an oppressed minority within the powerful Roman empire.

In the chapters that follow, I consider Maria Stewart's approach to scripture and her race- and gender-specific concerns, allowing each to interpret the other just as jazz improvisation interprets a melodic line. I inquire into the hermeneutics of a woman "with [her] back against the wall." Stewart's choices of biblical allusions reflect not only her concerns but also her self-understanding, her social location, and her view of history. I let the mirror of those choices reflect her theology and ideology, and as I examine the image those choices form, I hope to see Stewart in even sharper focus. Finally, I analyze Maria Stewart's performance of the Bible—both as glossolalia and as heteroglossia—so that her deeper meanings might be interpreted, heard, and understood by successive generations.

The Bible is more than a touchstone for black culture; it is its Rosetta stone: the key to interpreting the meaning African Americans have made of their lives in the New World. Just as the Rosetta stone provided the key to interpreting an unknown African language because it contained tongues both known (Greek) and unknown (Egyptian hieroglyphs) to its European interpreters, so the Bible provides one key to interpreting the deeper meanings of many of the cultural productions of African Americans. Most often, from the earliest slave narratives to Toni Morrison's novels,[86] from the spirituals to gospel or even some rap music,[87] from the political mani-

---

84. Howard Thurman, *Jesus and the Disinherited* (Richmond, IN: Friends United, 1981), 13.

85. Ibid., 15.

86. Morrison's novels frequently expand upon biblical themes or allusions. See, for example, A. Smith, "Toni Morrison's *Song of Solomon*," 107–15.

87. Numerous authors have analyzed the use of biblical themes in African American music. See, for example, Gilkes, "'Go and Tell Mary and Martha,'" 536–81; James Abbington, "Biblical Themes in the R. Nathaniel Dett Collection: Religious Folk-

festos of David Walker to those of Martin Luther King Jr. and even those of Louis Farrakhan,[88] that meaning is expressed scripturally.[89]

David Walker's Appeal, like the later writings of Walker's student Maria Stewart, alternates between references to scripture and republican rhetoric in constructing his case for the rights of black people,[90] in ways foreshadowing the work of Martin Luther King Jr. and almost every subsequent black political activist. Again and again, it is to the Bible that they make recourse. It is touchstone; it is the Rosetta stone. As I show in the coming chapters, it is the fount from which many cultural, political, theological, and literary streams flow.

Songs of the Negro," in Wimbush and Rosamond, *African Americans and the Bible*, 281–96; Horace Clarence Boyer, "African American Gospel Music," in Wimbush and Rosamond, *African Americans and the Bible*, 464–88; Keith D. Miller, "City Called Freedom: Biblical Metaphor in Spirituals, Gospel Lyrics, and the Civil Rights Movement," in Wimbush and Rosamond, *African Americans and the Bible*, 546–57; Mellonee Burnim, "Biblical Inspiration, Cultural Affirmation: The African American Gift of Song," in Wimbush and Rosamond, *African Americans and the Bible*, 603–15; Farah J. Griffin, "Adventures of a Black Child in Search of Her God: The Bible in the Works of Me'shell N'degeocello," in Wimbush and Rosamond, *African Americans and the Bible*, 773–81; Cheryl Kirk-Duggan, "Hot Buttered Soulful Tunes and Cold Icy Passionate Truths: The Hermeneutics of Biblical Interpolation in R & B (Rhythm & Blues)," in Wimbush and Rosamond, *African Americans and the Bible*, 782–803; and Charise Cheney, "Representin' God: Masculinity and the Use of the Bible in Rap Music," in Wimbush and Rosamond, *African Americans and the Bible*, 804–16.

88. Interestingly, in his address to the Million Man March in Washington, DC, in the fall of 1995, Nation of Islam leader Louis Farrakhan made more frequent references to the Bible than he did to the Qur'an. While Muslims claim the Bible as well as the Qur'an as sacred scripture, the frequency of Farrakhan's many quotations from the Bible may have had more to do with his audience's overwhelming familiarity with the Bible, and with the Bible's central place and unquestioned authority in African American culture, than with any concerns about the sacred canon.

89. For example, in his autobiography, itself generously sprinkled with Bible verses, Olaudah Equiano argued for the nobility of his African people on the basis of their similarities to the ancient Israelites. Olaudah Equiano, "The Interesting Narrative of the Life of Olaudah Equiano, or Gustavus Vassa, the African, Written by Himself," in *The Norton Anthology of African American Literature*, ed. Henry Louis Gates and Nellie Y. McKay (New York: W. W. Norton, 1997), 138–64.

90. David Walker, *David Walker's Appeal to the Coloured Citizens of the World*, ed. Peter P. Hinks (University Park: Pennsylvania State University Press, 2000).

CHAPTER I

"Religion and the Pure Principles of Morality"

*T*o MAKE THE CASE that Maria Stewart's use of biblical allusions in her speeches and essays is both plentiful and thoughtful, it is helpful to track such allusions in a representative sample of her work. Stewart's essay "Religion and the Pure Principles of Morality" is printed here, along with a running commentary on her use of the Bible throughout that text. The commentary in my footnotes will take note of Stewart's biblical allusions along with unusual phrases and ideas and important points in her theology and political ideology.

At times, Stewart's scriptural allusions seem almost utilitarian, as when she appears to have chosen to include a particular idea or phrase from the Bible in her essay merely because the Bible verse contains an idea or phrase that is consonant with her broader themes. Sometimes, Stewart's choice of scripture points to an idea she has stressed repeatedly and probably indicates that the text is one to which she has returned again and again in her devotional reading of the Bible. At times, however, Stewart's choice of scripture underscores a point where her political ideology and theology intersect. In identifying the scripture to which Stewart alludes, I hope to note not only the mundane appropriations but also the momentous ones that highlight connections between Stewart's political ideology and her theological concerns. While noting the mundane allusions only tells us how frequently Stewart repaired to scripture, the more momentous texts unlock important aspects of Stewart's political and theological program.

In the course of this essay, and by her appropriation of particular scripture verses and phrases, Stewart outlines several broad themes that I explore in greater detail in subsequent chapters. Stewart's concerns for black uplift and self-determination are on display here, as is her personal sense of vocation for the public career she has undertaken. At times, Stewart blurs the lines between religion and politics, as when she calls "independence" (as found in America's founding documents) a God-given gift. Frequently, Stewart chooses texts describing Israel's covenantal relationship with God as a means of making her case, as grounded in Psalms 68:31, that people of African descent are also people of a special covenant with God. Here and there, Stewart will playfully rearrange words or phrases as they appear in the biblical text to create her own emphases. Again and again, Stewart adamantly eschews violent actions on the part of her followers; this is a distinct difference from the work of her mentor, David Walker.

Through her biblical appropriations and her own words, Stewart demonstrates that her view of the role of women is the least well-developed or consistent aspect of her thought. When this first essay was written, Stewart clearly accepted the traditional view that a woman's place was (mainly or entirely) in the home, caring for her husband and raising her children. While she is sometimes inconsistent in this view, as when she advises the women in her audience to raise the money to build a high school, she nevertheless reinforces it by quoting parts of Proverbs 31, which is a fairly traditional description of a woman's work serving her household. In a later chapter, I track the evolution of Stewart's thought on questions of gender. Eventually, she comes to view women's social activism as biblically mandated, or at least historically mandated, by the deplorable conditions under which blacks lived in the United States in the nineteenth century. In this first speech, however, most of her ideas about women's equality remain undeveloped or inconsistently applied.

Ultimately, identifying Stewart's use of scripture throughout this essay allows us to approach it as a biblically literate nineteenth-century listener might have approached it: we can see Stewart's text, but at the same time, we can recognize the biblical texts upon which she relies. For Stewart, the Bible speaks not only to the historical moment about which the text was written but also to her historical moment. In her appropriation of scripture, Stewart draws analogies between the lives of the people in the Bible and the lives of her people.

As an evangelical, Stewart collapses biblical time into her present, so that the Bible, as an ancient text, can speak to her contemporary political and social situation because she believes that the same sorts of political or social situations existed in biblical times. Moreover, the biblical text is, for Stewart, also prophetic: it predicts an imminent judgment upon the slave regime and an ultimate Judgment Day for all who have ever lived. In both the imminent and the ultimate judgment, God is the actor who will bring justice. In this, by repeating the words of scripture, Stewart hopes to be heard speaking after God rather than calling down fire on her own authority.

For Stewart, to speak the words of God is to speak that which is eternally true and forever correct. In her appropriation of scripture and her predictions of coming judgment, Stewart speaks eschatologically: her hopes and expectations for her people break radically into the present, as she speaks hopefully and expectantly of a time that is yet to come. Even as she repeats the words of the ancient text, she is calling them into being over her listeners as prophetic declaration that is forever true (both in antiquity and in Stewart's day).

For evangelical believers like Stewart, the Bible is timeless in that its origin is in God and God is beyond time. As such, the entire biblical text can speak to that which is already and to that which is not yet. Indeed, the same verse can speak to that which is already and to that which is not yet. Past, present, and future are collapsed. Therefore, the ancient text can, for Stewart, also speak to her contemporary realities. Indeed, by comparing Stewart's choices of scripture and the situations to which she applies them, we can discern the contours of what she felt about her historical moment and what she expects to come of her words.

What Stewart believed about the Bible is of crucial importance here. In order to understand her deeper meanings, we must take her faith seriously and interrogate how she deployed the biblical texts, which she regarded as sacred, in works that we might otherwise be tempted to see as merely secular. Until we can read Stewart well—by taking her valuing of the Bible seriously even as she outlines her political ideology—we will hear only a political voice. When we read Stewart well, we can also appreciate her theological voice as she challenges the injustice she sees and calls down God's justice for her people.

My commentary—at times descriptive and at other times analytic—seeks to highlight both the political and theological in Stewart's words. They are, at times, intertwined and indivisible. My goal is to allow Stewart's political voice and her theological voice to be heard by taking her sources—including scripture—seriously. Not merely a rote recitation of Stewart's appropriation of scripture, the following essay and commentary lay the foundation for the analysis to come in subsequent chapters. Here I identify Stewart's biblical references; later I will analyze the more significant references to better understand Stewart's theology. Here, then, is Maria Stewart's essay "Religion and the Pure Principles of Morality," which was printed in Boston in October of 1831.

"Religion and the Pure Principles of Morality, the Sure Foundation[1] on Which We Must Build"

INTRODUCTION.

Feeling a deep solemnity of soul, in view of our wretched and degraded situation, and sensible of the gross ignorance that prevails among us,[2] I have thought proper thus publicly to express my sentiments before you.[3]

---

1. Isaiah 28:16: "Therefore thus saith the Lord GOD, Behold, I lay in Zion for a foundation a stone, a tried stone, a precious corner stone, *a sure foundation:* he that believeth shall not make haste." This selection shows Stewart's preference for Hebrew Bible references over those of the New Testament. She might easily have written that this was the "rock" upon which one must build or have alluded to any number of New Testament scriptures (Matthew 7:24, Luke 6:48, or Matthew 16:18, for example) that liken this rock of the revelation of faith in Jesus to a stone foundation for the purposes of building. She might even have chosen to make reference to any of the other New Testament uses of "foundation" (such as 1 Timothy 6:19 or 2 Timothy 2:19). Instead, however, Stewart chooses a reference from the Hebrew Bible, for which she seems to have a marked preference.

2. Here Stewart is probably referring to the "gross ignorance" that prevails among African Americans of her acquaintance. I believe that she is referring to an ignorance of their true potential as a people.

3. While Stewart may have thought it "proper" to give public speeches, there were many who did not. Indeed, her increasing insistence that she has a God-given charge to deliver these messages demonstrates that she felt the need to justify her activities.

I hope my friends will not scrutinize these pages with too severe an eye, as I have not calculated to display either elegance or taste in their composition,[4] but have merely written the meditations of my heart[5] as far as my imagination led; and have presented them before you, in order to arouse you to exertions, and to enforce upon your minds the great necessity of turning your attention to knowledge and improvement.

I was born in Hartford, Connecticut, in 1803; was left an orphan at five years of age; was bound out in a clergyman's family; had the seeds of piety and virtue early sown in my mind; but was deprived of the advantages of education, though my soul thirsted for knowledge. Left them at 15 years of age; attended Sabbath Schools until I was 20; in 1826, was married to James W. Steward [sic]; was left a widow in 1829; was, as I humbly hope and trust, brought to the knowledge of the truth, as it is in Jesus, in 1830; in 1831, made a public profession of my faith in Christ.[6]

From the moment I experienced the change,[7] I felt a strong desire, with the help and assistance of God, to devote the remainder of my days to piety and virtue, and now possess that spirit of independence,[8] that, were I called upon, I would willingly sacrifice my life for the cause of God and my brethren.

All the nations of the earth[9] are crying out for Liberty and Equality.

4. Despite her rather formulaic denial of ability, Stewart goes on to demonstrate considerable "taste [and] elegance" as well as a remarkable facility with the Bible.

5. Psalms 19:14: "Let the words of my mouth, and *the meditation of my heart*, be acceptable in thy sight, O LORD, my strength, and my redeemer." As the psalmist wrote, so Stewart repeats: may these words find favor with God. Having given a more formulaic apologia for her lack of ability, Stewart goes on to ask God's help in framing her text.

6. As this brief recitation shows, Stewart had been on her own most of her life. She was orphaned at a young age, and at fifteen she left the family of the clergyman who had taken her in. She was briefly married and soon left a widow. It is in this context — lacking the support of family — that Stewart declares her reliance upon her faith in Christ.

7. The "change" to which Stewart refers is her experience of salvation.

8. Stewart describes her receipt of a "spirit of independence." This idea is not found in the King James Version of the Bible and can only be Stewart's elevation of the democratic rhetoric of American civil religion to the level of God-given gift. If the Declaration of Independence is an object of holy writ in the American mythos, then God can similarly bless its citizens with a "spirit of independence."

9. For "all the nations of the earth," see Genesis 18:18: "Seeing that Abraham shall

Away, away with tyranny and oppression! And shall Afric's[10] sons be silent any longer? Far be it from me to recommend to you, either to kill, burn or destroy.[11] But I would strongly recommend to you, to improve your talents; let not one lie buried in the earth.[12] Show forth your powers of mind. Prove to the world, that

> Though black your skins as shades of night,
> Your hearts are pure, your souls are white.

This is the land of freedom. The press is at liberty. Every man has a right to express his opinion. Many think, because your skins are tinged with a sable hue, that you are an inferior race of beings; but God does not

---

surely become a great and mighty nation, and *all the nations of the earth* shall be blessed in him?" The phrase is also in Genesis 22:18, Genesis 26:4, Deuteronomy 14:2, Deuteronomy 28:1, Jeremiah 26:6, Jeremiah 33:9, and Jeremiah 44:8. Each occurrence is found in a text mentioning God's special relationship with Israel, as differentiated from the other nations. Ultimately, Stewart will argue that a similar covenant exists between God and those of African descent.

10. "Afric" seems to be a common nineteenth-century poetic spelling; Stewart uses it on several occasions. See, for example, Sarah Wentworth Morton, "The African Chief," or Herman Melville, "The Swamp Angel." Both contain "Afric" as a shortened form of Africa.

11. John 10:10: "The thief cometh not, but for *to steal, and to kill, and to destroy:* I am come that they might have life, and that they might have it more abundantly." Again, Stewart seems to repudiate the use of physical violence. In this text, only the enemies of Christ "kill" and "destroy." Stewart has omitted "steal" and inserted "burn." She apparently does not object to stealing, perhaps because it was considered by some to be stealing when a slave escaped his master's control. Instead of a prohibition against stealing, Stewart warns against "burn[ing]," which was a common element of slave uprisings. Here, then, she is against violence such as burning or destroying but not against self-preservation (as when one escaped from slavery).

12. Matthew 25 (and parallels): the parable of the talents. The good servant increased his talents; the poor servant merely buried his. In the original context of the Bible, the "talent" was money. However, over the years, it has come to mean any God-given ability. Stewart's use of the parable here underscores her insistence that blacks make use of their own talents and abilities rather than wait for whites to treat them fairly. She states elsewhere that she believes such behavior on the part of blacks will ultimately force whites to treat them more fairly. Unlike those who questioned blacks' abilities, Stewart believes that they have many but their talents are underutilized.

consider you as such.[13] He hath formed and fashioned[14] you in his own glorious image,[15] and hath bestowed upon you reason and strong powers of intellect.[16] He hath made you to have dominion over the beasts of the field, the fowls of the air, and the fish of the sea.[17] He hath crowned you with glory and honor; hath made you but a little lower than the angels;[18] and according to the Constitution of these United States, he

13. This is likely an oblique reference to the Ethiopian prophecy, Psalms 68:31: "Princes shall come out of Egypt; Ethiopia shall soon stretch out her hands unto God." Stewart also repudiates the idea that blackness is evidence of a curse from God, as some of the slavocracy argued in an effort to enlist scripture to justify the domination of people of African descent. In answer to accusations that the so-called mark of Cain (Genesis 4:1–16) and curse of Ham (Genesis 9:18–27) indicate God's displeasure with Africans, Stewart responds with the Ethiopian prophecy. With it, she argues that a special relationship exists between God and the people of Africa.

14. Psalms 119:73: "Thy hands have *made me and fashioned me:* give me understanding, that I may learn thy commandments."

15. Genesis 1:26: "And God said, Let us make man *in our image,* after our likeness." Here, Stewart inserts "glorious" to further describe the image in which Africans were formed. Refuting those who argued that Africans were the result of a second, inferior creation, Stewart includes them among those created by God "in the beginning"—as described in Genesis 1.

16. In response to those Enlightenment thinkers (like Thomas Jefferson) who questioned African Americans' ability to participate fully in literate civilization, Stewart argues that they are possessed not only of "reason" but of "strong powers of intellect." Here as elsewhere, Stewart continues her thesis that those of "sable hue" are in no way inferior to those of other races.

17. Genesis 1:26: "And God said, Let us make man in our image, after our likeness: and let them have *dominion over the fish of the sea, and over the fowl of the air,* and *over the cattle,* and over all the earth, and over every creeping thing that creepeth upon the earth." Stewart brackets her claim that people of African descent have "strong powers of intellect" with two references to the creation as detailed in Genesis 1, thereby underscoring her contention that people of African descent shared that moment of creation with those of the other races of the earth. This shared creation imparts a shared dominion over the earth. Although as slaves they are ruled by others, this was not God's intention. Rather, people of African descent ought to share rulership and dominion over the earth with all of the other peoples of the earth.

18. Psalms 8:5: "For thou hast made him *a little lower than the angels, and hast crowned him with glory and honour.*" Also, Hebrews 2:9: "But we see Jesus, who was made *a little lower than the angels for* the suffering of death, *crowned with glory and honour;* that he by the grace of God should taste death for every man." In these biblical texts and in Stewart's use of them, humanity's place is an exalted one.

hath made all men free and equal.[19] Then why should one worm say to another, "Keep you down there, while I sit up yonder; for I am better than thou?"[20] It is not the color of the skin that makes the man, but it is the principles formed within the soul.[21]

Many will suffer for pleading the cause of oppressed Africa, and I shall glory in being one of her martyrs;[22] for I am firmly persuaded, that the

19. Here Stewart mistakes the reference. The Constitution makes no use of the term "slavery" until it is abolished by amendment, and the promise of equality that she has in mind was not to be found there at the time that her words were written. But rather than the United States Constitution, Stewart has the Declaration of Independence in mind: "We hold these truths to be self-evident, that all men are created equal, that they are endowed by their Creator with certain unalienable Rights, that among these are Life, Liberty and the pursuit of Happiness." Thomas Jefferson, "Declaration of Independence," July 4, 1776, http://www.archives.gov/exhibit_hall/charters_of_freedom/declaration/declaration_transcription.html.

Note that Stewart has added "free" to the sentence. All, in her mind, are created both equal and free by God. Again, one is reminded of the "spirit of independence" that Stewart felt she had received from God. If independence is given by God, then no human has the right to enslave another. According to this line of reasoning, slavery is in fact a sin not only against the enslaved but also against God, who gives freedom to all. As is often the case, Stewart has combined republican rhetoric with scripture, blurring the line between political and religious concerns.

20. Job 25:6: "How much less man, that is *a worm?* and the son of man, which is *a worm?*" Also, James 2:3: "And ye have respect to him that weareth the gay clothing, and say unto him, *Sit thou here in a good place; and say to the poor, Stand thou there, or sit here under my footstool.*" Here Stewart alludes to these texts rather than quoting them outright, combining a reference from the Hebrew Bible with another from the New Testament. The text from James is a rebuke to those who treat rich believers better than poor ones. Stewart extends this rebuff beyond class to race, adding (by her allusion to the text from James) that "it is not the color of the skin that makes the man." It is also interesting that, having just described humans as "a little lower than angels," Stewart now calls them "worms." They are, on the one hand, God-like in their abilities, while at the same time, worm-like in their mistreatment of one another.

21. Notice how similar this statement is to Martin Luther King Jr.'s dream that his "children will one day live in a nation where they will not be judged by the color of their skin but by the content of their character." Yet more than a century after Stewart expressed this idea as fact, it was still primarily a dream to the African Americans to whom King spoke. Martin Luther King Jr., "I Have a Dream," in *I Have a Dream: Writings and Speeches that Changed the World,* ed. James Melvin Washington, 101–6 (San Francisco: HarperSanFranciso, 1992). In this context, Stewart's pronouncement is both prescriptive and prophetic.

22. The theme of potential martyrdom is repeated frequently in Stewart's writings.

God in whom I trust is able to protect me from the rage and malice of mine enemies, and from them that will rise up against me;[23] and if there is no other way for me to escape, he is able to take me to himself, as he did the most noble, fearless, and undaunted David Walker.[24]

NEVER WILL VIRTUE, KNOWLEDGE, AND TRUE POLITENESS BEGIN TO FLOW, TILL THE PURE PRINCIPLES OF RELIGION AND MORALITY ARE PUT INTO FORCE.

MY RESPECTED FRIENDS,

I feel almost unable to address you; almost incompetent to perform the task; and, at times, I have felt ready to exclaim, O that my head were waters, and mine eyes a fountain of tears, that I might weep day and night,

---

She was very sensitive to the dangers of proclaiming her message and very aware of the dangers of continued activism.

23. Similar to Psalms 18:48: "He delivereth me from *mine enemies:* yea, thou liftest me up above *those that rise up against me:* thou hast delivered me from the violent man." This is a common theme of deliverance in the scriptures. See, for example, Psalms 27:1–3: "The LORD is my light and my salvation; whom shall I fear? the LORD is the strength of my life; of whom shall I be afraid? When the wicked, even *mine enemies* and my foes, came upon me to eat up my flesh, they stumbled and fell. Though an host should encamp against me, my heart shall not fear: though war should rise against me, in this will I be confident." Such allusions to the unjust opposition suffered by biblical patriarchs underscore Stewart's point that she is fighting on the side of God.

24. David Walker, who taught Stewart, died in 1830. Peter P. Hinks, introduction to Walker, *Appeal to the Coloured Citizens,* xxiii. Stewart began public speaking in 1831. The circumstances of Walker's death were mysterious, but it occurred at about the same time that his radical abolitionist publication, *David Walker's Appeal to the Coloured Citizens of the World,* reached the South. He was found dead not long afterward, sparking speculation that the two events were connected.

This reference is similar to the proclamation of the three Hebrew boys in response to King Nebuchadnezzar's threats in Daniel 3:16–18: "Shadrach, Meshach, and Abednego, answered and said to the king, O Nebuchadnezzar, we are not careful to answer thee in this matter. If it be so, our God whom we serve *is able to deliver us* from the burning fiery furnace, and he will deliver us out of thine hand, O king. *But if not,* be it known unto thee, O king, that we will not serve thy gods, nor worship the golden image which thou hast set up." Though Stewart proclaims God's ability to deliver her out of trouble, she acknowledges that it may be God's will for her to die for this cause as David Walker did.

for the transgressions of the daughters of my people.[25] Truly, my heart's desire and prayer is, that Ethiopia might stretch forth her hands unto God.[26] But we have a great work to do. Never, no, never will the chains of slavery and ignorance burst,[27] till we become united as one, and cultivate among ourselves the pure principles of piety, morality, and virtue. I am sensible of my ignorance; but such knowledge as God has given to me, I impart to you.[28] I am sensible of former prejudices;[29] but it is high time for prejudices and animosities to cease from among us. I am sensible of

25. Jeremiah 9:1: *"Oh that my head were waters, and mine eyes a fountain of tears, that I might weep day and night for the slain of the daughter of my people!"* Note that Stewart replaces "slain" with "transgressions"—that is, that she has wept over the sins of her people. Stewart has assumed the mantle of a prophet here.

26. Psalms 68:31: "Princes shall come out of Egypt; *Ethiopia shall soon stretch out her hands unto God."* This reference was the central text of Ethiopianism. Here it is Stewart's prayer.

27. For Stewart, slavery and ignorance are intertwined in that they are both part of the same problem—the failure to recognize the true status of people of African descent. Stewart believes that both her people and the slavocracy are ignorant of this true status before God.

28. Stewart's protests that she has little or no knowledge to impart sound strikingly like the disciples' comments when approached for money in Acts 3:6: "Then Peter said, Silver and gold have I none; *but such as I have give I thee:* In the name of Jesus Christ of Nazareth rise up and walk." They had no money per se but something infinitely more desirable to the one making the entreaty. No doubt Stewart believes her message is of similar import to her audience.

She may also want to suggest her own impecuniosity. In the 1879 reprinting of her speeches, *Meditations from the Pen of Maria Stewart,* Stewart complains forthrightly about her poverty (and the occasional failure of those who had benefited from her teaching ministry to support her financially) in ways that she had not done in the previously printed version of her corpus. While, by the use of the text from Acts 3:6, she only hints that she does not have "silver and gold," she protests her lack of money quite clearly in her later version. See, for example, Richardson, *Maria W. Stewart,* 98–99, 104.

29. To what prejudices is she referring? They could be race or gender related. As a black woman, she would have faced both. However, I believe that she is referring to intraracial or intragender jealousies and to opposition from those she regards as her people. She notes that it is time for these "prejudices and animosities . . . among us" to end. That is, they should end among her people.

In her call for unity among people of African descent, Stewart is striking a protonationalist theme. In calling for black unity and self-sufficiency, she shares the central aims of what would later be expressed as Black Nationalism and, in the international context, Pan-Africanism.

exposing myself to calumny and reproach;[30] but shall I, for fear of feeble man who shall die, hold my peace?[31] Shall I for fear of scoffs and frowns, refrain my tongue? Ah, no! I speak as one that must give an account at the awful bar of God;[32] I speak as a dying mortal, to dying mortals.[33] O, ye daughters of Africa,[34] awake! Awake![35] Arise! No longer sleep nor

30. In taking the stage to speak publicly, Stewart was indeed taking a risk. She was doing what was not a commonly accepted activity for women.

31. In measuring her fear of people's opposition against her obligation to God, Stewart suggests Acts 5:27–29, where leaders of the early church are persecuted for preaching the Gospel: "And when they had brought them, they set them before the council: and the high priest asked them, Saying, Did not we straitly command you that ye should not teach in this name? . . . Then Peter and the other apostles answered and said, *We ought to obey God rather than men.*" Stewart also perhaps suggests two parallel verses from the Gospels, Matthew 10:28, "And fear not them which kill the body, but are not able to kill the soul: but rather fear him which is able to destroy both soul and body in hell," and Luke 12:5, "But I will forewarn you whom ye shall fear: Fear him, which after he hath killed hath power to cast into hell; yea, I say unto you, Fear him." That is to say, she ought to fear more for her soul in the next life than for her popularity in this one.

32. The "awful bar of God" is the bar, or place of God's judgment, of humanity, "awful" in the sense of "inspiring awe." This makes reference to what is elsewhere called the "great and terrible day of the Lord." It will be great for those whom God vindicates and terrible for all others. In calling the bar "awful," Stewart is not saying that she has anything to fear from it. Clearly, she expects to be among the vindicated elect.

33. Here Stewart accepts no gender-, class-, or race-based impediment to her message. Her credentials are her humanity. In this, she claims equality with other mortal humans on the basis of her own humanity and mortality.

34. Stewart invokes this imagery, similar to *"daughters of Zion"* (Song of Solomon 3:11, Isaiah 3:16, 3:17, 4:4), *"daughters of Judah"* (Psalms 48:11, 97:8), or *"daughters of Israel"* (Deuteronomy 20:17, Judges 11:40, 2 Samuel 1:24), when she calls out to the *"daughters of Africa"* as a new chosen people, a people of promise before God. Indeed, her many references to "her people" suggest that she intends to address African Americans with these phrases. In this she follows her mentor, David Walker, whose *Appeal* was addressed to the "Coloured" citizens of the world, particularly those in the United States. Here and throughout her texts, Stewart refers to her people (meaning African Americans) as the *"daughters of Africa,"* the *"daughters of [her] people,"* and the *"daughters of our land,"* while referring to white men and women as "Americans." In so doing, she continues the theological distinction she hopes to draw between America, as Babylon—place of sin—and Africa, which, according to Psalms 68:31, was the locus of God's ultimate redemption.

35. *"Awake, awake"* is found in several places. Judges 5:12: *"Awake, awake, Deborah: awake, awake, utter a song: arise, Barak, and lead thy captivity captive, thou son of*

slumber,[36] but distinguish yourselves. Show forth to the world that you are endowed with noble and exalted faculties. O, ye daughters of Africa! What have ye done to immortalize your names beyond the grave?[37] What examples have ye set before the rising generation? What foundations have ye laid for generations yet unborn? Where are our union and

---

Abinoam." Isaiah 51:9: "*Awake, awake*, put on strength, O arm of the LORD; awake, as in the ancient days, in the generations of old. Art thou not it that hath cut Rahab, and wounded the dragon?" Isaiah 51:17: "*Awake, awake*, stand up, O Jerusalem, which hast drunk at the hand of the LORD the cup of his fury; thou hast drunken the dregs of the cup of trembling, and wrung them out." Isaiah 52:1: "*Awake, awake*; put on thy strength, O Zion; put on thy beautiful garments, O Jerusalem, the holy city: for henceforth there shall no more come into thee the uncircumcised and the unclean."

This is a cry of alarm and a call to battle, as one might rouse an army. However, Stewart's battle cry is not to slay the slavocracy but for her people to "distinguish yourselves." Stewart does not continue the quotation to include "*put on your strength,*" which might be understood as a call to arms, or to dress in battle garb. Stewart always stops short of making a call to physical arms (unlike her mentor, David Walker). Instead, she seems here to call for a mental or moral wakefulness. Even when she uses scripture referring to battle, she qualifies it so that it is clearly a moral (rather than physical) battle to which she refers.

36. Psalms 121:4: "Behold, he that keepeth Israel shall *neither slumber nor sleep.*" Psalms 132:4: "I will not give *sleep* to mine eyes, or *slumber* to mine eyelids." Proverbs 6:4: "Give not *sleep* to thine eyes, *nor slumber* to thine eyelids." Proverbs 6:10: "Yet a little *sleep*, a little *slumber*, a little folding of the hands to sleep." Proverbs 24:33: "Yet a little *sleep*, a little *slumber*, a little folding of the hands to sleep." Isaiah 5:27: "None shall be weary nor stumble among them; none shall *slumber nor sleep*; neither shall the girdle of their loins be loosed, nor the latchet of their shoes be broken." That Stewart puts "sleep" before "slumber" in her text (which is the reverse of the word order in the biblical references) suggests that at times Stewart may have been working from memory rather than from a printed Bible. While the first of these texts notes that God does not sleep on the job of guarding Israel, the subsequent texts listed here all tell the believer not to be caught sleeping. God does not sleep; the people of God are also called to be alert, watchful, lest they be overtaken. Stewart has extended her "Awake, awake" metaphor with some antisleeping allusions. Clearly, Stewart believes that her people have fallen asleep on the job.

37. Stewart may refer to her own immortality in these words. Producing, proclaiming, and then publishing this text are the ways that she has "immortalized [her] name beyond the grave." Despite her coy protestations elsewhere, given her exertions to have these words disseminated widely, and given her frequent comments on the risk of martyrdom because of them, it seems likely that she is well aware of the potential effect of her words, both spoken and written.

love? And where is our sympathy, that weeps at another's wo,[38] and hides the faults we see? And our daughters, where are they? Blushing in innocence and virtue?[39] And our sons, do they bid fair to become crowns of glory to our hoary heads?[40] Where is the parent who is conscious of having faithfully discharged his duty, and at the last awful day of account, shall be able to say, here, Lord, is thy poor, unworthy servant, and the children thou hast given me?[41] And where are the children that will arise, and call them blessed?[42] Alas, O God! Forgive me if I speak amiss; the minds of our tender babes are tainted as soon as they are born; they go

38. This is probably meant to be "woe." The instruction to weep at others' woes suggests Romans 12:15: "Rejoice with them that do rejoice, and weep with them that weep."

39. Here Stewart seems to expect African American women to fulfill at least some of the tenets of the Cult of True Womanhood in their "innocence and virtue." Nevertheless, in her defenses of her own forthrightness, she argues that the expectations of the Cult of True Womanhood should not extend to her because she is on a mission from God.

40. Here Stewart combines the ideas of two scriptures, Proverbs 16:31, "The *hoary head* is a *crown of glory*, if it be found in the way of righteousness," and Proverbs 17:6, "Children's children are the *crown* of old men; and *the glory* of children are their fathers." By combining elements of the two texts, Stewart suggests that it is good to have gray hair (a "hoary head") if that hair indicates that one's life has been spent raising children (and grandchildren) who serve God.

41. Again and again, Stewart refers to Judgment Day, when God will judge each person's life. Here, even parents are judged based upon their care of the children God has given them. Such references to the Judgment Day only serve to intensify Stewart's apocalyptic tone.

Stewart's words also resemble those of Luke 17:7, "So likewise ye, when ye shall have done all those things which are commanded you, say, We are *unprofitable servants:* we have done that which was our duty to do." Although these parents have arrived safely at the judgment and have managed to bring their children with them (that is, they have led their children into the faith), they are but unprofitable or unworthy servants because they have done only that which was their duty.

42. Regarding parents (particularly mothers) blessed by children who rise up to praise them, see Genesis 30:13: "And Leah said, Happy am I, for the daughters will *call me blessed:* and she called his name Asher"; Proverbs 31:28: "Her children *arise* up, and *call her blessed;* her husband also, and he praiseth her"; and Luke 1:48: "For he hath regarded the low estate of his handmaiden: for, behold, from henceforth all generations *shall call me blessed.*" Note, however, that Stewart uses the gender-inclusive "parent" rather than the more gender-specific "mother" or "father." Regarding an inheritance of blessing, see Psalms 72:17: "His name shall endure for ever: his name shall be con-

astray, as it were, from the womb.[43] Where is the maiden who will blush at vulgarity? And where is the youth who has written upon his manly brow a thirst for knowledge; whose ambitious mind soars above trifles, and longs for the time to come,[44] when he shall redress the wrongs of his father, and plead the cause of his brethren?[45] Did the daughters of our land[46] possess a delicacy of manners, combined with gentleness and

---

tinued as long as the sun: and men shall be blessed in him: all nations shall *call him blessed*." Malachi 3:12: "And all nations shall *call you blessed*: for ye shall be a delightsome land, saith the LORD of hosts."

43. Psalms 58:3: "The wicked are estranged *from the womb: they go astray as soon as they be born*, speaking lies." Note that while Stewart reverses the word order, she restates most of this text. This reversal doesn't seem significant, however. Also Isaiah 53:6: "All we like sheep have *gone astray*; we have turned every one to his own way; and the LORD hath laid on him the iniquity of us all."

44. The reference to the *"time to come"* is not always apocalyptic in scripture. Sometimes it refers to a vague or indeterminate future time, not necessarily associated with the end of time or with the time of judgment. However, the phrase appears quite frequently. See, for example, Genesis 30:33, Exodus 13:14, Deuteronomy 6:20, Joshua 4:6, Joshua 4:21, Joshua 22:24, Joshua 22:27, Joshua 22:28, Proverbs 31:25, Isaiah 30:8, Isaiah 42:23, and 1 Timothy 6:19. (Though this phrase occurs in the New Testament, it is primarily associated with the Hebrew Bible. Most of Stewart's references and imagery are from the Hebrew Bible rather than the New Testament.) Here, however, Stewart indicates her expectation that there will be a "time to come" when the wrongs of her people are redressed. As in any eschatological tableau, Stewart expects this time will come for both those who are ready for the judgment and those who are not. For Stewart, women demonstrate their readiness by moral superiority—by "blush[ing] at vulgarity"—and men show their readiness by their "manly thirst for knowledge" and soaring ambition. The gender roles that Stewart describes here are quite traditional.

45. For *"plead . . . cause,"* see 1 Samuel 24:15; Psalms 35:1, 43:1, 74:22, and 119:154; Proverbs 22:23, 23:11, and 31:9; Jeremiah 30:13 50:34, and 51:36; and Micah 7:9. It is the righteous who plead the cause of the unjustly accused. In this case, blacks are expected to plead the cause of those being unfairly treated in their community.

46. Stewart uses phrases like *"daughters of our land,"* and *"daughters of my people,"* interchangeably with *"daughters of Africa"* to distinguish them from whites, whom she simply calls Americans. Interestingly, here Stewart calls for men to have ambitious minds longing for knowledge, while she calls for women to have delicate manners, gentleness, and dignity. Did she not possess both? (Would she have argued for gentleness of manners in others, for example, if she didn't believe that she possessed it?) Despite the evidence of her life and writings, which strongly suggests that Stewart sought and received some education, she nevertheless resorts to a fairly trite separation of sex roles in this passage. If women receive education, it is for the sake of the next generation: the children must be taught. Over time, and over the course of her

dignity; did their pure minds hold vice in abhorrence and contempt, did they frown when their ears were polluted with its vile accents, would not their influence become powerful? Would not our brethren fall in love with their virtues? Their souls would become fired with a holy zeal for freedom's cause.[47] They would become ambitious to distinguish themselves. They would become proud to display their talents. Able advocates would arise in our defense.[48] Knowledge would begin to flow, and the

---

speeches, her view of what is appropriate for women will expand, slightly and slowly. It is, at times, uneven.

47. Although there is little extant evidence of Stewart's direct Methodist or Holiness Church involvement, this passage sounds strongly influenced by Wesleyan theology on sanctification. Stewart argues that should African American women live more virtuous and holy lives, they would influence others who would become *"fired with a holy zeal."* "Fire" and "zeal" are both ideas deeply imbedded in Holiness teaching and its emphasis upon the action of the fire of the Holy Spirit to inspire, cleanse, and empower believers. Stewart's mentor, David Walker, was a Methodist, first at the African Church in Charleston, South Carolina, which was part of the nascent African Methodist Episcopal denomination. Later, Walker joined a Methodist church in Boston. Perhaps the Wesleyan theology suggested by this passage is evidence of Walker's influence. Hinks, introduction to Walker, *Appeal to the Coloured Citizens,* xix–xxiii.

This passage also shows the tenets of sentimentalism, which emphasized the role of women as the "gentler sex," whose influence was expected to produce gentility in the men and children who were exposed to them. Sentimentalism, as described in the popular fiction of the day, "emphasized the cultivation of sensibility, the glorification of virtue, the preservation of family life, the revival of religion, and the achievement of a utopian society." Frances Smith Foster, *Witnessing Slavery: The Development of Ante-Bellum Slave Narratives,* Contributions in Afro-American and African Studies (Westport, CT: Greenwood, 1979), 64.

Finally, Stewart advocates a "holy zeal for freedom's cause," again intermingling categories others might see as separate: she joins the religious ("holy zeal") to the political ("freedom"). For her, the pursuit of a political virtue, freedom, is an element of spiritual vocation.

48. The Cult of True Womanhood argued that women, as the sensitive sex, had a responsibility to inspire men and train children in the appreciation of virtue and culture. The perverse logic of the scheme is what Stewart is arguing here: if society lacks an appreciation for virtue and culture, then women must not be doing their jobs to inspire and promote them. The flaw in her circular thinking is that she must blame those same women who are without "able advocates," since the advocates' absence must be the fault of these same women and of their inability to inspire others by their strong character. The Cult of True Womanhood was ultimately a trap for women, for whom it provided more penalties than protections. Unfortunately, however, it was a trap into which Stewart occasionally fell.

chains of slavery and ignorance would melt like wax before the flames. I am but a feeble instrument. I am but as one particle of the small dust of the earth.[49] You may frown or smile.

After I am dead, perhaps before, God will surely raise up those[50] who will more powerfully and eloquently plead the cause of the virtue and the pure principles of morality than I am able to do. O virtue! How sacred is thy name! How pure are thy principles! Who can find a virtuous woman? For her price is far above rubies.[51] Blessed is the man who shall call her

---

49. *"Dust of the earth"* in the following texts refers to that which is small, insignificant, commonly available, and too numerous to count. Interestingly, however, it is often used in reference to the children of Abraham, the first people of the covenant with God. Genesis 13:16: "And I will make thy seed as *the dust of the earth*: so that if a man can number *the dust of the earth*, then shall thy seed also be numbered." See also Genesis 28:14, Exodus 8:17, 2 Samuel 22:43, 2 Chronicles 1:9, Job 14:19, Isaiah 40:12, Daniel 12:2, Amos 2:7. To describe her people as *"dust of the earth"* is an interesting rhetorical flourish typical of Stewart. On the one hand, it suggests that she sees herself as small and even meaningless—like dust. It suggests finitude. (Genesis 3:19: "for *dust* thou art, and unto *dust* shalt thou return.") On the other hand, it also conjures up imagery of a numberless army: ubiquitous and too numerous to be counted or ignored. *"Dust of the earth,"* sands of the seashore, and stars of the heavens are all biblical images linked to the children of Abraham—children of the covenant with God—who begin small in number and strength (in the case of Abraham, having begun of a single offspring, Isaac) but grow into a mighty nation. Is Stewart likewise suggesting that she, and her abolitionist army, will similarly grow?

Here, as elsewhere, Stewart links the plight of African Americans to that of the people of Israel, suggesting that African Americans are also people with a special relationship to God.

50. The idea that God will raise up someone to take up her crusade should she fall is a common one in scripture. See, for example, Deuteronomy 18:15: "The LORD thy God will raise up unto thee a Prophet from the midst of thee, of thy brethren, like unto me; unto him ye shall hearken." This passage also suggests the image of John the Baptist, predicting (of Jesus) that someone greater than himself would come. In context, this reinforces the speaker's claim to prophetic insight and the importance of the speaker's mission. It suggests that Stewart is a prophet whose mission is too important to be allowed to languish simply because of her own death; God will continue the mission after her by raising up others to take it up when she has fallen. Earthly powers cannot prevent the fulfillment of her mission; even if they kill her, God will raise up others to finish the crusade she has begun.

51. Proverbs 31:10: *"Who can find a virtuous woman? for her price is far above rubies."* From her discussion of women's roles and responsibility, Stewart jumps nimbly to this often-quoted text describing womanly virtue.

his wife; yea, happy is the child who shall call her mother. O, woman, woman, would thou only strive to excel in merit and virtue; would thou only store thy mind with useful knowledge,[52] great would be thine influence. Do you say, you are too far advanced in life now to begin? You are not too far advanced to instill these principles into the minds of your tender infants.[53] Let them by no means be neglected. Discharge your duty faithfully, in every point of view: leave the event with God. So shall your skirts become clear of their blood.[54]

52. What sort of knowledge would Stewart think was useful? At the dawn of the twentieth century (over seventy years after Stewart wrote these words), the debate in the African American community over what sorts of knowledge were "useful" continued to be a heated one. Often, even today, commentators reduce the two major schools of thought on this topic to a discussion of the personalities and philosophies of the two best-known proponents: Booker T. Washington and W. E. B. Du Bois. Du Bois, for his part, championed the idea of the "talented tenth" (first articulated by Henry Morehouse, field secretary of the American Baptist Home Mission Society), arguing that an educated African American elite would simultaneously impress hostile whites by their accomplishments while concurrently inspiring and improving the lot of less gifted blacks. Washington, on the other hand, advocated for African Americans to be educated in the industrial arts and make themselves useful by putting their hands to whatever work is made available to them rather than aspire to more elite and esoteric talents. By encouraging African Americans to pursue "useful knowledge" was Stewart anticipating, or even supporting, one or both of these arguments? For Morehouse as source of the term "talented tenth," see Higginbotham, *Righteous Discontent*, 25; Elliott Rudwick, "W. E. B. Du Bois: Protagonist of the Afro-American Protest," in *Black Leaders of the Twentieth Century*, ed. John Hope Franklin and August Meier, Blacks in the New World (Urbana: University of Illinois Press, 1982), 63–83; Louis R. Harlan, "Booker T. Washington and the Politics of Accommodation," in Franklin and Meier, *Black Leaders*, 1–18.

53. Stewart posits a multigenerational strategy. She has earlier argued that she believes God will raise up others to take on her quest for equality for African Americans after her death. Here, she counsels parents not to consider their age a bar to their participation; instead, they can teach their children to take up the fight. Apparently, her expectation is that the battle for equality will take time, and she wants her hearers to be prepared for a lengthy siege.

54. Jeremiah 2:34: "Also *in thy skirts is found the blood* of the souls of *the poor innocents*: I have not found it by secret search, but upon all these." This picture is a violent one: it conjures up the idea of those who sweep by innocent victims bleeding in the street. The only evidence that they have even seen the stricken is that some of the blood of the stricken has marred the hem of the bystander's clothing. Unlike the Good Samaritan of Luke 10:33, who helped a fallen stranger when others had unfeelingly passed by the wounded man, the one whose skirts are found with blood has coldly turned his/her back upon the plight of the needy. This indictment (of a sin of

When I consider how little improvement has been made the last eight years; the apparent cold and indifferent state of the children of God; how few have been hopefully brought to the knowledge of the truth as it is in Jesus;[55] that our young men and maidens are fainting and drooping, as it were, by the way-side, for the want of knowledge;[56] when I see how few care to distinguish themselves either in religious or moral improvement, and when I see the greater part of our community following vain bubbles of life with so much eagerness, which will only prove to them like the serpent's sting upon the bed of death,[57] I really think we are in as wretched and miserable a state as was the house of Israel[58] in the days of Jeremiah.[59]

---

omission) is leveled against those who have done nothing, when they should have, by all means, done something to help. Stewart seems to suggest that it is not enough to have, or even raise, children well if they are not also enlisted in the battle for equality that she continually describes.

55. *"Knowledge of the truth"*: 1 Timothy 2:4: "Who will have all men to be saved, and to come unto *the knowledge of the truth.*" 2 Timothy 3:7: "Ever learning, and never able to come to *the knowledge of the truth.*" Hebrews 10:26: "For if we sin wilfully after that we have received *the knowledge of the truth,* there remaineth no more sacrifice for sins." In evangelical parlance, *"the knowledge of the truth"* means the knowledge that brings one to an experience of salvation in Jesus, just as Stewart has linked these ideas by adding "as it is in Jesus" to the phrase "knowledge of the truth" in her text.

56. This is very similar to Hosea 4:6: "My people are *destroyed for lack of knowledge:* because thou hast rejected knowledge, I will also reject thee, that thou shalt be no priest to me: seeing thou hast forgotten the law of thy God, I will also forget thy children." Stewart uses "want of knowledge" rather than "lack of knowledge," describing the young people as "fainting and drooping" rather than being "destroyed," but the sentiments are strikingly similar. By substituting "fainting and drooping" for "destroyed" Stewart has toned down the violence in the text.

57. In *"serpent's sting upon the bed of death,"* Stewart inverts 1 Corinthians 15:55–56: "O death, where is thy sting? O grave, where is thy victory? The *sting of death* is sin; and the strength of sin is the law." Here, the serpent's sting is the sting of sin and its consequence is death.

58. Stewart compares African Americans with the Israelites: "wretched," "miserable," and fallen, perhaps, but still a chosen people. Ethiopianism was the nineteenth-century school of thought that conflated all of Africa with Ethiopia and, in particular, biblical references to Ethiopia. Chief among these references was Psalms 68:31. Ethiopianists took this text to prophesy a sweeping Christian revival in Africa and a specific role for Africans in diaspora, in bringing the word of God to the rest of the world. Ethiopianists thought Africans particularly sensitive to spiritual matters. As Israel was never far from the heart of God (despite its continual sinning), so Ethiopia

I suppose many of my friends will say, "Religion is all your theme,"[60] I hope my conduct will ever prove me to be what I profess, a true follower of Christ; and it is the religion of Jesus alone, that will constitute your happiness here, and support you in a dying hour.[61] O, then, do not trifle with God and your own souls any longer. Do not presume to offer him the very dregs of your lives; but now, whilst you are blooming in health and vigor, consecrate the remnant of your days to him.[62] Do you wish to become useful in your day and generation? Do you wish to promote the welfare and happiness of your friends, as far as your circle extends? Have you one desire to become truly great? O, then, become truly pious,[63] and God will endow you with wisdom and knowledge from on high.

> Come, turn to God, who did thee make,
> And at his presence fear and quake;
> Remember him now in thy youth,
> And let thy soul take hold of truth.
>
> The devil and his ways defy,
> Believe him not, he doth but lie;

---

and, by extension, all Africans and people of African descent were never far from God's plans.

59. The jeremiad as genre is named after the biblical prophet Jeremiah, who warned of coming destruction if God's people did not repent. Jeremiah was also known as the "Weeping Prophet." He was brought to tears by the deplorable state of his people.

60. Stewart addresses a political program in her speeches but also acknowledges their heavily religious content. She is perhaps also anticipating a criticism of her words: that she is too religious.

61. Like the evangelical that she is, Stewart must note the efficacy of faith in Christ. It is Jesus who "will constitute your happiness here, and support you in a dying hour."

62. Although Stewart called them "speeches," her words often have the ring of an altar call about them. She seems intent not only on enlisting others in her fight for equality but also on inviting them to give their lives to Jesus. What differentiates a "speech" from a "sermon"? For Stewart, there is no dividing line between the two types of address, as she jumps from what we might identify as sacred concerns to secular ones. For her, the two are linked; there are no purely secular concerns. Everything has a spiritual dimension, and God is sovereign over all. If her people became true followers of Christ, she believes, they would also enlist in her fight for people of African descent. Because the battle for equality is, for her, a holy cause, it is a cause that all true Christians would willingly join.

63. For Stewart, piety is greatness.

His ways seem sweet: but youth, beware!
He for thy soul hath laid a snare.[64]

Religion is pure; it is ever new; it is beautiful; it is all that is worth living for; it is worth dying for: O, could I but see the church built up in the most holy faith;[65] could I but see men spiritually minded,[66] walking in the fear of God,[67] not given to filthy lucre,[68] not holding religion in one hand and the world in the other, but diligent in business, fervent in the spirit, serving the Lord,[69] standing upon the walls of Zion,[70] crying to passers by, "Ho, every one that thirsteth, come ye to the waters,

64. "A Dialogue between Christ, a Youth, and the Devil," in *The New England Primer*, 1777 ed., http://www.sacred-texts.com/chr/nep/1777/index.htm. Here, perhaps, is a tiny hint of the materials Stewart was taught in Sabbath school.

65. Jude 1:20: "But ye, beloved, *building up yourselves on your most holy faith*, praying in the Holy Ghost." Stewart omits the part of the verse that would be most important later to Pentecostals, who view the text as a reference to praying in tongues.

66. Romans 8:6: "For to be carnally minded is death; but to be *spiritually minded* is life and peace."

67. *"Fear of God"* appears in multiple scriptures, while "walking in the fear of" is found in Acts 9:31: "Then had the churches rest throughout all Judaea and Galilee and Samaria, and were edified; and *walking in the fear of* the Lord, and in the comfort of the Holy Ghost, were multiplied."

68. This listing of qualifications is similar to those in 1 Timothy 3:3, "Not given to wine, no striker, not greedy *of filthy lucre*; but patient, not a brawler, not covetous," which lists qualifications for deacons, elders, etc. See also 1 Timothy 3:8. "Filthy lucre": money, wealth. As does this text from 1 Timothy, Stewart seems to delineate the characteristics required for leaders in her movement.

69. Romans 12:11: *"Not slothful in business; fervent in spirit; serving the Lord."* By echoing the requirements found in scripture, Stewart underscores that what she is looking for is godly conduct and character.

70. Isaiah 62:6: "I have set watchmen *upon thy walls*, O Jerusalem, which shall never hold their peace day nor night: ye that make mention of the LORD, keep not silence." While the idea of a watchman on the wall is a martial one, it is a defensive (rather than aggressive) stance. Again, Stewart eschews violence.

71. Isaiah 55:1: *"Ho, every one that thirsteth, come ye to the waters, and he that hath no money; come ye, buy, and eat; yea, come, buy wine and milk without money and without price."* An enduring picture of the kingdom of God is one of feasting. For the subsistence farmers of antiquity, this picture of abundance was particularly resonant. The kingdom that Stewart imagines shares that abundance. No one goes hungry there. Every slave narrative described the poverty of the slave existence. Even as they provided wealth for their masters, slaves suffered want of clothing, food, and every necessity. In the picture of abundance that she has drawn by her use of this scripture,

and he that hath no money; yea, come and buy wine and milk without money and without price;[71] Turn ye, turn ye, for why will ye die?"[72] Could I but see mothers in Israel,[73] chaste, keepers at home, not busy bodies, meddlers in other men's matters,[74] whose adorning is of the in-

---

Stewart proposes a radical realignment in which the slave does not want but instead has plenty.

72. Ezekiel 33:11: "Say unto them, As I live, saith the Lord GOD, I have no pleasure in the death of the wicked; but that the wicked turn from his way and live: *turn ye, turn ye* from your evil ways; *for why will ye die*, O house of Israel?" Here Stewart returns to her evangelistic call to her listeners to turn to Christ for salvation. Significantly, this salvation is "without money and without price"—it is freely available, so that only a fool would refuse it. According to this metaphor as Stewart has deployed it, salvation is a thing as necessary to the human as food. Interestingly, however, although she has previously argued that it is in the religion of Jesus alone that one finds happiness and peace, Stewart has nevertheless chosen a text from the Hebrew Bible to make this point. Among others, both James Cone and James H. Evans Jr. have noted this tendency among African Americans to move back and forth quite freely between the Hebrew Bible and the New Testament. Evans sees "the need to see the Bible as a unified text" as having its basis in evangelical theology, but he nonetheless agrees with Cone that the ultimate reason for such movement is to highlight liberative biblical texts, irrespective of the place (Hebrew Bible or New Testament) where such texts are found. Evans, *We Have Been Believers*, 45; Cone, *The Spirituals and the Blues.*

73. Judges 5:7: "The inhabitants of the villages ceased, they ceased in Israel, until that I Deborah arose, that I arose *a mother in Israel.*" It is interesting that the text refers to Deborah, a warrior prophetess and judge/ruler in Israel, and not just a mother. Also 2 Samuel 20:19, "I am one of them that are peaceable and faithful in Israel: thou seekest to destroy a city and *a mother in Israel*: why wilt thou swallow up the inheritance of the LORD?" Although Stewart is still talking about her people, she wants them to be like the mothers in Israel. Again, this allusion strengthens the metaphoric ties Stewart has drawn between the people of the covenant in the Bible, the Israelites, and her people, the sons and daughters of Africa.

74. 1 Peter 4:15: "But let none of you suffer as a murderer, or as a thief, or as an evildoer, or as *a busybody in other men's matters.*" Unfortunately the allusion here does not suit her meaning. Elsewhere, especially in 1 Timothy 5: 13, idle women are denounced as "busybodies." Stewart seems to have combined the references to ill effect. She ends up calling for "mothers" who aren't meddling in "other men's matters." Are the matters they meddle in men's matters at all? Does she mean "men's" matters, or "humanity's" matters? Elsewhere, she has been very careful with gender, so it is surprising that she is so imprecise here, describing "men's" rather than "people's" matters. She calls for mothers to be "keepers at home" by alluding to a text about Deborah, who judged Israel and definitely did not stay at home. Was this allusion unintentional? Or does it reflect Stewart's own inner conflict over the role of women?

"Religion and the Pure Principles of Morality" ✳ 59

ward man,[75] possessing a meek and quiet spirit,[76] whose sons are like olive-plants,[77] and whose daughters were as polished corner-stones;[78] could I but see young men and maidens turning their feet from impious ways, rather choosing to suffer affliction with the people of God rather than to enjoy the pleasures of sin for a season;[79] could I but see the rising youth blushing in artless innocence,[80] then could I say, now, Lord, let

75. *"Adorning of the inward man"* is perhaps an allusion to 1 Peter 3:3–5: "Whose adorning let it not be that outward adorning of plaiting the hair, and of wearing of gold, or of putting on of apparel; But let it be *the hidden man of the heart*, in that which is not corruptible, even the even the ornament of a meek and quiet spirit, which is in the sight of God of great price. For after this manner in the old time the holy women also, who trusted in God, *adorned* themselves, being in subjection unto their own husbands." (Although the biblical text reads *"hidden man of the heart,"* not "inward man," as Stewart writes, the ideas are very close.) This is definitely a scripture touting the benefits of women's submission to their husbands. It doesn't fit with her earlier allusion to Deborah, but it is in line with the admonition against "busybodies" (i.e., women who do not keep at home). *"Inward man"*: Romans 7:22: "For I delight in the law of God after *the inward man"*; and 2 Corinthians 4:16, "For which cause we faint not; but though our outward man perish, yet *the inward man* is renewed day by day." Here, the text differentiates between the "outward man," or physical body, and the "inward man," or spirit.

76. 1 Peter 3:4: "But let it be the hidden man of the heart, in that which is not corruptible, even the ornament of *a meek and quiet spirit*, which is in the sight of God of great price."

77. Psalms 128:3: "Thy wife shall be as a fruitful vine by the sides of thine house: *thy children like olive plants* round about thy table." Here, surprisingly, Stewart specifies "sons" when the biblical text she is quoting uses the less gender-specific "children." Perhaps this is because she chooses "daughters" for use in her next phrase.

78. Psalms 144:12: "That our sons may be as plants grown up in their youth; that *our daughters may be as corner stones, polished* after the similitude of a palace."

79. Hebrews 11:25: "*Choosing rather to suffer affliction with the people of God, than to enjoy the pleasures of sin for a season."* To serve God is to care for eternal things; to enjoy the pleasures of sin is to enjoy temporary pleasures.

80. *"Artless innocence"* is innocence that is unfeigned and natural, innocence that is neither artificial nor superficial.

81. Luke 2:29: "Lord, now lettest *thou thy servant depart in peace*, according to thy word." Stewart has probably substituted "handmaiden" for "servant" because she is a woman. This is perhaps to make it clear that, in this case, she is referring to herself. (Then she adds the deferential "unworthy" as well.) She would be free to "depart in peace," that is, to die, if she knew that her crusade would be continued by young men and women of righteousness such as she has here described. Here Stewart is quoting the words of Simeon, a righteous and devout man who was waiting in the Jerusalem temple to see the Messiah. Once he had seen the baby Jesus, he was satisfied, and, after

thine unworthy handmaiden depart in peace,[81] for I have seen the desire
of mine eyes,[82] and am satisfied.

PRAYER.[83]

O, Lord God, the watchmen of Zion have cried peace, peace, when there
is no peace;[84] they have been, as it were, blind leaders of the blind.[85]
Wherefore hast thou so long withheld from us the divine influences of
thy Holy Spirit?[86] Wherefore hast thou hardened our hearts and blinded

---

blessing Jesus and his parents and prophesying about the child's significance, he spoke
the words Stewart has quoted. Again, she likens herself to a prophet by appropriating
Simeon's words to describe herself. However, to guard against any accusation of self-
aggrandizement, Stewart also inserts "unworthy" in this self-description.

82. Psalms 92: 11: "Mine *eye* also shall see *my desire* on mine enemies, and mine ears
shall hear my desire of the wicked that rise up against me." Also Psalms 54:7: "For
he hath delivered me out of all trouble: and *mine eye hath seen his desire* upon mine
enemies." Interestingly, both these texts attribute to the "eye" the ability to see one's
"desire" of vengeance upon one's enemies.

Once the army of righteous young men and women ("artless" innocents) has been
formed, the judgment that Stewart expects will befall the slavocracy. In this sense,
Stewart blames not only the slavocracy for the wretched state of affairs for blacks
but also the blacks themselves. The "desire of [Stewart's] eyes"—vengeance upon the
slave regime—cannot occur until a righteous army of blacks has arisen to effect or,
perhaps, to provoke it.

83. Although Stewart's venue for this speech is secular, her prayer here (and a hymn
later) suggest that she intended to create an atmosphere of worship. In this context,
her words represent a sermon being presented between an opening prayer and a clos-
ing hymn.

84. Jeremiah 6:14: "They have healed also the hurt of the daughter of my people
slightly, *saying, Peace, peace; when there is no peace.*" Jeremiah 8:11: "For they have healed
the hurt of the daughter of my people slightly, *saying, Peace, peace; when there is no
peace.*" No justice, no peace. Stewart seems to say that as long as the injustices against
black people continue, others may declare peace but will never achieve it. There is no
peace as long as there is no justice.

85. Matthew 15:14: "Let them alone: *they be blind leaders of the blind.* And if the blind
lead the blind, both shall fall into the ditch." In its context, this verse excoriates the
supposed leaders of the people as blind. If these are the watchmen, then the difficulty
that the people are in becomes clear. Their leaders and their watchmen are blind, and
as such, are totally unable either to lead them or foresee approaching danger. Indeed,
the doom is so clearly presented that Stewart doesn't even need to include its description, from the end of Matthew 15:14, that "both shall fall into the ditch."

86. Later in this same speech, Stewart notes that God has not deprived the children

our eyes?[87] It is because we have honored thee with our lips, when our hearts were far from thee.[88] We have polluted thy Sabbaths,[89] and even our most holy things have been solemn mockery to thee. We have regarded iniquity in our hearts, therefore thou wilt not hear.[90] Return again unto us, O Lord God, we beseech thee, and pardon this the iniquity of thy servants. Cause thy face to shine upon us, and we shall be saved.[91] O visit us with thy salvation.[92] Raise up sons and daughters unto Abraham,[93] and grant that there might come a mighty shaking of dry bones

---

of Africa of the influence of the Holy Spirit. Here, she complains that they have not sufficiently experienced its influence. It is a rare inconsistency for Stewart.

87. John 12:40: "He hath *blinded their eyes*, and *hardened their heart*; that they should not see with their eyes, nor understand with their heart, and be converted, and I should heal them." Not only are the leaders blind; the people are too. Were they able to see clearly, they would know what to do in the current crisis. However, this is a moral rather than physical blindness that the people suffer, having been provoked because of a lack of the "divine influences of the Holy Spirit."

88. Isaiah 29:13: "Wherefore the Lord said, Forasmuch as this people draw near me with their mouth, and *with their lips do honour me, but have removed their heart far from me*, and their fear toward me is taught by the precept of men." The people have a form of religion that they have been taught but have not experienced real transformation. If they had, they would not, according to Stewart, be in the present predicament.

89. "*Polluted . . . Sabbaths*" occurs many times in Exodus 20:12–24. It suggests having failed to do one's duty to God on the Lord's Day, having committed inappropriate acts on that day, or having failed in one's most basic obligation: to worship God on the Lord's Day. This goes along with Stewart's accusation that their religious practice is empty and fatally flawed.

90. Psalms 66:18: "If I *regard iniquity in my heart, the Lord will not hear me*." Stewart believes that the people know they ought to do better than they have done. God is justified in ignoring their prayers and staying the hand of judgment (against their oppressors) as long as the people continue willfully sinning.

91. Psalms 80:3 (and similar refrains at 80:7 and 19): "Turn us again, O God, and *cause thy face to shine; and we shall be saved*." As soon as the people of God repent of their phony devotions and empty practices and turn to God, God can unleash the promised and long-awaited vengeance upon the slavocracy.

92. Psalms 106:4: "Remember me, O LORD, with the favour that thou bearest unto thy people: *O visit me with thy salvation*." By replacing "me" with "us," Stewart calls for a corporate salvation—salvation for her entire people and not herself alone.

93. Matthew 3:9: "And think not to say within yourselves, We have Abraham to our father: for I say unto you, that God is able of these stones to *raise up children unto Abraham*." See also Luke 3:8: "Bring forth therefore fruits worthy of repentance, and begin not to say within yourselves, We have Abraham to our father: for I say unto

among us,[94] and a great ingathering of souls.[95] Quicken thy professing children.[96] Grant that the young may be constrained to believe that there is a reality in religion, and a beauty in the fear of the Lord.[97] Have mercy on the benighted sons and daughters of Africa.[98] Grant that we may soon

---

you, That God is able of these stones to *raise up children unto Abraham.*" In raising up children unto Abraham, Stewart is calling for children of the covenant with God to enlist in her crusade. For her, these are the sons and daughters of Africa. If God can create a chosen people out of stones, it is certainly not too great a thing for God to create a chosen people out of the sons and daughters of Africa.

94. Ezekiel 37:4–10 (esp. verse 7): "Again he said unto me, Prophesy upon these bones, and say unto them, O ye *dry bones,* hear the word of the LORD. Thus saith the Lord GOD unto these bones; Behold, I will cause breath to enter into you, and ye shall live: And I will lay sinews upon you, and will bring up flesh upon you, and cover you with skin, and put breath in you, and ye shall live; and ye shall know that I am the LORD. So I prophesied as I was commanded: and as I prophesied, there was a noise, and behold *a shaking, and the bones came together,* bone to his bone. And when I beheld, lo, the sinews and the flesh came up upon them, and the skin covered them above: but there was no breath in them. Then said he unto me, Prophesy unto the wind, prophesy, son of man, and say to the wind, Thus saith the Lord GOD; Come from the four winds, O breath, and breathe upon these slain, that they may live. So I prophesied as he commanded me, and the breath came into them, and they lived, and stood up upon their feet, an exceeding great army."

From her discussion of God's creating sons and daughters of Abraham from stones, Stewart moves to the creation of whole armies out of the bleached bones of the long dead. This text is often preached in black churches, even today, as the archetypical example of life from death. Dry bones—that is, the desiccated bones of those who are long dead—are reanimated by God. It is a miracle of the impossible, even of the extremely impossible. God takes that which is utterly lifeless—and has been lifeless for quite a while—and builds of it an army. So it is that this text suggests the value of hope against hope.

"Can these bones live?" God asks the prophet (Ezekiel 37:3). And the prophet answers, "O Lord GOD, thou knowest." Only God knows if, and when, the impossible will become possible. Therefore, no matter how desperate (or how dead) the situation (or the object), God holds the secret of life from death, of resurrection, and of the most unimaginable springing from the most unlikely. In the context of a Bible passage where long-dead bones become living, breathing beings, Stewart's hope that African Americans, now downtrodden servants and enslaved chattel, would become a mighty nation agitating for equality is not particularly far fetched. "Can these bones live?" "O Lord GOD, thou knowest." Only God may know, but Stewart believes.

95. This phrase combines the ideas of the "*ingathering,*" or harvest, with the work of the evangelist, who gathers souls to Christ. Exodus 23:16: "And the feast of harvest, the firstfruits of thy labours, which thou hast sown in the field: and the feast of *ingather-*

become so distinguished for our moral and religious improvements, that the nations of the earth may take knowledge of us;[99] and grant that our cries may come up before thy throne like holy incense.[100] Grant that every daughter of Africa may consecrate her sons to thee from birth. And do

_____

ing, which is in the end of the year, when thou hast gathered in thy labours out of the field"; and Exodus 34:22: "And thou shalt observe the feast of weeks, of the firstfruits of wheat harvest, and the feast of *ingathering* at the year's end." Here Stewart likens the salvation of many to the gathering of the harvest. This passage also suggests Jesus's words: "Then saith he unto his disciples, The harvest truly is plenteous, but the labourers are few; Pray ye therefore the Lord of the harvest, that he will send forth labourers into his harvest" (Matthew 9:37). This text (because of its context with the verse preceding it) has often been taken as referring to a harvest of souls. Here harvest functions as a kind of *eschaton*, or end time, when the laborers' work is revealed. Those who have worked well will receive a good harvest, while those who have not will go without. The judgment Stewart expects will also be an *eschaton* of sorts, revealing the diligent work of some and the sloth of others. She is very concerned that her people get about the work of righteousness because the time of the harvest is coming.

96. *"Quicken"* is used many times, especially in the Psalms (71:20; 80:18; 119:25, 37, 40, 88, 107, 149, 154, 156, 159; and 143:11), and in Romans 8:11. It means to be made alive. This use is interesting, following as it does the reference to the dry bones that are reanimated in Ezekiel. Stewart asks God to "quicken thy professing children." She wants them to be spiritually alive to God and not just "professing" or claiming to be so. For Stewart, even those who claim to be Christian need a reawakening similar to that which occurred in the valley of dry bones.

97. Psalms 96:9: "O worship the LORD in *the beauty of* holiness: *fear before him*, all the earth."

98. Stewart never forgets her two favorite causes: black men and women, whom she calls the "sons and daughters of Africa" here.

99. If the sons and daughters of Africa were distinguishing themselves as Stewart suggests, the world would take notice of their plight. By this reasoning, blacks are at least partially to blame for their situation; were they behaving differently, the cry for their equality would arise not only from them but from the whole earth. This is not significantly different from the reasoning of the Cult of True Womanhood that all of society would be provoked to virtue by the behavior of its virtuous women. While on the one hand it suggests tremendous agency on the part of blacks or women, it also blames them (rather than their oppressors) for the oppression they endure.

100. For a passage referring not to "cries" but "prayers" and "incense," see Revelation 8:3–4: "And another angel came and stood at the altar, having a golden censer; and there was given unto him much *incense*, that he should offer it with the *prayers* of all saints upon the golden altar which was before the throne. And the smoke of the incense, which came with the *prayers* of the saints, *ascended up before God* out of the angel's hand." By substituting "cries" for "prayers," Stewart makes the pleas more des-

thou, Lord, bestow upon them wise and understanding hearts.[101] Clothe
us with humility of soul,[102] and give us a becoming dignity of manners:[103]
may we imitate the character of the meek and lowly Jesus;[104] and do
grant that Ethiopia may soon stretch forth her hands unto thee.[105] And
now, Lord, be pleased to grant that Satan's kingdom may be destroyed;

---

perate in tone. In this text, evangelicals typically understand "saints" to refer to those
(otherwise ordinary believers) who have been sanctified by the blood of the Lamb.

101. According to 1 Kings 3:12, a wise and understanding heart was one of King
Solomon's God-given attributes: "Behold, I have done according to thy words: lo, I
have given thee *a wise and an understanding heart;* so that there was none like thee
before thee, neither after thee shall any arise like unto thee." Stewart doesn't just want
ordinary wisdom for her people; she wants them to possess miraculous and extraordinary wisdom.

102. This seems to be an amalgamation of 1 Peter 5:5 and Acts 20:19. 1 Peter 5:5:
"Likewise, ye younger, submit yourselves unto the elder. Yea, all of you be subject one
to another, and be *clothed with humility:* for God resisteth the proud, and giveth grace
to the humble." Acts 20:19: "Serving the Lord with all *humility of mind,* and with many
tears, and temptations, which befell me by the lying in wait of the Jews."

103. "Dignity of manners" suggests Evelyn Brooks Higginbotham's conception of
the "politics of respectability." Higginbotham notes that among black Baptist women
in the late nineteenth and early twentieth centuries, there was a strong emphasis upon
respectability because "they felt certain that 'respectable' behavior in public would earn
their people a measure of esteem from white America, and hence they strove to win
the black lower class's psychological allegiance to temperance, industriousness, thrift,
refined manners, and Victorian sexual morals." Such deportment, then, constituted
more than a moral statement; it represented a political statement of resistance to racism: a kind of politics of respectability. The politics of respectability was in one sense
conservative, in its rigid social regimentation of conduct and dress, for example, but
it was also progressive, in its emphasis upon black uplift and in its "attack on the
failure of America to live up to its liberal ideals of equality and justice." However, it
also drove a wedge between these proponents of middle-class virtues and many other
African Americans. Higginbotham, *Righteous Discontent,* 14–15. Although she lived
much earlier than the women in Higginbotham's study, Stewart also seems convinced
of the power of black respectability to impress whites and thus further blacks' fight
for equality.

104. Matthew 11:29–30: "Take my yoke upon you, and learn of me; for I am *meek
and lowly* in heart: and ye shall find rest unto your souls. For my yoke is easy, and my
burden is light."

105. Psalms 68:31, "Princes shall come out of Egypt; *Ethiopia shall soon stretch out her
hands unto God.*" Of all the mentions of Ethiopia in the King James Version, why was
this verse so favored? (Ethiopia is mentioned by name twenty times.) For Stewart, this

that the kingdom of our Lord Jesus Christ may be built up;[106] that all nations, and kindreds, and tongues, and people[107] may be brought to the knowledge of the truth, as it is in Jesus,[108] and we at last meet around thy throne, and join in celebrating thy praises.[109]

---

text becomes a kind of prophetic call. Ethiopia becomes shorthand for all of Africa, and by extension, all of Africa's children, throughout the diaspora. In this context (juxtaposed against several allusions to Revelation and the end of time that follow in Stewart's speech), the turning of Ethiopia to God becomes a kind of apocalyptic sign of the defeat of Satan's kingdom and the coming of the kingdom of God.

106. This line is very similar to Revelation 11:15: "And the seventh angel sounded; and there were great voices in heaven, saying, *The kingdoms of this world are become the kingdoms of our Lord*, and of his *Christ; and he shall reign for ever and ever.*"

107. Revelation 14:6: "And I saw another angel fly in the midst of heaven, having the everlasting gospel to preach unto them that dwell on the earth, and to *every nation, and kindred, and tongue, and people.*" This is also an allusion to the vision of racial inclusiveness found in Revelation 7:9–17: "After this I beheld, and, lo, a great multitude, which no man could number, *of all nations, and kindreds, and people, and tongues,* stood before the throne, and before the Lamb, clothed with white robes, and palms in their hands; And cried with a loud voice, saying, Salvation to our God which sitteth upon the throne, and unto the Lamb. And all the angels stood round about the throne, and about the elders and the four beasts, and fell before the throne on their faces, and worshipped God, Saying, Amen: Blessing, and glory, and wisdom, and thanksgiving, and honour, and power, and might, be unto our God for ever and ever. Amen. And one of the elders answered, saying unto me, What are these which are arrayed in white robes? and whence came they? And I said unto him, Sir, thou knowest. And he said to me, These are they which came out of great tribulation, and have washed their robes, and made them white in the blood of the Lamb. Therefore are they before the throne of God, and serve him day and night in his temple: and he that sitteth on the throne shall dwell among them. They shall hunger no more, neither thirst any more; neither shall the sun light on them, nor any heat. For the Lamb which is in the midst of the throne shall feed them, and shall lead them unto living fountains of waters: and God shall wipe away all tears from their eyes." This is a picture of the ultimate equality. Every people and language group is gathered in unity, in peace, and in worship. It can only be the *eschaton*, when the kingdom of God has finally come in all of its fullness.

108. 1 Timothy 2:4: "Who will have all men to be saved, and to *come unto the knowledge of the truth.*" 2 Timothy 3:7: "Ever learning, and never able *to come to the knowledge of the truth.*" However, Stewart has modified the phrase so that it is not just the "knowledge of the truth"—but specifically the knowledge of the truth in Jesus, or salvation by faith in Jesus.

109. Again, Revelation 7:9–17 is suggested, with its picture of contented, unified worshippers from every nation, tribe, and tongue, gathered around the Lamb of God.

I have been taking a survey of the American people[110] in my own mind, and I see them thriving in arts, and sciences, and in polite literature. Their highest aim is to excel in political, moral and religious improvement.[111] They early consecrate their children to God, and their youth indeed are blushing in artless innocence;[112] they wipe the tears from the orphan's eyes, and they cause the widow's heart to sing for joy![113] [A]nd their poorest ones, who have the least wish to excel, they promote! And those that have but one talent, they encourage.[114] But how very few are there among them that bestow one thought upon the benighted sons and daughters of Africa,[115] who have enriched the soils of America with their tears and blood: few to promote their cause, none to encourage their talents. Under these circumstances, do not let our hearts be any longer discouraged; it is no use to murmur nor to repine; but let us promote ourselves and improve our own talents.[116] And I am rejoiced to reflect that there are many able and talented ones among us, whose names might be

110. After Stewart has spent several pages complaining about the ignorance of her own people, there can be little doubt that those she considers her people are different from those she calls the "American people" whose intelligence and industry she here commends. Her people are the sons and daughters of Africa; they are people of African descent in the United States. The American people, on the other hand, are the European Americans.

111. The religious and political are given a kind of equivalence here.

112. If black youth lack "artless innocence," Stewart believes that white youth do not.

113. To argue that the Americans care for their widows is to suggest that the African Americans do not. Stewart was both an orphan and a widow who would have benefited from such support.

114. Stewart commends the Americans for demonstrating the racial unity and self-determination that she would love to see flourish among her own people. One positive thing she does say about the Americans is that they look after their own.

115. "Daughters of Africa": here Stewart draws an analogy between the "Daughters of Zion" (that is, the women of the covenant) and the "Americans" (that is, European Americans). African Americans are always "Africans" as contrasted with the "Americans." African Americans are not Americans but something higher: they are people of the covenant. The Americans' failure in all this, according to Stewart, is that they look out for one another but not for the sons and daughters of Africa. Even after black people have enriched them, the Americans do nothing to reciprocate.

116. This is nascent Black Nationalism. Stewart always advises self-sufficiency and self-determination in answer to the slights that blacks experience at the hands of the Americans. That is, she argues, if the Americans will not do for you, do for yourself!

recorded on the bright annals of fame. But, "I can't," is a great barrier in the way. I hope it will soon be removed, and "I will," resume its place.[117]

Righteousness exalteth a nation, but sin is a reproach to any people.[118] Why is it, my friends, that our minds have been blinded by ignorance, to the present moment? 'Tis on account of sin. Why is it that our church is involved in so much difficulty? It is on account of sin. Why is it that God has cut down, upon our right hand and upon our left,[119] the most learned and intelligent of our men? O, shall I say, it is on account of sin![120] Why is it that thick darkness is mantled upon every brow, and we, as it were, look sadly upon one another? It is on account of sin. O, then, let us bow before the Lord our God, with all our hearts, and humble our very souls in the dust before him; sprinkling, as it were, ashes upon our heads[121] and

117. Stewart accepts no excuses for failure. As she perseveres, so she calls her people to persevere.

118. Proverbs 14:34: "*Righteousness exalteth a nation: but sin is a reproach to any people.* The king's favour is toward a wise servant: but his wrath is against him that causeth shame." Stewart omits the next verse, which mentions wise servants. It might have been in keeping with her present theme, that blacks should develop their own talents, given that whites are developing theirs, but she interestingly omits it instead. Perhaps she would prefer not to link African Americans to servanthood in any context.

119. Multiple attestations: Genesis 24:49: "And now if ye will deal kindly and truly with my master, tell me: and if not, tell me; that I may turn *to the right hand, or to the left.*" Exodus 14:22: "And the children of Israel went into the midst of the sea upon the dry ground: and the waters were a wall unto them *on their right hand, and on their left.*" Deuteronomy 2:27 even has the "unto": "Let me pass through thy land: I will go along by the high way, I will neither turn *unto the right hand nor to the left.*" Also Numbers 20:17 and 22:26 and many other places as well.

120. This is probably an allusion to the death of Stewart's mentor, David Walker, and perhaps to the death of her husband as well. Note that she attributes these deaths to God, who she states has "cut down . . . the most learned and intelligent" among her people because of the sin of her people. Stewart doesn't attribute these losses to the sins of the Americans against the sons and daughters of Africa; instead she seems here to attribute the deaths to God's reaction against the sin of the sons and daughters of Africa.

121. This is a typical act of mourning or contrition and repentance. See 2 Samuel 13:19: "And Tamar put *ashes on her head,* and rent her garment of divers colours that was on her, and laid her hand on her head, and went on crying." Esther 4:1: "When Mordecai perceived all that was done, Mordecai rent his clothes, and put on sackcloth *with ashes,* and went out into the midst of the city, and cried with a loud and a bitter cry." Esther 4:3, "And in every province, whithersoever the king's commandment and his decree came, there was great mourning among the Jews, and fasting, and weep-

awake to righteousness and sin not.[122] The arm of the Lord is not shortened, that it cannot save; neither is his ear heavy, that it cannot hear; but
it is your iniquities that have separated you from me, saith the Lord.[123]
Return, O ye backsliding children,[124] and I will return unto you, and ye
shall be my people, and I will be your God.[125]

O, ye mothers,[126] what a responsibility rests on you! You have souls

---

ing, and wailing; and many lay in sackcloth and *ashes.*" Job 2:8: "And he took him a
potsherd to scrape himself withal; and he *sat down among the ashes.*" Job 42:6: "Wherefore I abhor myself, and *repent in* dust and *ashes.*" Jeremiah 6:26: "O daughter of my
people, gird thee with sackcloth, and *wallow thyself in ashes:* make thee mourning, as
for an only son, most bitter lamentation: for the spoiler shall suddenly come upon us."
Particularly Daniel 9:3, where the act is an intercession for the whole of Israel: "And I
set my face unto the Lord God, to seek by prayer and supplications, with fasting, and
sackcloth, *and ashes.*" Stewart expects black people to repent when presented with the
laundry list of their sins that she has provided.

122. 1 Corinthians 15:34: "*Awake to righteousness, and sin not;* for some have not the
knowledge of God: I speak this to your shame."

123. Isaiah 59:1–2: "*Behold, the* LORD'*s hand is not shortened, that it cannot save;
neither his ear heavy, that it cannot hear: But your iniquities have separated between you
and your God, and your sins have hid his face from you, that he will not hear.*" Here
Stewart sharpens the allegation into a direct address from God by adding "*Saith the
Lord.*" Delivering such direct address from God to the people of God is the job of a
prophet.

124. Jeremiah 3:14: "*Turn, O backsliding children, saith the* LORD; *for I am married
unto you: and I will take you one of a city, and two of a family, and I will bring you to
Zion.*" Jeremiah 3:22: "*Return, ye backsliding children, and I will heal your backslidings.
Behold, we come unto thee; for thou art the* LORD *our God.*"

125. Jeremiah 24:7: "And I will give them an heart to know me, that I am the LORD:
and *they shall be my people, and I will be their God:* for they shall return unto me
with their whole heart." Here, in Stewart's rendering, it is God who returns, not the
wandering backslider (as is usually the case in verses using the word "return"). God
returns because these are a people with whom God has a covenantal relationship.
Also, Leviticus 26:12, "And I will walk among you, and *will be your God, and ye shall
be my people.*"

126. Again, Stewart makes a specific address to mothers concerning the heavy responsibility they bear in raising children. Her many references to the responsibility
of a mother are despite the fact that she has no children of her own. Perhaps this also
reflects her own regret that she is childless. Like many people without children of their
own, she may feel that she could do a better job of raising young than she has seen in
her community. However, as any parent will attest, the job of raising children is infinitely more difficult than it may appear to those who are not parents themselves.

committed to your charge, and God will require a strict account of you.[127] It is you that must create in the minds of your little girls and boys a thirst for knowledge,[128] the love of virtue, the abhorrence of vice, and the cultivation of a pure heart.[129] The seeds thus sown will grow with their growing years; and the love of virtue thus early formed in the soul will protect their inexperienced feet from many dangers. O, do not say, you cannot make any thing of your children; but say, with the help and assistance of God, we will try. Do not indulge them in their little stubborn ways; for a child left to himself, bringeth his mother to shame.[130] Spare not, for their crying; thou shalt beat them with a rod, and they shall not die; and thou shalt save their souls from hell.[131] When you correct them, do it in the fear of God, and for their own good. They will not thank you for your false and foolish indulgence; they will rise up, as it were, and curse you in this world, and in the world to come,[132] condemn you. It is no use to say, you can't do this, or, you can't do that; you will not tell your Maker so, when you meet him at the great day of account.[133]

127. To Stewart, the role of mothers is one of authority and of stewardship. Parents will have to give account to God for the way they have raised their children.

128. The thirst for knowledge is not just for boys but for girls, too. Education is important for both sexes.

129. *"Pure heart"*: Psalms 24:4, 1 Timothy 1:5, 2 Timothy 2:22, 1 Peter 1:22. This is one of many biblical metaphors that Stewart uses freely.

130. Proverbs 29:15: "The rod and reproof give wisdom: *but a child left to himself bringeth his mother to shame.*" An undisciplined child brings shame upon his or her parents.

131. Proverbs 23: 13–14: "Withhold not correction from the child: for *if thou beatest him with the rod, he shall not die. Thou shalt beat him with the rod, and shalt deliver his soul from hell.*" How many times has this text been misused by Bible-quoting parents to justify excessive corporal punishment of their own children? Stewart joins that throng with this reference.

132. *"World to come"*: Matthew 12:32, Mark 10:30, Luke 18:30, Hebrews 2:5, Hebrews 6:5. Here and elsewhere, this is an apocalyptic reference to the coming judgment resulting either in eternal life or in condemnation.

133. *"Great day of account"*: i.e., Judgment Day. See, for example, Romans 14:11–12: "For it is written, As I live, saith the Lord, every knee shall bow to me, and every tongue shall confess to God. So then every one of us shall *give account* of himself to God"; and 1 Peter 4:5: "Who shall *give account to him* that is ready to judge the quick and the dead." "Great day" is also evocative of Joel 2:31: "The sun shall be turned into darkness, and the moon into blood, before *the great and the terrible day of the* LORD come." Also Zephaniah 1:14–17, another apocalyptic reference: "The *great day of the* LORD is near,

And you must be careful that you set an example worthy of following, for you they will imitate. There are many instances, even among us now, where parents have discharged their duty faithfully, and their children now reflect honor upon their gray hairs.[134]

Perhaps you will say, that many parents have set pure examples at home, and they have not followed them. True, our expectations are often blasted; but let not this dishearten you. If they have faithfully discharged their duty, even after they are dead, their works may live; their prodigal children may then return to God,[135] and become heirs of salvation;[136]

---

it is near, and hasteth greatly, even the voice of the day of the LORD: the mighty man shall cry there bitterly. That day is a day of wrath, a day of trouble and distress, a day of wasteness and desolation, a day of darkness and gloominess, a day of clouds and thick darkness, A day of the trumpet and alarm against the fenced cities, and against the high towers. And I will bring distress upon men, that they shall walk like blind men, because they have sinned against the LORD: and their blood shall be poured out as dust, and their flesh as the dung." Jude 1:6: "And the angels which kept not their first estate, but left their own habitation, he hath reserved in everlasting chains under darkness unto the *judgment of the great day*." Revelation 6:17: "For *the great day of his wrath is come*; and who shall be able to stand?" Revelation 16:14: "For they are the spirits of devils, working miracles, which go forth unto the kings of the earth and of the whole world, to gather them to the battle *of that great day of God Almighty*."

In John 7:37, the reference is not to judgment: "In the last day, that *great day* of the feast, Jesus stood and cried, saying, If any man thirst, let him come unto me, and drink." However, every other reference to "great . . . day" refers to coming judgment and the chaos that will accompany it — including apocalyptic images of battle, etc. Stewart makes it clear that she is describing an apocalypse when she combines "great day" with "of account."

134. For *"Gray hairs"* (not *gray heads*), see Genesis 44:31: "It shall come to pass, when he seeth that the lad is not with us, that he will die: and thy servants shall bring down *the gray hairs* of thy servant our father with sorrow to the grave." Similarly, Genesis 44:29 and 42:38.

135. Luke 15:11–32, the parable of the *prodigal* son. By adding that "prodigal children may return to God," Stewart emphasizes that they are prodigals not only from their families but from God.

136. Hebrews 1:14: "Are they not all ministering spirits, sent forth to minister for them who shall *be heirs of salvation*?" In other words, to be an heir of salvation is to become an inheritor of salvation. In the parable of the prodigal son, the prodigal squandered his inheritance, turning his back on his father and family. By combining the idea of the prodigal with that of the "heir of salvation," Stewart suggests that the real inheritance all prodigals squander is the invitation to salvation.

if not, their children cannot rise and condemn them[137] at the awful bar of God.

Perhaps you will say, that you cannot send them to high schools and academies. You can have them taught the first rudiments of useful knowledge,[138] and then you can have private teachers,[139] who will instruct them in the higher branches; and their intelligence will become greater than ours, and their children will attain to higher advantages, and their children still higher;[140] and then, though we are dead, our works shall live: though we are mouldering, our names shall not be forgotten.[141]

137. Matthew 12:41–42: "The men of Nineveh shall *rise* in judgment with this generation, *and shall condemn* it: because they repented at the preaching of Jonas; and, behold, a greater than Jonas is here. The queen of the south shall *rise* up *in the judgment* with this generation, and *shall condemn it:* for she came from the uttermost parts of the earth to hear the wisdom of Solomon; and, behold, a greater than Solomon is here." Also parallels in Luke 11:31–32. One frightening element of the Judgment Day that Stewart envisions is that those you fail in life will be present to condemn you in death.

138. Always, Stewart recommends self-help, despite whatever obstacles exist—in this case, the lack of schools available for African American students. The ultimate concern is never what whites try to prevent but what blacks must do despite these hindrances.

139. Did Stewart have a private teacher? She must have been instructed somewhere. Are these private teachers to be black? Or is she recommending starting alternative schools if other existing schools will not admit black children? Did she serve as a private teacher? Is this sentence a kind of advertisement for her teaching services? Stewart tells us little to nothing about her own education. Instead, she demonstrates in the course of these speeches that she is educated.

140. This is the typical goal of black uplift: it is reminiscent of the slogan of black women's clubs of the twentieth century: "Lifting as we climb." That is, that attainment is never only personal but also for the benefit of the whole of black people. As in the old hymn "We Are Climbing Jacob's Ladder," every round goes higher, higher; each generation's attainment is the starting point for the next generation's ascent. Each generation is to stand on the shoulders of the previous generations, making their ancestors' ending point their starting point.

141. One of the cruelest penalties of slavery was the loss of name, identity, even birthplace. Frederick Douglass, in his autobiography, lamented that few slaves knew their own birthdays: "I have no accurate knowledge of my age, never having seen any authentic record containing it. By far the larger part of the slaves know as little of their age as horses know of theirs, and it is the wish of most masters within my knowledge to keep their slaves thus ignorant. I do not remember to have ever met a slave who could tell of his birthday." Frederick Douglass, *Narrative of the Life of Frederick Douglass, an American Slave,* ed. David W. Blight, Bedford Books in American History

Finally, my heart's desire and prayer to God is, that there might come a thorough reformation among us. Our minds have too long groveled in ignorance and sin.[142] Come, let us incline our ears to wisdom, and apply our hearts to understanding;[143] promote her and she shall exalt thee; she shall bring thee to honor when thou dost embrace her.[144] An ornament of grace shall she be to thy head, and a crown of glory shall she deliver to thee.[145] Take fast hold of instruction; let her not go; keep her, for she is thy life.[146] Come, let us turn unto the Lord our God,[147] with all our heart and

---

(Boston: Bedford Books of St. Martin's Press, 1993), 39. Alex Haley's *Roots* documented one black family's struggle to recover the names and personal histories of its African ancestors—a difficult task given the lack of documentation of slaves' lives. Alex Haley, *Roots*, 1st ed. (Garden City, NY: Doubleday, 1976).

Stewart suggests here that the sheer nobility of her people's deeds will constitute a kind of recovered memory—that no more generations of African Americans will be nameless; rather, they will be remembered. This is in keeping with the themes of Ethiopianism—as a way of recovering Africa as a noble place of origin, Stewart suggests that African Americans prove this nobility by their deportment in the Americas. This theme of remembrance is one to which Stewart has turned before. As a childless widow, how was she to be remembered? Stewart hopes to immortalize her name by means of the message she is preaching to her people.

142. Although "reformation" is a term heavy with theological meaning (as in the Protestant Reformation), here Stewart means it to include civic and educational renewal as well as spiritual restoration. To be sure, Stewart believes that the civic and spiritual are wedded and that one reformation cannot take place without the other. "Ignorance" is tied to "sin."

If, as Ethiopianism teaches, African Americans have a noble heritage, they can escape the ignobility of their American condition by recovering that heritage and living up to it. What whites do to keep blacks down is therefore no real obstacle; as a noble people, Stewart calls African Americans to rise, irrespective of obstacles. They are to be motivated by knowledge: knowledge of the coming judgment of God, and knowledge of who they really are.

143. Proverbs 2:2: "So that *thou incline thine ear unto wisdom, and apply thine heart to understanding.*"

144. Proverbs 4:8: "*Exalt her, and she shall promote thee: she shall bring thee to honour, when thou dost embrace her.*" Here, Stewart inverts the order of the proverb—that is, she suggests that although wisdom is *promoted*, African Americans will be *exalted*.

145. Proverbs 4:9: "She shall give *to thine head an ornament of grace: a crown of glory shall she deliver to thee.*"

146. Proverbs 4:13: "*Take fast hold of instruction; let her not go: keep her; for she is thy life.*"

147. Deuteronomy 4:30 and 30:10: "*turn unto the* LORD *thy God.*" Joel 2:13: "*turn unto the* LORD *your God.*" Luke 1:16: "*turn to the Lord their God.*" Again, Stewart has inserted

soul,[148] and put away[149] every unclean and unholy thing from among us, and walk before the Lord our God,[150] with a perfect heart,[151] all the days of our lives; then we shall be a people with whom God shall delight to dwell;[152] yea, we shall be that happy people whose God is the Lord.[153]

---

a familiar biblical phrase and has adjusted the pronoun ("our") to indicate that she is speaking of the God of her people.

148. Deuteronomy 4:29: "with *all thy heart and with all thy soul*"; Deuteronomy 6:5: "And thou shalt love the LORD thy God *with all thine heart, and with all thy soul*"; Deuteronomy 10:12 and elsewhere, particularly throughout Deuteronomy, and in Joshua 22:5, 1 and 2 Kings, 1 and 2 Chronicles, and in the Gospels, quoting the Ten Commandments.

149. "*Put . . . away*" is used quite a bit, particularly in the Hebrew Bible and in the New Testament when referring to the Hebrew Bible (as in discussions of the Mosaic code on divorce, for example). Variously, *put away* evil, *put away* whoredom, *put away* sin, *put away* [your] wife (i.e., in divorce), *put away* [your] idols, etc. In other words, to have nothing else to do with something/someone with which/whom one was previously involved or associated.

150. "*Walk before . . . God*" or "*. . . the Lord*" is also quite common. Psalms 116:9: "I will *walk before the* LORD in the land of the living." 2 Chronicles 7:17–18: "And as for thee, if thou wilt *walk before me*, as David thy father walked, and do according to all that I have commanded thee, and shalt observe my statutes and my judgments; Then will I stablish the throne of thy kingdom." Usually part of a covenantal agreement: one "*walk[s] before*" God (i.e., lives according to God's law); God blesses one in some specific way. Again, Stewart is reinforcing the idea of a covenant with God.

151. "*Perfect heart*": 1 Kings 8:61: "Let your *heart* therefore *be perfect* with the LORD our God, to walk in his statutes, and to keep his commandments, as at this day." Often used as an indicator of the individual's obedience to, or love for, God. See 1 Kings 15:3: "And he walked in all the sins of his father, which he had done before him: and *his heart was not perfect* with the LORD his God, as the heart of David his father." 1 Kings 15:14, "But the high places were not removed: nevertheless Asa's *heart was perfect* with the LORD all his days."

The fulfillment of the covenant God has struck with the people of African descent requires that God return (as Stewart has earlier suggested) to the people. God cannot return to them as long as they continue in sin. As a result, their salvation and the achievement of equality require the same repentance. Then God, who gives both freedom and salvation, can restore the people of African descent to their rightful state.

152. This is similar to Zechariah 8:8: "And I will bring them, and they *shall dwell* in the midst of Jerusalem: and *they shall be my people, and I will be their God*, in truth and in righteousness"; and Revelation 21:3: "And I heard a great voice out of heaven saying, Behold, the tabernacle of God is with men, and *he will dwell with them, and they shall be his people, and God himself shall be with them, and be their God*." This is just a restatement of Stewart's contention that it is God who must return.

I am of a strong opinion,[154] that the day on which we unite, heart and soul, turn our attention to knowledge and improvement, that day the hissing and reproach among the nations of the earth against us will cease. And even those who now point at us with the finger of scorn, will aid and befriend us. It is of no use for us to sit with our hands folded, hanging our heads like bulrushes,[155] lamenting our wretched condition; but let us make a mighty effort, and arise; and if no one will promote or respect us, let us promote and respect ourselves.

The American ladies have the honor conferred on them, that by prudence and economy in their domestic concerns, and their unwearied attention if forming the minds and manners of their children, they laid the foundation of their becoming what they now are. The good women of Wethersfield, Conn.[156] toiled in the blazing sun, year after year, weeding onions, then sold the seed and procured money enough to erect them a house of worship; and shall we not imitate their examples, as far as they

153. Psalms 144:15: "*Happy is that people, that is in such a case: yea, happy is that people, whose God is the* LORD."

154. Stewart was nothing if not a woman of strong opinions. However, one can see how those opinions might have gotten her into trouble with her audiences. If one follows her reasoning carefully, one sees that she thinks that *everyone* has failed God except her and David Walker. Black women have not done their jobs to raise their children properly and to inspire their men; black men have not done their jobs to distinguish themselves and demonstrate "manly ambition." And whites have just exploited black men and women—but that's no excuse for blacks, who are still responsible for gaining economic power and education, despite how whites oppress them. (Stewart hasn't yet had anything particularly negative to say about whites, either. Instead, she's complemented their racial solidarity.) Stewart isn't pleased with anyone. Not surprisingly, listening audiences were not particularly pleased with her or her message.

155. Isaiah 58:5: "Is it such a fast that I have chosen? a day for a man to afflict his soul? is it to *bow down his head as a bulrush*, and to spread sackcloth and ashes under him? wilt thou call this a fast, and an acceptable day to the LORD?"

Folded hands are empty hands. Stewart says that her people should unfold their hands and put them to work. When her people take up the work of self-improvement, Stewart optimistically believes that their "reproach among the nations of the earth" will end. Her hope (which was generally disproven by history) is that whites will fairly credit blacks with whatever they achieve by their own efforts.

156. Stewart is apparently referring to the "good [white] women of Wethersfield," Connecticut, since she then tells her people that they should "imitate [the whites'] examples, as far as they are worthy of imitation." Whites are American; she and her people are of African descent—"sons and daughters of Africa."

are worthy of imitation?[157] Why cannot we do something to distinguish ourselves, and contribute some of our hard earnings that would reflect honor upon our memories, and cause our children to arise and call us blessed?[158] Shall it any longer be said of the daughters of Africa, they have no ambition, they have no force? By no means. Let every female heart become united, and let us raise a fund ourselves;[159] and at the end of the one year and a half, we might be able to lay the corner-stone for the building of a High School, that the higher branches of knowledge might be enjoyed by us; and God would raise us up,[160] and enough to aid us in our laudable designs. Let each one strive to excel in good house wifery, knowing that prudence and economy are the road to wealth. Let us not say, we know this, or we know that, and practise nothing; but let us practise what we do know.

How long shall the fair daughters of Africa be compelled to bury their minds and talents beneath a load of iron pots and kettles? Until union, knowledge and love begin to flow among us.[161] How long shall a mean set of men flatter us with their smiles, and enrich themselves with our hard

157. Stewart does not believe that everything European Americans do is worthy of imitation—only those acts that preserve racial solidarity, value education, and promote virtue.

158. Proverbs 31:28: "*Her children arise up, and call her blessed*; her husband also, and he praiseth her."

159. Stewart calls for collective economic action among her people. This would later become a tenet of Black Nationalism.

160. This is a common expression. See, for example, Deuteronomy 18:15: "*The* LORD *thy God will raise up unto thee* a Prophet from the midst of thee, of thy brethren, like unto me; unto him ye shall hearken"; or Acts 2:24: "Whom *God hath raised up*, having loosed the pains of death: because it was not possible that he should be holden of it." Here, Stewart makes the point that despite the work that blacks may do to build schools or to improve their educations, it is God who will ultimately cause their efforts to succeed. Moreover, the great difficulty of the task for humans is negated by the fact that God will complete it.

161. "*Union, knowledge and love*": Stewart argues that whites are able to continue to exploit blacks because blacks lack love for one another (or perhaps self-love), are ignorant, and are not united. Until blacks develop self-determination and unity, whites will be able to continue to exploit them, forcing them to "bury their minds and talents beneath a load of iron pots and kettles." The picture here is particularly one of the exploitation of black women, who were more likely to be found in kitchens working among "iron pots and kettles."

earnings; their wives' fingers sparkling with rings, and they themselves laughing at our folly?[162] Until we begin to promote and patronize each other.[163] Shall we be a by-word among the nations any longer? Shall they laugh us to scorn forever? Do you ask, what can we do? Unite and build a store of your own, if you cannot procure a license. Fill one side with dry goods, and other with groceries. Do you ask, where is the money? We have spent more than enough for nonsense,[164] to do what building we should want. We have never had an opportunity of displaying our talents; therefore the world thinks we know nothing. And we have been possessed of by far too mean and cowardly a disposition, though I highly disapprove of an insolent or impertinent one. Do you ask the disposi-

162. Stewart paints a grim but realistic picture here. Black women work, consigned to manual and domestic chores, while white women reap the material benefits. However, there is an even more sinister aspect to the situation Stewart describes. There are "men [who] flatter us with their smiles, and enrich themselves with our hard earnings." I believe that here Stewart is alluding to the fact that black women domestic servants were never safe from the sexual attentions of the white men of the household. They smiled at the daughters of Africa, while giving the ill-gotten gains to their white (American) wives (whose "fingers sparkle with rings"). With a final note of anger, Stewart denounces the white men who are "laughing at" the "folly" of the black women in such a situation. However, Stewart is also slyly denouncing the black women who are deceived by the flattering smiles of white men.

163. Stewart's program of economic empowerment requires her people to "promote and patronize" black businesses.

164. Even today, commentators sometimes bemoan the lack of black buying power. Stewart does not accept the excuse that blacks do not have enough money. Instead, she thinks that blacks have been spending their money on the wrong things, failing to pool their resources to collective effect, or failing to support other blacks' businesses. Further, Stewart chides her audience for having spent their limited finances on "nonsense." One can only speculate as to what Stewart considers to be a nonsensical purchase, but I suspect that she would reject expenditures that benefit the individual person rather than the whole people, or spending that does not promote education or virtue. However, achieving black economic advancement was not as simple as organizing the sort of black collective action Stewart proposed, even after the Civil War. As Ida B. Wells noted, black economic empowerment sometimes provoked a violent reaction from whites. Wells identified perceived economic competition against whites as one of the factors inciting whites to lynch blacks in the post–Civil War South. Paula Giddings, *When and Where I Enter: The Impact of Black Women on Race and Sex in America*, 1st ed. (New York: W. Morrow, 1984), 17–31.

tion I would have you possess? Possess the spirit of independence. The Americans do,[165] and why should not you?

Possess the spirit of men, bold and enterprising, fearless and undaunted.[166] Sue for your rights and privileges.[167] Know the reason that you cannot attain them. Weary them with your importunities.[168] You can but die, if you make the attempt; and we shall certainly die if you do not.[169] The Americans have practiced nothing but head-work these 200 years,

165. The Americans possess the spirit of independence, as does Maria Stewart. She would have her people possess it, too.

166. After all of her exhortations to the women in her audience, to possess manners and "artless innocence" while avoiding "meddling" in others' business, Stewart now tells them not only to possess the "spirit of independence" but also to possess the "spirit of men." She has exhorted women to excel at "housewifery." Now, she encourages them to be "bold and enterprising, fearless and undaunted"—all characteristics she identifies as distinguishing the "spirit of men." Obviously, the line she has drawn to differentiate the sexes is at best somewhat flexible and at worst inconsistent. At this early stage in her political and theological development, Stewart is not clear what she wants with regard to issues of gender. Eventually, such inconsistencies will push Stewart to abandon some elements of her more traditional thinking about women's roles in society.

167. Stewart sued for her rights to her husband's estate. She did not win the case, but she did prosecute it, nonetheless. In her speeches, she never speaks directly of this court defeat but instead advocates that others also sue for their rights. See Richardson, *Maria W. Stewart*, 7. In suing for her rights, did Stewart then possess the "spirit of men" as she understood it? Did one have to possess the "spirit of men" to venture thus out into the marketplace, or into the machinery of government and justice?

168. Luke 11:5–9: "And he said unto them, Which of you shall have a friend, and shall go unto him at midnight, and say unto him, Friend, lend me three loaves; For a friend of mine in his journey is come to me, and I have nothing to set before him? And he from within shall answer and say, Trouble me not: the door is now shut, and my children are with me in bed; I cannot rise and give thee. I say unto you, Though he will not rise and give him, because he is his friend, yet *because of his importunity* he will rise and give him as many as he needeth. And I say unto you, Ask, and it shall be given you; seek, and ye shall find; knock, and it shall be opened unto you." Jesus gives this instruction as part of a larger teaching on prayer and persistence in prayer. Stewart uses it to encourage persistence on the part of her audience. Of this text from Luke, verse 9 was probably familiar to most in her audience.

169. Why fear death? Stewart argues that you're going to die whether you do anything or not. You might as well do something. Stewart is aware that for her crusade to succeed, others must join her cause. She states pointedly that "*we* shall certainly die if *you* do not" join the struggle for African American liberation and advancement.

and we have done their drudgery.[170] And is it not high time for us to imitate their examples, and practise head-work too, and keep what we have got, and get what we can? We need never to think that any body is going to feel interested for us, if we do not feel interested for ourselves. That day we, as a people, hearken unto the voice of the Lord our God, and walk in his ways and ordinances, and become distinguished for our ease, elegance and grace, combined with other virtues, that day the Lord will raise us up, and enough to aid and befriend us,[171] and we shall begin to flourish.

Did every gentleman in America realize, as one, that they had got to become bondmen, and their wives, their sons, and their daughters, servants forever, to Great Britain, their very joints would become loosened, and tremblingly would smite one against another; their countenance would be filled with horror, every nerve muscle would be forced into action, their souls would recoil at the very thought, their hearts would die within them, and death would be far more preferable. Then why have not Africa's sons a right to feel the same? Are not their wives, their sons, and their daughters, as dear to them as those of the white man's?[172] Certainly, God has not deprived them of the divine influences of his Holy Spirit, which is the greatest of all blessings, if they ask him.[173] Then why should

170. Stewart complains that the Americans have had the leisure to develop politics, literature, and religion because they have had the sons and daughters of Africa to do their manual labor.

171. Ultimately, unlike the more militant Black Nationalists of the twentieth century, Stewart does not exclude other races or peoples from joining her fight. She expects the Lord to raise up not only her people but also "enough [others] to aid and befriend" her people.

172. In the rhetoric of the American Revolution, continued political allegiance to Great Britain was often equated with slavery. The irony is that while demanding freedom for themselves, the Americans kept Africans in slavery. Here Stewart takes note of that irony. As a New Englander, and as a resident of Boston, she would have been well aware of the Americans' rhetoric on the need for independence, as well as their likening of British rule to slavery. Because she believes independence to be a gift to every human given by God, she does not limit the need for freedom only to whites but extends it to her people as well. For references to "slavery" to Great Britain dating from the period of the American Revolution, see for example, Thomas Paine's "Common Sense," http://www.earlyamerica.com/earlyamerica/milestones/commonsense/text .html.

173. In a continuation of an earlier allusion to Luke 11, Stewart now notes God's gift of the Holy Spirit (and its influence) as evidence of God's acknowledgment of

man any longer deprive his fellow-man of equal rights and privileges? Oh, America, America, foul and indelible is thy stain! Dark and dismal is the cloud that hangs over thee, for thy cruel wrongs and injuries to the fallen sons of Africa. The blood of her murdered ones[174] cries to heaven for vengeance against thee.[175] Thou art almost become drunken with the blood of her slain;[176] thou hast enriched thyself through her toils and la-

---

the children of Africa as his children. (This is despite the fact that she has earlier in this same speech complained—in prayer—that they have not experienced the Holy Spirit's influence.) One of the lynchpins of the slavocracy was the contention that Africans needed or deserved slavery because of their innate inferiority. Stewart uses this text to demonstrate that Africans are not inferior before God. The scripture to which she alludes compares a father who gives his children good gifts to God, who gives his children the Holy Spirit. The extension of the analogy is this: as the Holy Spirit is a good gift, so God is a good father. Therefore, receipt of the Holy Spirit serves as evidence of membership in the family of God, and nothing less than membership in the human family as well. Luke 11:9–13: "And I say unto you, Ask, and it shall be given you; seek, and ye shall find; knock, and it shall be opened unto you. For every one that asketh receiveth; and he that seeketh findeth; and to him that knocketh it shall be opened. *If a son shall ask bread of any of you that is a father, will he give him a stone? or if he ask a fish, will he for a fish give him a serpent? Or if he shall ask an egg, will he offer him a scorpion? If ye then, being evil, know how to give good gifts unto your children: how much more shall your heavenly Father give the Holy Spirit to them that ask him?"*

Interestingly, in the book of Acts, receipt of the Holy Spirit was taken as evidence of membership in the Jesus movement. This was of particular interest in the case of Gentiles, since receipt of the Holy Spirit indicated that God had allowed them to enter into the covenant relationship previously believed to have been the exclusive purview of the Jews. (See Acts 10:48 and 19:1–6.)

174. Here Stewart avoids a rather obvious allusion: *"blood of the slain"* is a common biblical expression. (See, for example, Leviticus 14:51, Numbers 23:24, Deuteronomy 32:42, 1 Samuel 1:22.) However, she chooses *"blood of . . . murdered ones."* Stewart doesn't always go for the obvious biblical allusion. This suggests a certain care in her application of the biblical text to her speeches.

175. This is similar to Genesis 4:10: "And he said, What hast thou done? the voice of thy brother's *blood crieth unto me from the ground.*"

176. Although the idea of becoming drunk with blood (as one would with wine) occurs several times (Deuteronomy 32:42, Isaiah 49:26, Jeremiah 47:10, Ezekiel 39:19), it is closest to Revelation 17:6: "And I saw the woman *drunken with the blood of the saints, and with the blood of the martyrs of Jesus:* and when I saw her, I wondered with great admiration." With this text, Stewart begins the turn to the heart of her accusation against America, by beginning (metaphorically) to link the nation's behavior to that of the opponents of Christ who are described in the book of Revelation. The harlot,

bors; and now thou refuseth to make even a small return. And thou hast caused the daughters of Africa to commit whordoms and fornications;[177] but upon thee be their curse.[178]

O, ye great and mighty men of America, you rich and powerful ones, many of you will call for the rocks and mountains to fall upon you,[179] and to hide you from the wrath of the Lamb,[180] and from him that sitteth

---

consort of the Antichrist, is she who becomes drunk with the blood of the saints and martyrs. The image is powerfully anti-Eucharistic, and it is utterly blasphemous.

177. This is almost certainly another reference to the sexual access and control that the slavocracy exercised over slaves—and particularly over female slaves. The slave regime regularly forced slaves into sexual encounters with whites or with one another. A slave might be told to breed with another slave for the purposes of producing more stock for the master. Women slaves, and especially those who worked in the master's house, were always in danger of rape by any of the white men in the household.

178. Although it is slaves who are involved in the sin of fornication, it is committed because their masters have forced them to it. Therefore, the "curse" or guilt of it remains on the masters rather than upon the slaves.

179. Revelation 6:16–17: "And *said to the mountains and rocks, Fall on us*, and hide us from the face of him that sitteth on the throne, and from the wrath of the Lamb: For the great day of his wrath is come; and who shall be able to stand?" This scripture is part of the inspiration for the Negro spiritual "No Hidin' Place." The refrain of the song is "Oh, I went to the rock to hide my face. / The rock cried out, 'No hidin' place'; / [There's] no hidin' place down [there]." When the great day of God's judgment comes, there will be no place for sinners to hide. The second verse proclaims, "Oh, de rock cried, 'I'm burnin' too, / I want-a go to [heaven] as well as you.' / [There's] no hidin' place down [there]." "No Hidin' Place," in *Songs of Zion*, ed. J. Jefferson Cleveland and Verolga Nix (Nashville: Abingdon, 1981), 141. The spiritual conjures up the same image that I believe Stewart intends here: when judgment finally comes, none of the guilty will be able escape it.

180. *"The wrath of the Lamb"* is an interesting image but also a paradoxical one. Lambs are not generally known for their anger. There is only one part of the Bible that describes the Lamb of God (Jesus) as being angry: the book of Revelation. See, for example, Revelation 6:16–17: "And said to the mountains and rocks, Fall on us, and hide us from the face of him that sitteth on the throne, and from *the wrath of the Lamb*: For the great day of his wrath is come; and who shall be able to stand?" (Compare this with, for example, John 1:29, where Jesus is described as the Lamb of God who takes away the sins of the world.) Ultimately, the sins of the world have become so egregious to the author of the book of Revelation that even the long-suffering, slow-to-anger Lamb of God is angry—and righteously so. This image of the "wrath of the Lamb" is another indication that Stewart has turned to the heart of her accusations against America and that she has begun an apocalyptic denunciation of it. Stewart

upon the throne;[181] whilst many of the sable-skinned Africans you now despise, will shine in the kingdom of heaven as the stars forever and ever.[182] Charity begins at home, and those that provide not for their own, are worse than infidels.[183] We know that you are raising contributions to aid the gallant Poles; we know that you have befriended Greece and Ireland; and you have rejoiced with France, for her heroic deeds of valor. You have acknowledged all the nations of the earth, except Hayti;[184] and

---

rarely turns to images of Jesus, but when she does, it is often to ones like this: of the *"wrath of the Lamb."* Even when she quotes the New Testament, she prefers texts like Luke 16:19–31, where Jesus tells a parable about a master punished in hell while his servant is rewarded in heaven. Stewart is angry, and she wants to evoke by her words an angry God as well.

181. The image of one *"sitt[ing] upon the throne"* is quite ubiquitous in scripture occurring six times in the book of Revelation alone. (See Revelation 3:21, 4:4, 6:16, 7:10, 7:15.) To sit upon the throne is to be invested with all of the power of state.

182. Daniel 12:3: "And they that be wise *shall shine as the brightness of the firmament; and they that turn many to righteousness as the stars for ever and ever."* A consequence of the judgment Stewart envisions is that the righteous inherit glory and eternal life, while the wicked receive only death.

183. 1 Timothy 5:8: "But if any *provide not for his own,* and specially for those of his own house, he hath denied the faith, and is *worse than an infidel."* Note that although Stewart begins the sentence with the fairly trite "Charity begins at home," she ends with scripture that disparages those whose charity has not begun at home. If, as Stewart has argued, blacks are in every human category equal to whites, then for whites to fail to provide for them (even the fair wages for their labor) is a sin. Stewart is here refuting the idea that the Americans are the most spiritual, most religious people on the earth, possessed of a biblical "city upon a hill." Instead, Stewart decries them as "worse than" infidels, or unbelievers. Only infidels would fail to notice the true people of the covenant—the people of Africa—in their midst.

184. "Hayti" is Stewart's alternate spelling of Haiti. The slave revolt in Haiti, which ended in 1804 with Haitian independence, was closely watched by blacks in Boston, and elsewhere in the United States, as was the thwarted slave revolt planned by Denmark Vesey in Charleston, South Carolina. Richardson, *Maria W. Stewart,* 4, 126. Because of David Walker's connections among the members of Charleston's African Church, where Vesey's plot was believed to have been hatched, some have speculated that Walker may have been aware of at least some elements of the plot or acquainted with some of the plotters. After Vesey's 1822 plot was foiled by a conspirator's confession, Charleston's officials seem to have run every black suspected of involvement (who wasn't hung) out of town. By 1825, Walker turned up in Boston, where Stewart lived. Slave revolts such as Gabriel Prosser's rain-thwarted plot in Richmond, Virginia, in August 1800, Denmark Vesey's planned attack, and the successful slave insurrection in

you may publish, as far as the East is from the West,[185] that you have two millions of negroes, who aspire no higher than to bow at your feet, and to court your smiles. You may kill, tyrannize, and oppress as much as you choose, until our cry shall come up before the throne of God;[186] for I am firmly persuaded, that he will not suffer you to quell the proud, fearless and undaunted spirits of the African forever; for in his own time, he is able to plead our cause against you,[187] and to pour out upon you the ten plagues of Egypt.[188] We will not come out against you with swords and

---

Haiti were increasingly frightening and threatening to the slave regime. Whites lived with the fear that their slaves might at any time turn against them in organized revolt. Hinks, introduction to Walker, *Appeal to the Coloured Citizens*, xvii–xxiii.

185. Psalms 103:12: "*As far as the east is from the west*, so far hath he removed our transgressions from us." The only contribution that this scripture seems to make to Stewart's overall theme is that it describes an infinite or at least (by ancient standards) immeasurable or unfathomable distance, or one that cannot be crossed. In the context of a round planet, east is an infinite distance from west.

186. Exodus 2:23: "And it came to pass in process of time, that the king of Egypt died: and the children of Israel sighed by reason of the bondage, and they cried, and *their cry came up unto God* by reason of the bondage." Interestingly here, the cry that went up was because the Israelites were being held as slaves in Egypt. Stewart expects the same sort of cry—for justice and for freedom—to arise from her people and to move God to action on their behalf.

187. For "*plead our [or my] cause*," see Psalms 35:1, Psalms 43:1, and various other locations throughout the Bible. However, in the context of the two quotations from Exodus (which come before and after this reference), Stewart's allusion to the one who pleads the cause of the children of Africa sounds very much like a Moses figure. Was she anticipating the coming of a new David Walker or another charismatic leader who could gather the children of Africa into an effective unit?

Elsewhere, Stewart has used the phrase "fearless and undaunted" to describe David Walker and as a characteristic of the spirit of men. Now, she uses the same phrase to describe the spirits of Africans. Might the Moses figure being evoked here symbolize a kind of corporate leadership as the sons and daughters of Africa come together as a mighty, unified force with a single goal? I believe that, rather than anticipating the return of another Walker, Stewart expects his spirit to animate the entire black populace.

188. In calling for God to pour out ten plagues upon America, Stewart continues her point that the slaveholding United States resembles the slaveholding Egypt of the book of Exodus, much more than it resembles the Israelites—the people of God's covenant. In fact, the United States is, like Egypt, oppressing the people of God's covenant.

staves, as against a thief;[189] but we will tell you that our souls are fired with the same love of liberty and independence with which your souls are fired. We will tell you that too much of your blood flows in our veins, and too much of your color in our skins,[190] for us not to possess your spirits. We will tell you, that it is our gold that clothes you in fine linen and purple, and causes you to fare sumptuously every day;[191] and it is the blood of our fathers, and the tears of our brethren that have enriched your soils. AND WE CLAIM OUR RIGHTS.[192] We will tell, you that we are not afraid of them that kill the body, and after that can do no more;[193] but we will tell you whom we do fear. We fear Him who is able, after he hath killed, to destroy both souls and body in hell forever.[194] Then, my brethren,

189. Luke 22:52, and parallels: "Then Jesus said unto the chief priests, and captains of the temple, and the elders, which were come to him, Be ye *come out, as against a thief, with swords and staves?*" Here, Jesus complains that those who have come to arrest him have come with weapons as though he were an armed revolutionary. Jesus's point is that he is unarmed. By this appropriation, Stewart makes clear that this is not a threat of physical violence so much as it is the promise of divine retribution.

190. Stewart notes the obvious here—although it is a fact that the slavocracy wished to deny—that the Africans and the Americans have been interbreeding. Although miscegenation would remain a crime in some states in the United States until the Supreme Court struck down such laws in its decision in *Loving v. Virginia* (1967), it was clear, even in Stewart's day, that many, many children had been born of mixed-race parentage. This fact makes the issue of slavery all the more inhumane. Ultimately, parents enslaved their own children and were protected by law in this because one of the child's parents was of African descent.

191. This is taken from the parable of the rich man and Lazarus, Luke 16:19: "There was a certain rich man, which was clothed in purple and fine linen, and fared sumptuously every day." The parable tells of a poor man, Lazarus, who dies and goes to heaven, and the rich man who presumably goes to hell because he never had mercy on Lazarus. The parallel between blacks/Lazarus, and whites/the rich man are clear. Stewart expects there to be eternal consequences for the whites who have mistreated blacks.

192. At the end of this recitation of the fact that blacks desire liberty and freedom as much as anyone else does, Stewart repeats her demand for rights, even more emphatically than before. (The emphasis in the text is in the original 1835 publication.)

193. Luke 12:4: "And I say unto you my friends, Be not afraid of them *that kill the body, and after that have no more that they can do.*"

194. Matthew 10: 28: "And fear not them which kill the body, but are not able to kill the soul: but rather *fear him which is able to destroy both soul and body in hell.*" Stewart has combined this scripture with its Lucan parallel cited in the previous note. This is a repetition of an idea she has stated previously: that one should fear God rather than other people.

sheath your swords,[195] and calm your angry passions. Stand still, and know that the Lord he is God.[196] Vengeance is his, and he will repay.[197] It is a long lane that has no turn. America has risen to her meridian. When you begin to thrive, she will begin to fall.[198] God hath raised you up a Walker[199] and a Garrison.[200] Though Walker sleeps,[201] yet he lives, and his name shall be had in everlasting remembrance.[202] I, even I, who am but a child,[203] inexperienced to many of you, am a living witness to testify unto you this day, that I have seen the wicked in great power, spreading

195. John 18:11: "Then said Jesus unto Peter, *Put up thy sword into the sheath*: the cup which my Father hath given me, shall I not drink it?" Here, as elsewhere, Stewart preaches a pacifism not found in David Walker's *Appeal*.

196. Psalms 46:10: "*Be still, and know that I am God*: I will be exalted among the heathen, I will be exalted in the earth." Stewart replaces the admonition of the text to "be still" with a more emphatic "stand still." She doesn't want her people to provoke a conflict. She believes that in God's own timing, God will do all that is necessary to set things right. It is a continuation of her antiviolence message.

197. Romans 12:19: "Dearly beloved, avenge not yourselves, but rather give place unto wrath: for it is written, *Vengeance is mine; I will repay,* saith the Lord." God is the ultimate source of justice; blacks do not have to provoke this justice by taking up arms.

198. The flip side of African ascendance, as the Ethiopian prophecy was believed to foretell, was the decline of the West. Here Stewart attests her belief that America had already reached its peak and must begin its inevitable decline as Africa and her people rise.

199. David Walker, author of *David Walker's Appeal to the Coloured Citizens of the World*.

200. William Lloyd Garrison, publisher of the abolitionist newspaper *The Liberator*, for which Stewart occasionally wrote articles.

201. Sleeping is a biblical euphemism for death. See, for example, 1 Kings 2:10: "So David slept with his fathers, and was buried in the city of David." See also Acts 7:60 and 1 Corinthians 15:6, 18.

202. Psalms 112: 5–6, 8, 10: "A good man showeth favour, and lendeth: he will guide his affairs with discretion. Surely he shall not be moved for ever: *the righteous shall be in everlasting remembrance*. . . . His heart is established, he shall not be afraid, until he see his desire upon his enemies. . . . The wicked shall see it, and be grieved; he shall gnash with his teeth, and melt away: the desire of the wicked shall perish." Here, "everlasting remembrance" takes place in the context of the life of a righteous man. By substituting "Walker" for "righteous" when she quotes the text, Stewart makes clear that she believes David Walker was a righteous man. In contrast, the wicked suffer the punishment their deeds have earned for them. So Walker's "everlasting remembrance" is the result not only of literary fame or even Christian resurrection but also of the eventual elimination (by the judgment of God) of all who opposed him.

203. Stewart was in her late twenties when she wrote this.

himself like a green bay tree,[204] and lo, he passed away; yea, I diligently sought him, but he could not be found;[205] and it is God alone that has inspired my heart to feel for Afric's woes.[206] Then fret not yourselves because of evil doers.[207] Fret not yourselves because of evil who bring wicked devices to pass; or they shall be cut down as the grass, and wither as the green herb.[208] Trust in the Lord, and do good; so shalt thou dwell in the land, and verily thou shalt be fed.[209] Encourage the noble-hearted Garrison.[210] Prove to the world that you are neither ourang-outangs,[211]

204. Psalms 37:35: "I have *seen the wicked in great power, and spreading himself like a green bay tree.*"

205. Psalms 37:36: "*Yet he passed away,* and, lo, he was not: yea, I sought him, *but he could not be found.*" The rich man prospered one moment, then disappeared the next. Using this juxtaposition, Stewart compares David Walker, whose body had died but whose words have lived on, with the United States, which appeared prosperous and healthy at that time. Stewart predicts the nation's demise and disappearance by likening it to the disappearance of the rich man, who prospered and spread like a bay tree only to die anonymously.

206. Again, Stewart attests that her concerns for her people originate with God: she is on a divine mission.

207. Psalms 37:1: "*Fret not thyself because of evildoers,* neither be thou envious against the workers of iniquity." Or Proverbs 24:19: "*Fret not thyself because of evil men,* neither be thou envious at the wicked; For there shall be no reward to the evil man; the candle of the wicked shall be put out."

208. Psalms 37:2: "For *they shall* soon *be cut down like the grass, and wither as the green herb.*" Because judgment is coming, evil is temporary; the righteous shall live forever. However, Stewart omits "soon." She's making no promises about how soon this judgment will come; her only promise is that it is indeed coming.

209. Psalms 37:3: "*Trust in the* LORD, *and do good; so shalt thou dwell in the land, and verily thou shalt be fed.*"

210. Stewart includes William Lloyd Garrison among the company of "good" whites who should be supported.

211. Here, Stewart takes issue with a point from Thomas Jefferson's *Notes on the State of Virginia.* In answering why he thought freed blacks should be deported to Africa rather than incorporated into the state as citizens, Jefferson notes "deep rooted prejudices entertained by whites; ten thousand recollections, by the blacks, of the injuries they have sustained" but then goes on to suggest that at the heart of the difficulty is what he calls "real distinctions which nature has made . . . which will probably never end but in the extermination of the one or the other race." Jefferson notes that his objection to the presence of blacks is not only political but also "physical and moral." He then suggests a hierarchy of races with whites on top and blacks just above the orangutan: "Add to these . . . [blacks'] own judgment in favor of the whites, declared by their preference of them, as uniformly as is the preference of the Oranootan [*sic*] for the black women over

nor a species of mere animals, but that you possess the same powers of intellect as those of the proud-boasting American.[212]

I am sensible, my brethren and friends, that many of you have been deprived of advantages, kept in utter ignorance, and that your minds are now darkened;[213] and if any of you have attempted to aspire after high and noble enterprises, you have met with so much opposition that your souls have become discouraged.[214] For this very cause, a few of us have

---

those of his own species." Jefferson goes on to state his belief in the general inferiority of blacks to whites, even to the point of questioning their capacity for literacy and literary achievement and, by extension, civilization: "Misery is often the parent of the most affecting touches in poetry.—Among the blacks is misery enough, God knows," Jefferson sniffs, "but no poetry." Thomas Jefferson, *Notes on the State of Virginia*, ed. William Harwood Peden (Chapel Hill: University of North Carolina Press, 1982), 138, 40.

Those comments infuriated David Walker. He fired back that to call people of African descent animals meant that American slavery was by far more inhumane than any slave regime of antiquity. Walker wrote, "But to prove farther that the condition of the Israelites was better under the Egyptians than ours under the whites. I call upon the professing Christians, I call upon the philanthropist, I call upon the very tyrant himself, to show me a page of history, either sacred or profane, on which a verse can be found, which maintains, that the Egyptians heaped the insupportable insult upon the children of Israel by telling them that they were not of the human family. Can the whites deny this charge? Have they not, after having reduced us to the deplorable condition of slaves under their feet, held us up as descending originally from the tribes of Monkeys or Orang-Outans [*sic*]? O! my God! I appeal to every man of feeling—is not this insupportable? . . . Has Mr. Jefferson declared to the world, that we are inferior to the whites, both in the endowments of our bodies and our minds?" Walker, *Appeal to the Coloured Citizens*, 12. Is the "tyrant" Walker calls upon a reference to Jefferson? If so, as seems likely, it is a daring charge. However, Walker reasons that men like Thomas Jefferson are tyrants in their support of an insupportable slave regime. Jefferson's comments were no less repugnant to Stewart than they had been to Walker.

212. Stewart does agree with Jefferson on one point: to demonstrate literacy is to demonstrate the ability to be included in the human family. (Interestingly, in *Notes on the State of Virginia*, Jefferson dismisses the work of African American poet Phillis Wheatley, whose name he misspells. He must make the point that blacks have no literature.) Stewart argues that black literacy is one of the most important achievements in the Africans' fight for equality with the Americans.

213. Ephesians 4:18: "Having the *understanding darkened*, being alienated from the life of God through the ignorance that is in them, because of the blindness of their heart." Here Stewart substitutes "mind" for "understanding."

214. Although Stewart acknowledges the difficulties blacks face, she does not regard those difficulties as an excuse to do nothing.

ventured to expose our lives in your behalf, to plead your cause against the great; and it will be of no use, unless you feel for yourselves and your little ones, and exhibit the spirits of men.[215] Oh, then, turn your attention to knowledge and improvement; for knowledge is power. And God is able to fill you with wisdom and understanding,[216] and to dispel your fears. Arm yourselves with the weapons of prayer.[217] Put your trust in the living God. Persevere strictly in the paths of virtue. Let nothing be lacking on your part; and, in God's own time, and his time is certainly the best, he will surely deliver you with a mighty hand and with an outstretched arm.[218]

I have never taken one step, my friends, with a design to raise myself in your esteem, or to gain applause. But what I have done, has been done with an eye single[219] to the glory of God, and to promote the good of souls. I have neither kindred nor friends. I stand alone in your midst,[220] exposed to the fiery darts of the devil, and to the assaults of wicked men.[221] But though all the powers of earth and hell were to combine

---

215. "To expose our lives" is to speak out in public. However, Stewart's speaking out will, she believes, be of no avail if the blacks on whose behalf she pleads do not join her and "exhibit the spirits of men"—join the struggle for justice.

216. Colossians 1:9: "For this cause we also, since the day we heard it, do not cease to pray for you, and to desire that ye *might be filled with* the knowledge of his will in *all wisdom and* spiritual *understanding*." Stewart doesn't limit her desire to "spiritual" understanding; she wants her people to have book learning, too.

217. This is similar but not identical to the admonitions of Ephesians 6, which recommend putting on the "whole armour of God" (verses 11 and 13) and "Praying always with all prayer and supplication in the Spirit" (verse 18). However, prayer is nowhere in the Bible described as a weapon. Even in this, Stewart selects a martial image that suggests not physical violence but vigilance for God's justice. The people are to pray, but God is to mete out justice.

218. Deuteronomy 4:34: "by a mighty hand, and by a stretched out arm." God is both "mighty" and willing to help in that God's arm is "outstretched."

219. Matthew 6:22: "The light of the body is the eye: if therefore *thine eye be single*, thy whole body shall be full of light." Also, Luke 11:34. In this case, Stewart indicates an undivided and unwavering purpose.

220. Stewart was both widow and orphan; she was also childless. Her mentor and model in this work, David Walker, was also dead. That she keeps mentioning these losses suggests that she felt them quite acutely.

221. Ephesians 6:16: "Above all, taking the shield of faith, wherewith ye shall be able to quench *all the fiery darts of the wicked*."

against me,[222] though all nature should sink into decay, still would I trust in the Lord, and joy in the God of my salvation.[223] For I am fully persuaded, that he will bring me off conqueror, yea, more than conqueror, through him who hath loved me and given himself for me.[224]

Boston, October, 1831.

HYMN.

God is a spirit, just and wise,
  He knows our inmost minds;
In vain to heaven we raise our cries,
  And leave our souls behind.

Nothing but truth before his throne,
  With honor can appear;
The painted hypocrites are known
  By the disguise they wear.[225]

222. Although this passage sounds remarkably like the words of Psalms 27, Stewart does not use them. Rather than quote the Psalms, which discuss earthly warfare, Stewart chooses instead to evoke a more cataclysmic, superhuman battle where she must battle "all the powers of earth and hell." Psalms 27:1–3: "The LORD is my light and my salvation; whom shall I fear? the LORD is the strength of my life; of whom shall I be afraid? When the wicked, even mine enemies and my foes, came upon me to eat up my flesh, they stumbled and fell. Though an host should encamp against me, my heart shall not fear: though war should rise against me, in this will I be confident."

223. Habakkuk 3:18: "Yet I will rejoice in the LORD, I will joy in the God of my salvation." Here Stewart has replaced "rejoice" with "trust." First comes faith ("trust"); then comes joy, as Stewart has reconfigured this text. Perhaps this reflects Stewart's own disposition: she may be indicating that she's experienced more of the need for trust than of the release of joy.

224. Stewart ends triumphantly. Romans 8:37: "Nay, in all these things we are *more than conquerors* through him that loved us. For I am persuaded, that neither death, nor life, nor angels, nor principalities, nor powers, nor things present, nor things to come, Nor height, nor depth, nor any other creature, shall be able to separate us from the *love* of God, which is in Christ Jesus our Lord."

225. Stewart inserted a prayer near the beginning of her remarks; here she ends with a hymn. By quoting this hymn by Isaac Watts, Stewart reinforces her contention that God, before whom "nothing but truth . . . with honor can appear," will be the ultimate judge on behalf of the sons and daughters of Africa. When the disguises of the slave owners are finally stripped away, the "painted hypocrites are known by the disguise they wear." God, who "knows our inmost minds" will know their sins and

Their lifted eyes salute the skies,
  Their bended knees the ground.
But God abhors the sacrifice,
  Where not the heart is found.[226]

Lord, search my heart, and try my reins,
  And make my souls sincere;
So shall I stand before thy throne,
  And find acceptance there.[227]

WATTS

---

judge them accordingly. They can pretend to be godly, but their treatment of the sons and daughters of Africa has betrayed them: only truly evil people could treat God's children as the slavocracy has treated blacks.

226. Here Watts seems to echo the often-quoted rebuke against empty sacrifices found in Micah 6:6–8: "Wherewith shall I come before the LORD, and bow myself before the high God? shall I come before him with burnt offerings, with calves of a year old? Will the LORD be pleased with thousands of rams, or with ten thousands of rivers of oil? shall I give my firstborn for my transgression, the fruit of my body for the sin of my soul? He hath shown thee, O man, what is good; and what doth the LORD require of thee, but to do justly, and to love mercy, and to walk humbly with thy God?" It is not enough to go through the motions before God. Stewart underscores her contention that it is the state of the heart that really matters. She's not convinced by high church attendance. Looking at the behavior of the Americans, and also of her own people, Stewart is convinced that they are lacking in real religion, which would have changed both their hearts and their actions.

227. For Stewart, Judgment Day is always looming. Her many references to judgment in this essay point to the importance—the eternal significance—she sees in her words.

CHAPTER 2

Maria Stewart's
Approach to Scripture

*T*HE PERIOD DURING which Maria Stewart gave her speeches, laden as they were with biblical references, was an important one for the battles of African Americans against slavery. (Although she was born free, Stewart regarded herself as having been enlisted in that battle.) Just as blacks were having their first encounters with the Bible on American shores, the slavocracy was using the Bible to construct defenses for slavery.[1] Nevertheless, African American exegetes were formulating from that same Bible refutations of the slavocracy and arguments for their own freedom.[2]

---

1. "African slaves in North America were introduced to the Bible at a point in history when the Bible was the main support in proslavery ideology. From about 1772 until 1850 the Bible was the primary source of authority and legitimation for the enslavement of Africans." Evans, *We Have Been Believers*, 35.

2. John Saillant, "Origins of African American Biblical Hermeneutics in Eighteenth-Century Black Opposition to the Slave Trade and Slavery," in Wimbush and Rodman, *African Americans and the Bible*, 236–50. Theophus H. Smith, *Conjuring Culture: Biblical Formations of Black America*, Religion in America (New York: Oxford University Press, 1994), 55–80.

The ability to read and understand the Bible was an undertaking of special significance among antebellum African Americans. What was at stake for blacks striving for literacy during the time of the slave regime was proof of their humanity in the face of Enlightenment arguments that conflated abilities to read and to reason while denying that Africans were capable of either.[3] In contrast to the age of reason's leading lights—men like Thomas Jefferson, David Hume, and Immanuel Kant, who questioned blacks' intellectual capacities—for African Americans "to read and to write was to transgress this nebulous realm of liminality"[4] into which slavery forced all blacks—a realm between humanity and commodity. The ideological underpinning of slavery was the assertion that Africa had no culture because blacks were incapable of it. Indeed, slavery was to be a "school for civilization"[5] for the slaves, and the only schooling of which they were capable. Such racist preconceptions were used to justify not only slavery but also the consequent mistreatment of all blacks, both slave and free. As Frederick Douglass and other former-slave authors proved to the great delight of the abolitionist movement and consternation of the slavocracy, the black man or woman who read and wrote confounded these demeaning assertions. As Henry Louis Gates observes, "The slave wrote not primarily to

3. See Gates, "The Trope of the Talking Book," 127–68. See also Henry Louis Gates and Nellie Y. McKay, "Preface: Talking Books," in *The Norton Anthology of African American Literature*, ed. Henry Louis Gates and Nellie Y. McKay (New York: W. W. Norton, 1997), xxvii–xxxvi.

4. Gates, "The Trope of the Talking Book," 128.

5. Ulrich Bonnell Phillips, *American Negro Slavery: A Survey of the Supply, Employment and Control of Negro Labor as Determined by the Plantation Regime*, 1st paperback ed. (Baton Rouge: Louisiana State University Press, 1966). In the foreword to this edition, historian Eugene D. Genovese reconsiders *American Negro Slavery*, which was originally published in 1918. Phillips argues that slavery was not particularly economically profitable but served the beneficial purpose of exposing "Negroes" to the civilizing presence of whites and of white culture. Although Phillips's work was regarded by many in the early years of the twentieth century as a classic history of the slave regime, it has subsequently been resoundingly refuted by scholars like Genovese, Richard Hofstadter, Stanley M. Elkins, and Kenneth M. Stampp, among others, who in the latter part of the twentieth century came to question not only the methods by which Phillips undertook his study, its conclusions, and the underlying racist and dismissive attitude he demonstrates toward the ostensible subjects of his study, the "American Negro Slaves."

demonstrate humane letters, but to demonstrate his or her own membership in the human community."[6]

For African American Christians, the Bible offered a powerful moti-
vation to learn to read and write. Blacks wanted to be able to read the
Bible because they were "distrustful of the white folks' interpretation of the
Scriptures and wanted to be able to search them for themselves,"[7] particularly given whites' tendency to preach only those Bible verses calculated to
produce more docile and obedient slaves. However, for those who could
not read, large passages of scripture were committed to memory through
oral traditions that repeated texts in lessons, stories, and songs. A missionary to former slaves in Beaufort, South Carolina, recounted a freed-
woman's description of her knowledge of the Bible: "'Oh! I don't know
nothing! I can't read a word. But oh! I read Jesus in my heart, just as you
read him in de book;' and drawing her forefingers across the other palm,
as if tracing a line: 'I read and read him here in my heart just as you read

6. Gates, "The Trope of the Talking Book," 128. Gates describes a topos of several
slave narratives that illustrates this sense of the Bible as written text and lived experience, as literature and vernacular. Gates calls it the "trope of the talking book," which
"between 1770 and 1815" appeared in "no fewer than five . . . slave narratives . . . as a
crucial scene of instruction to dramatize the author's own road to literacy." Ibid., 130.
According to this trope, the Bible speaks, somehow miraculously, to whites, but is
silent when an African holds his ear to it. Nevertheless, as he reports in his memoir,
former slave John Jea does not accept the silence of the book; when it will not speak
to his ears, he nevertheless perseveres until God reveals its mysteries to his eyes and
mind. Jea's narrative demonstrates his humanity not by an appeal to reason but by an
appeal to divinity. As Jea tells it, it is God who has sovereignly bestowed upon him the
ability to read—but it is only the Bible that he can comprehend. Clearly, Jea understands the miracle of his literacy and thorough knowledge of the Bible to demonstrate
divine favor bestowed upon one who has been otherwise demeaned and enslaved by
society. Indeed, by virtue of his salvation and baptism, Jea is freed from slavery even
before God teaches him to read the Bible. Ibid., 158–66. Jea's narrative suggests that
his salvation and baptism resulted in his freedom after magistrates had ascertained
the validity of his experience. According to Albert Raboteau, "One of the principal
reasons for the refusal of English planters to allow their slaves to receive instructions
was the fear that baptism would emancipate the slaves. The notion that if slaves were
baptized, 'they should, according to the laws of the *British* nation, and the canons of
its church,' be freed was legally vague but widely believed." Albert J. Raboteau, *Slave
Religion: The "Invisible Institution" in the Antebellum South* (New York: Oxford University Press, 1978), 98.

7. Raboteau, *Slave Religion*, 239.

him in the Bible. O, . . . my God! I got Him! I hold him here all de time! He stay with me!'"[8] It is this sense of the Bible as Word: as spoken and lived, as recited text and oral tradition, as ancient history and present reality, as written word but also word made flesh, that has animated African Americans' engagements with the scriptures.

Henry Louis Gates Jr. and Nellie Y. McKay suggest that this movement between written and oral traditions is essential to understanding all black literature, not only that which relates to the Bible:

> Historically, anonymous vernacular literature certainly preceded the tradition of written letters among African Americans. . . . In the instance of our literary tradition, the oral, or the vernacular, is never far from the written. Oral expression . . . surrounds the written tradition rather as a Möbius strip intertwines above and below a plane, in the traditional antiphonal 'call/response' structures peculiar to African and African American expressive cultural forms. Not only has the vernacular tradition served as the foundation of the written tradition, but it continues to nurture it, comment upon it, and criticize it in a dialectical, reciprocal relation that surely obtained historically in every major literary tradition.[9]

In moving between the written text and oral recitation of the Bible, African American exegetes like Maria Stewart laid the groundwork for such "dialectical, reciprocal" relations between written traditions and vernacular culture in the African American community in much the same way that sermons and spirituals did. In sermons and spirituals, as in the speeches of Maria Stewart, scriptures were not just recited or, re-membered[10] but were also commented upon in an interesting interplay between the written and the spoken or performed Word.

Webs of Meaning

Here is a typical passage from Stewart. The text invokes the King James Version of the Bible and intertwines quotations, near quotations (where

8. Ibid., 242.

9. Gates and McKay, "Preface: Talking Books," xxxviii.

10. By this I mean to play on the word *remembered* to suggest another meaning: "to be given members." In her performances of the biblical text, Stewart embodied them: she gave the members of her own body to the interpretive enterprise.

perhaps a word or two is changed), and allusions (where Stewart uses an idea from scripture but significantly changes the way it is expressed):

> This is the land of freedom. The press is at liberty. Every man has a right to express his opinion. Many think, because your skins are tinged with a sable hue, that you are an inferior race of beings; but God does not consider you as such. He hath formed and fashioned[11] you in his own glorious image,[12] and hath bestowed upon you reason and strong powers of intellect. He hath made you to have dominion over the beasts of the field, the fowls of the air, and the fish of the sea.[13] He hath crowned you with glory and honor; hath made you but a little lower than the angels;[14] and according to the Constitution of these United States, he hath made all men free and equal.[15] Then why should one worm say to another, "Keep you down there, while I sit up yonder; for I am better than thou?"[16] It is not the color of the skin that makes the man, but it is the principles formed within the soul.[17]

11. Psalms 119:73: "Thy hands have made me *and fashioned me*: give me understanding, that I may learn thy commandments."

12. Genesis 1:26: "And God said, Let us make man *in our image*, after our likeness."

13. Genesis 1:26: "And God said, Let us make man in our image, after our likeness: and let them have *dominion over the fish of the sea, and over the fowl of the air, and over the cattle, and over all the earth, and over every creeping thing that creepeth upon the earth.*"

14. Psalms 8:5: "*For thou hast made him a little lower than the angels, and hast crowned him with glory and honour.*" Also Hebrews 2:9: "But we see Jesus, who was *made a little lower than the angels* for the suffering of death, crowned with glory and honour; that he by the grace of God should taste death for every man."

15. "We hold these truths to be self-evident, that *all men are created equal,* that they are endowed by their Creator with certain unalienable Rights, that among these are Life, Liberty and the pursuit of Happiness." Thomas Jefferson, "Declaration of Independence," http://www.archives.gov/exhibit_hall/charters_of_freedom/declaration/declaration_transcription.html. Note that Stewart has added "free" to the sentence. All men, in her mind, are created both *equal* and *free* by God. However, she is referring to the Declaration of Independence, rather than the US Constitution, as she has erroneously stated here.

16. Job 25:6: "How much less man, that is a *worm?* and the son of man, which is a *worm?*" Also James 2:3: "And ye have respect to him that weareth the gay clothing, and say unto him, Sit thou here in a good place; and say to the poor, Stand thou there, or sit here under my footstool."

17. Stewart, "Productions of Maria Stewart," 4–5.

Note that Stewart intersperses the republican rhetoric of American civil religion with her biblical quotations and allusions. In this way, she lifts the democratic ideals of liberty and freedom as articulated in the Declaration of Independence (ideals that were being denied to large portions of the black populace of the United States at the time) to the level of the sacred and God-given.[18]

The genius of Stewart's word choice is that, by invoking scripture and appropriating its voice as her own, she is able to manipulate not only the words themselves but also the semiotic webs in which the biblical metaphors and images are embedded. In this way, her words become multivalent, meaning one thing to those who know only what she has spoken but able to mean something (slightly or perhaps greatly) different to those familiar with the webs of meaning enmeshed with the biblical ideas she has strung together. In that way, the words of Stewart's speeches become exactly the phenomenon that Mae Gwendolyn Henderson describes as "speaking in tongues."[19] Stewart's words can be understood on one level by all who hear them, as heteroglossia, and on another level by those who are also familiar with the biblical texts she is quoting, as glossolalia.

In order to understand Stewart's words as both heteroglossic and glossolalic, one must understand speech as a social phenomenon. As a social phenomenon, the meaning of spoken language lies not only in the speaker's intended meaning but also in the hearer's perceptions of those meanings. M. M. Bakhtin writes, "The linguistic significance of a given utterance is understood against the background of language, while its actual meaning is understood against the background of other concrete utterances on the same theme, a background that is made up of contradictory opinions, points of view and value judgments—that is, precisely that background that, as we see, complicates the path of any word toward its object."[20]

Bakhtin continues, "In the actual life of speech, every concrete act of understanding is active: it assimilates the word to be understood into its own conceptual system filled with specific objects and emotional expressions, and is indissolubly merged with the response, with a motivated agreement

---

18. I return to the question of Stewart's use of republican rhetoric in chapter 4.

19. Henderson, "Speaking in Tongues," 16–37.

20. M. M. Bakhtin, *The Dialogic Imagination: Four Essays by M. M. Bakhtin*, ed. Michael Holquist, trans. Caryl Emerson and Michael Holquist (Austin: University of Texas Press, 1981), 281.

or disagreement."[21] By rooting her speech in biblical allusions and images, Stewart was able to surround her words with all the potential meanings that those same allusions brought with them. For those who not only understood her words but could identify the sources of her biblical allusions, entire new vistas of meaning and context were opened.

Perhaps you have had the experience of listening to a piece of music that took you back in your memory to a particular moment in your life. The music swept in its wake all of those memories associated with it as you had first or most memorably heard it. It invoked sights, sounds, emotions, and sensations associated with it. In the same way, texts can sweep meaning in their wake, drawing up associations made when the text was first or most memorably encountered. Maria Stewart's use of scripture demonstrates one very great power of biblical allusion: its ability to sweep in its semiotic web not only images from its present usage in a sermon or speech but also echoes of its previous usages in the biblical text being quoted. Like a fishing net, the semiotic web of biblical appropriation drags with it all that it touches and all that is in its path: the words recall their original situation in text as well as their new use in speech. By invoking scripture, Stewart speaks to the present situation while nevertheless drawing in her semiotic web resonances of the metaphors as they were first used in the Bible.

For example, when she quotes a verse that speaks of the prophetess Deborah, the audience members who recognize the verse hear Stewart speaking but may think of Deborah ruling Israel and perhaps even Stewart representing Deborah as she stands before them. In this respect, Stewart's allusion is multivalent: it reinforces her present point, it invokes in her audience all the layers of meaning and emotion they experienced when they heard or read the text previously and personally, and, not coincidentally, it reinforces Stewart's authority as biblical interpreter because it reminds her audience of other occasions when the Bible has been interpreted in their presence. The biblical allusion therefore is also able to draw in its web all of the ways that the text had been previously interpreted in sermon and song, for example. Multiple layers of potential meaning-making resonate in every allusion.

Although Bakhtin cautions that the background of every word "is made up of contradictory opinions, points of view and value judgments" and that it "complicates the path of any word toward its object,"[22] Stewart's

21. Ibid., 282.
22. Ibid., 281.

use of scripture is ingenious because of the care with which she selects the texts she uses—selecting carefully their metaphors while remaining fully aware of their meanings in scripture. In this way, her words operate on various levels: they mean one thing to someone deciphering the words alone but contain a wide spectrum of possible and compatible meanings for those who understand not only the words but the theological, historical, or cultural meanings of those words as they were used in the Bible. Indeed, Stewart's genius lies in her ability to find compatible biblical allusions that fit with the overall points she seeks to make in her speeches. Stewart's scripture selections are very significant, particularly regarding texts to which she returns again and again, like the Ethiopian prophecy, Psalms 68:31.[23] Her near quotations and allusions are also significant. Knowing scripture as she does, Stewart occasionally changes words in her appropriation. Those word changes can be telling.

In this context, it is also important to note that it is possible to quote or allude to the Bible quite carelessly—something that Stewart almost never seems to do.[24] It is not enough to match words: that a portion of scripture

23. Psalms 68:31, "Princes shall come out of Egypt; *Ethiopia shall soon stretch out her hands unto God.*"

24. Perhaps this might be the appropriate moment to give an example of what I regard as a noncomplementary use of a literary allusion. In his State of the Union address delivered on January 29, 2003, President George W. Bush said the following: "Our fourth goal is to apply the compassion of America to the deepest problems of America. For so many in our country—the homeless and the fatherless, the addicted—the need is great. Yet there's power, wonder-working power, in the goodness and idealism and faith of the American people" (http://www.whitehouse.gov/news/releases/2003/01/20030128-19.html). Journalists had begun to note the increasing use of biblical and evangelical imagery in President Bush's public statements in the days and weeks leading up to the Second Gulf War. Some speculated that it represented, at least in part, an attempt to galvanize the support of evangelical and conservative Christians, whose votes would also be essential to Bush's successful reelection bid. Howard Fineman, "Bush and God," *Newsweek*, March 10, 2003, 22–30. Certainly, it was a reference to something that would be quite familiar to quite a few Americans. "Wonder-working power" is taken from the refrain of a well-known Gospel hymn called "There Is Power in the Blood." Lewis E. Jones, "There Is Power in the Blood," in *African American Heritage Hymnal: 575 Hymns, Spirituals and Gospel Songs*, ed. Rev. Dr. Delores Carpenter and Rev. Nolan E. Williams Jr. (Chicago: GIA Publications, 2001), 258.

If all that the president intended was to give a wink and a nod to evangelicals around the nation, then the usage was successful, for they would surely have recognized it. If

uses the same words as are desired in a particular speech or text does not mean that it will form an appropriate allusion or quotation when inserted into that speech or text. It must invoke the same ideas in ways that are aesthetically and hermeneutically harmonious. It is not enough to know what the *words* mean. The meanings of the *metaphors* must also be complementary. Stewart's biblical references and imagery almost always seem to work on almost every imaginable level. They almost never distract from the meaning of her overall text, but instead, they magnify it.

Sumptuous Fare

Maria Stewart's use of scripture seems to invite endless examination, but on almost every level, the meaning grows richer as the scripture complements and illuminates the text into which it has been set. An example of the elegance of Stewart's masterful knowledge and use of the Bible is clear in five little words with which she powerfully frames a new exegetical paradigm. She states simply of those Americans who have grown rich at the expense of the labor of slaves and oppressed blacks, "you . . . fare sumptuously every day."[25] The biblical allusion is clear: Stewart is quoting Luke 16:19, from the parable of Lazarus and the rich man.[26] In the parable, Jesus tells of a

---

the intention was merely to suggest a generalized theme of the possibility of redemption for "the homeless and the fatherless, the addicted," for example, then the use of the tag line from the hymn was appropriate in the context of the speech. However, the speech juxtaposes the sunny "goodness and idealism and faith of the American people" against a song invoking the death of Jesus on the Cross. "There Is Power in the Blood" is, after all, a song about bloodshed, about atonement, about death and resurrection, about the power of faith in Jesus to turn lives around. It suggests a victory for the believer, but one purchased at unfathomable cost. It seems a disproportionately heavy allusion abutting a hopeful reference to "goodness . . . idealism and faith" in the midst of a generally upbeat presidential speech.

Placing the metaphor of the hymn in the speech works on some levels, but is unsatisfactory on others. The metaphor of the hymn and the meaning of the speech are not a perfect match, although, as the work of perhaps a small army of speech writers whose ideas were being vetted by a gauntlet of political advisors, probably represented a safe, if ultimately unsatisfying reference-by-committee.

25. Stewart, "Productions of Maria Stewart," 20.

26. Luke 16:19–31: "There was a certain rich man, which was clothed in purple and fine linen, and *fared sumptuously every day*: And there was a certain beggar named Lazarus, which was laid at his gate, full of sores, And desiring to be fed with the crumbs

rich man who dies after a life of ease in which he "fared sumptuously every day,"[27] only to end up in hell. While in torment in hell, he looks up to heaven and sees the old beggar, Lazarus, who used to sit at his door. Lazarus sits in heaven being comforted by none other than the patriarch Abraham. The rich man asks Abraham to send Lazarus to hell with some water for him to drink. Hell is apparently too hot for the rich man's comfort, and he is a man quite used to being made comfortable, even at the expense of others' comfort. Abraham refuses the request, noting that the final ends of the two men are justified because of the lives they lived while on earth.

The text itself is subversive and Stewart's use of it doubly subversive. In a reversal of the usual way of things, this translation of the parable forgets the rich man's proper name and records only the name of the poor man, Lazarus.[28] In a further reversal of the men's stations in life, the poor man is comforted in heaven after a miserable life on earth, while the rich man is tormented in hell after a comfortable life on earth. Moreover, the rich man believes, even in hell, that Lazarus will still fetch and carry for him as poor men did while he was on earth—even in hell, he doesn't fully comprehend that his and Lazarus's circumstances have radically changed. Lazarus is no longer the poor servant, and the rich man is no longer his master. But

---

which fell from the rich man's table: moreover the dogs came and licked his sores. And it came to pass, that the beggar died, and was carried by the angels into Abraham's bosom: the rich man also died, and was buried; And in hell he lift up his eyes, being in torments, and seeth Abraham afar off, and Lazarus in his bosom. And he cried and said, Father Abraham, have mercy on me, and send Lazarus, that he may dip the tip of his finger in water, and cool my tongue; for I am tormented in this flame. But Abraham said, Son, remember that thou in thy lifetime receivedst thy good things, and likewise Lazarus evil things: but now he is comforted, and thou art tormented. And beside all this, between us and you there is a great gulf fixed: so that they which would pass from hence to you cannot; neither can they pass to us, that would come from thence. Then he said, I pray thee therefore, father, that thou wouldest send him to my father's house: For I have five brethren; that he may testify unto them, lest they also come into this place of torment. Abraham saith unto him, They have Moses and the prophets; let them hear them. And he said, Nay, father Abraham: but if one went unto them from the dead, they will repent. And he said unto him, If they hear not Moses and the prophets, neither will they be persuaded, though one rose from the dead."

27. Luke 16:19.

28. The rich man is named elsewhere. For example, in the Latin Vulgate Bible, he is called "Dives," from the Latin for "rich man." Dives is what the rich man is called in the spiritual "Poor Man Lazrus."

Stewart's retelling, in context, does not merely describe a rich man punished and a poor man rewarded but rather former servants in heaven and
former masters in hell.

Stewart's words "you . . . fare sumptuously every day" can be taken at face
value as an indictment of those who live well, particularly those of the slavocracy whose leisure was wrought from the forced labor of others. However,
in the context of Luke 16, the parable becomes a broader, more stark and
eternal judgment against all those who live well on the backs of others' suffering, since the parable is set in the context of final judgment with the ultimate consequence of heaven or hell. Stewart's accusation that "you . . . fare
sumptuously every day" invokes recollection of one earthly banquet, where
Lazarus must content himself with its crumbs, and a later celestial banquet,
where he reclines in Abraham's bosom while his rich and hard-hearted master's thirst goes unabated. As a result, Stewart's invocation of the parable carries with it some of those same apocalyptic implications of judgment as social reversal that are central to its original telling in Luke. It suggests wealthy
slave owners' forgotten and nameless slaves comforted and applauded—
the rich hungry but the poor filled. It suggests God's clear advocacy for and
ultimate rewarding of Lazarus, the putative underdog of the story.

Hear Stewart's words of indictment against the slave system: "We will
tell you, that it is our gold that clothes you in fine linen and purple, and
causes you to fare sumptuously every day; and it is the blood of our fathers, and the tears of our brethren that have enriched your soils. AND
WE CLAIM OUR RIGHTS."[29] Her words ring of apocalyptic expectation;
they burn with anticipation of a soon-coming justice similarly kindled in
the original parable in Luke. What are the rights that she claims? In the
context of the apocalyptic parable she has cited, their scope is expanded
far beyond that of legal rights: she demands human rights by invocation of
divine imprimatur. It is God who will enforce her demands for justice.

In this appropriation of Luke 16, however, Stewart has not made an
explicit threat against the slavocracy. No violence is described other than
that which God will cause. Later in the same paragraph, she writes, "Then,
my brethren, sheath your swords, and calm your angry passions. Stand
still, and know that the Lord he is God.[30] Vengeance is his, and he will

---

29. Stewart, "Productions of Maria Stewart," 20. (Emphasis is in the 1835 text.)
30. Psalms 46:10: "Be still, and know that I am God: I will be exalted among the
heathen, I will be exalted in the earth."

repay."[31] Stewart suggests that justice is as sure as that which the rich man receives in Luke 16 and that African Americans' claim to that same justice is as clear as Lazarus's claim to heaven. This interpretation is both revolutionary and deeply subversive: classic counterhegemonic discourse. And all it took was five little words: "you . . . fare sumptuously every day."

However, to understand the use of scripture in Stewart's writings fully, it is not enough to identify which texts are being alluded to or quoted. One must also understand the context into which Stewart had dropped the biblical text. The parable of Lazarus and the rich man was obviously a favorite of Stewart's. She returns to the theme in one of her meditations, as she describes the deathbed scene of a nonbeliever still unrepentant of his sins. (For Stewart, as for most evangelicals, this would have meant certain judgment and eternal damnation for this dying soul.) Note the difference in tone between this and the previous use of the parable:

> "What shall it profit a man if he gain the whole world and lose his own soul?"[32] . . . And he had no God to look to! Heart-rending scene! Who can describe it! . . . And what gratification will it be to you, my friends, to think that you have been able to be decked in fine linen and purple, and to fare sumptuously every day,[33] if you are not decked in the pure robes of Christ's righteousness?[34]

31. Romans 12:19: "Dearly beloved, avenge not yourselves, but rather give place unto wrath: for it is written, *Vengeance is mine; I will repay*, saith the Lord." Stewart, "Productions of Maria Stewart," 20.

32. Mark 8:36–38: "For what shall it profit a man, *if he shall gain the whole world, and lose his own soul?* Or what shall a man give in exchange for his soul? Whosoever therefore shall be ashamed of me and of my words in this adulterous and sinful generation; of him also shall the Son of man be ashamed, when he cometh in the glory of his Father with the holy angels."

33. Luke 16:19: "There was a certain rich man, which was *clothed in* purple and *fine linen*, and *fared sumptuously every day*."

34. Revelation 7:13–17: "And one of the elders answered, saying unto me, What are these which are arrayed in *white robes?* and whence came they? And I said unto him, Sir, thou knowest. And he said to me, These are they which came out of great tribulation, and have *washed their robes, and made them white in the blood of the Lamb*. Therefore are they before the throne of God, and serve him day and night in his temple: and he that sitteth on the throne shall dwell among them. They shall hunger no more, neither thirst any more; neither shall the sun light on them, nor any heat. For the Lamb

Here the text from Luke 16:19 is used not as an indictment of economic inequality but rather as an indication of the finality of the judgment against the rich man. By eliding the Lucan story of the rich man and Lazarus with the warning from Mark 8:26 ("For what shall it profit a man, if he shall gain the whole world, and lose his own soul?") and situating them within a deathbed scene of an unidentified friend, Stewart has turned these texts into a prediction of certain doom for those who put wealth and comfort before their duties to God. By contrasting earthly clothing of the rich ("fine linen and purple") against those garments purchased with Christ's blood ("the pure robes of Christ's righteousness"), Stewart's images again suggest radical reversal, the great theme of the parable of the rich man and Lazarus. The wealthy man's rich apparel lands him in hell, while being clothed in Christ's righteousness delivers the poor man to heaven. Indeed, it is almost a lament here, as Stewart is not calling down fire but tears. Yet the same text from Luke 16 is used in each case.

The Fire This Time

Like many evangelicals, Stewart reads the entire Bible as a unified whole. Uninfluenced by currents from European academies of higher biblical criticism, which would evaluate every biblical text according to strict exegetical standards that resisted harmonizing Bible verses with those found elsewhere in the Bible, Stewart links verses from various books of the Bible, sometimes harmonizing texts spanning the testaments, from old to new. Evangelical belief that the entire Bible was held together by the intention and inspiration of God undergirds such usage. Evangelicals like Stewart see the whole Bible as the story of Jesus: the Hebrew Bible tells of his heritage, but the New Testament tells of his life, death, and resurrection while predicting his imminent return.

An excellent example of Stewart's tendency to harmonize texts across testaments is found in one of her many meditations upon biblical themes:

---

which is in the midst of the throne shall feed them, and shall lead them unto living fountains of waters: and God shall wipe away all tears from their eyes." Here Stewart has alludes to (rather than quoting outright) a text from Revelation that describes the reward of those God has clothed in righteousness; they experience peace and joy in the presence of God. Stewart, "Productions of Maria Stewart," 40–41.

My friends, I have been brought to consider that it is because the Lord he is God,[35] that I have not been consumed.[36] It is because that his tender compassion fails not, that I am not now in hell lifting up my eyes in torments,[37] where the worm dieth not, and where the fire is not quenched.[38] And I cannot help but exclaim, glory to God that I am yet a prisoner of hope.[39] I rejoice that I have been formed a rational and accountable creature, and that ever I was born to be born again.[40] I rejoice that the Lord God omnipotent reigneth,[41] and that he searches the hearts and tries the reins of the children of men.[42] When I sin, I feel that I have an

35. Deuteronomy 4:35: "Unto thee it was shown, that thou mightest know that *the* LORD *he is God*; there is none else beside him." Deuteronomy 4:39: "Know therefore this day, and consider it in thine heart, that *the* LORD *he is God* in heaven above, and upon the earth beneath: there is none else." Psalms 100:3: "Know ye that *the* LORD *he is God*: it is he that hath made us, and not we ourselves; we are his people, and the sheep of his pasture."

36. Consumption as if by fire—particularly the fire of God—occurs frequently in scripture. See, for example, Genesis 19:15, Exodus 3:2, Leviticus 6:10, Numbers 11:1, and particularly Numbers 16:35 ("And there came out a fire from the LORD, and *consumed* the two hundred and fifty men that offered incense") or 1 Kings 18:38 ("Then the fire of the LORD fell, and *consumed* the burnt sacrifice, and the wood, and the stones, and the dust, and licked up the water that was in the trench"). However, in this context, Stewart is probably referring to Daniel 3, where Shadrach, Meshach, and Abednego are protected by God from the fire of King Nebuchadnezzar's furnace. Precisely because of God's protection, neither Stewart nor the exiles in Daniel are consumed in the fires kindled by the enemies of God and the people of God. The fire of God falls upon the sinful, but God protects the innocent, who are not consumed.

37. Luke 16:23: "And *in hell he lift up his eyes, being in torments*, and seeth Abraham afar off, and Lazarus in his bosom." This is yet another reference to the parable of Lazarus and the rich man, discussed earlier in this chapter.

38. Isaiah 66:24; Matthew 9:44, 46, and 48. Matthew 9:48: "Where *their worm dieth not, and the fire is not quenched.*"

39. Zechariah 9:12: "Turn you to the strong hold, *ye prisoners of hope*: even today do I declare that I will render double unto thee."

40. John 3:7: "Marvel not that I said unto thee, *Ye must be born again.*" For evangelicals, to be born again is to experience salvation from sin by virtue of belief in Jesus.

41. Revelation 19:6: "And I heard as it were the voice of a great multitude, and as the voice of many waters, and as the voice of mighty thunderings, saying, Alleluia: for *the Lord God omnipotent reigneth.*"

42. Revelation 2:23: "And I will kill her children with death; and all the churches shall know that I am *he which searcheth the reins and hearts*: and I will give unto every one of you according to your works." Notice that the inclusion of "reins" differentiates

advocate with the Father, even Jesus Christ the righteous,[43] who was in all points tempted like unto ourselves, yet without sin.[44] He knows what sore temptations mean, for he has felt the same; and with his supporting grace, I am determined to resist the lusts of the world, the flesh and the devil, and to fight the good fight of faith,[45] and win the crown and by my Father's side sit down.[46] Choose ye this day, therefore, whom ye will serve; but as for me, I am determined to serve the Lord.[47]

Note how many of the texts that Stewart has chosen invoke fiery judgment in their original pericopes (Numbers 16:35; 1 Kings 18:38). The majority

---

this text from two similar texts: 1 Chronicles 28:9 states, "And thou, Solomon my son, know thou the God of thy father, and serve him with a perfect heart and with a willing mind: for the LORD *searcheth all hearts*, and understandeth all the imaginations of the thoughts: if thou seek him, he will be found of thee; but if thou forsake him, he will cast thee off for ever." Romans 8:27 states, "And he that *searcheth the hearts* knoweth what is the mind of the Spirit, because he maketh intercession for the saints according to the will of God." Of the three texts, the citation from Revelation that Stewart chose carries the strongest connotations of judgment, even judgment upon the children of the wicked.

43. 1 John 2:1: "My little children, these things write I unto you, that ye sin not. *And if any man sin, we have an advocate with the Father, Jesus Christ the righteous.*"

44. Hebrews 4:15: "For we have not an high priest which cannot be touched with the feeling of our infirmities; but *was in all points tempted like as we are, yet without sin.*"

45. 1 Timothy 6:12: "*Fight the good fight of faith*, lay hold on eternal life, whereunto thou art also called, and hast professed a good profession before many witnesses." 2 Timothy 4:7 is similar but not exactly the same: "I have *fought a good fight*, I have finished my course, I have kept *the faith*." It is perhaps interesting that Stewart chose the allusion that was purely military (likening keeping faith to a "good fight"), as in 1 Timothy, rather than using the nearly identical metaphor from 2 Timothy, which waters down the martial implications by further likening keeping faith to running a race. Stewart seems to have preferred the reference to battle over that of competition, friendly or otherwise.

46. Revelation 3:21: "To him that overcometh will I grant to sit with me in my throne, even as I also overcame, and am *set down with my Father* in his throne."

47. Joshua 24: 15, "And if it seem evil unto you to serve the LORD, *choose you this day whom ye will serve*; whether the gods which your fathers served that were on the other side of the flood, or the gods of the Amorites, in whose land ye dwell: but *as for me and my house, we will serve the LORD.*" Note that Stewart, a widow, does not speak for her household but only for herself when she writes, "but as for me, I am determined to serve the Lord" rather than "for me and my house, we will serve the LORD" as the text from Joshua states. Stewart, "Productions of Maria Stewart," 28.

of the texts she has chosen take place in situations of judgment upon the wicked and vindication of the just (Luke 16:23; Zechariah 9:12; Revelation 2:23) or at points of life-and-death decisions for the people of God (1 Timothy 6:12; Joshua 24:15; John 3:7). They frequently take place in hell (Isaiah 66:24; Matthew 9:44, 46, and 48; Matthew 9:48) or in the presence of God (Revelation 19:6; Revelation 3:21). And while Stewart encourages her audience to choose correctly, reminding them of God's readily available mercy for those who choose to serve God (1 John 2:1; Hebrews 4:15), as she has chosen to do (Joshua 24:15), we are left with incredibly vivid word pictures depicting the consequences of failing to choose to serve God. The word picture Stewart has drawn here is not without images of mercy, but it is also full of dire warnings about judgment. And in a typically evangelical usage that draws from both testaments, harmonizing all the way, Stewart invokes a judgment and mercy that are equally available and dependent upon the choices of the believer.

A Spirit of Independence

Maria Stewart understood her public speaking and writing very much as a religious vocation. Near the very beginning of her first public address, she outlines her Christian credentials in far greater detail than that of the scant biographical information she provides. She not only notes her birth in 1803 and her marriage in 1829, but for the purpose of establishing her credibility as a religious voice, she also points to having been raised by a pastor and his family, to her attendance of Sabbath schools (as the only formal education she mentions having received), to her experience of salvation in 1830, and to her "public profession of . . . faith in Christ" in 1831.[48]

Stewart goes on to proclaim her public career as having been dedicated to God; she is willing, she states, even to go to the point of death if need be to fulfill her charge. Stewart further states that her mission began at the moment of her Christian conversion: "From the moment I experienced the change [of Christian conversion], I felt a strong desire, with the help and assistance of God, to devote the remainder of my days to piety and virtue, and now possess that spirit of independence, that, were I called upon, I would willingly sacrifice my life for the cause of God and my brethren."[49]

48. Stewart, "Productions of Maria Stewart," 3–4.
49. Ibid., 4.

Here and elsewhere in her writing, Stewart indicates that she realizes such a public crusade might cost her life.

Because she discusses it so frequently, Stewart seems fascinated by her own death.[50] This morbid fixation is probably the consequence of her many experiences of death and loss. Stewart's writing and speaking career began in 1831; her mentor, David Walker, had died in 1830. Stewart's husband, James Stewart, had died in 1829. Both widow and orphan, Stewart despaired, "I have neither kindred nor friends."[51] In the context of so much personal loss, it is not surprising that Stewart mentions the possibility of her own death frequently.

Stewart cites the "spirit of independence" as having empowered her to do the work to which God and her experience of salvation have called her. This phrase is interesting because its origin is not the Bible.[52] She does not use terms like *liberty* or *freedom*, which she might easily have invoked, or biblical references to them. *Liberty* and *freedom* are words and ideas found in the King James Bible.[53] Independence is not a virtue much lauded in scripture. Obedience is lauded in scripture; independence was lauded in the rhetoric of the American Revolution and in its subsequent nation building. By prefacing this gift of independence with the descriptor "spirit of," Stewart suggests that its origin is divine, even if it is not listed as a biblical charism. Here, as elsewhere in her writing, Stewart seems to be combining evangelical theology (in her descriptions of salvation and vocation, for example, and in her use of scripture) with the republican rhetoric at the foundation of the United States. In the midst of her mission statement, her declaration of vocation, she inserts the "spirit of independence" and links it to her willingness to sacrifice herself for God and for her people. In

50. Moody, *Sentimental Confessions*, 38.

51. Stewart, "Productions of Maria Stewart," 21.

52. The word "independence" does not appear anywhere in the King James Version of the Bible, which was undoubtedly the version that Stewart used. She quotes quite frequently from it, and it was, and perhaps remains, the version most commonly found in African American churches. Only in recent years have versions such as the New International or New Revised Standard begun to appear beside the hymnals in the backs of African American churches' pews.

53. Stewart might, for example, have quoted 2 Corinthians 3:17: "Now the Lord is that Spirit: and where the Spirit of the Lord is, there is liberty." However, Stewart, who demonstrates marvelous dexterity with the Bible, chose to use a term not found there. I believe that this choice was intentional.

so doing, she equates independence with the rest of her mission, thereby elevating independence from its moorings in republican rhetoric to the level of charism. Independence becomes not only a republican virtue but also a gift from God and a key element of Stewart's vocation. Moreover, as she is one of a class of people relegated to involuntary servitude by virtue of the color of their skin, Stewart's proclamation that independence is a God-given gift serves as an accusation leveled by God against the United States, which purported to embrace independence as a virtue while denying it to large portions of its population.

I am persuaded that Stewart did not select the term "independence" carelessly. The term on the one hand invokes the very origins of the United States as a nation, from its Declaration of Independence onward. Yet Stewart proclaims that it is her "spirit of independence" that has allowed her to fight against the shackles that held African Americans, both literally and figuratively. In her speeches, Stewart decries both the institution of slavery and the ignorance and immorality that supported and enabled it.

However, although she describes her Christian experiences in terms of evangelical theology (such as "having been brought to the knowledge of the truth, as it is in Jesus")[54] that would have been quite familiar to many in her listening audience, she does not mention specifics, such as denominational affiliation or other sectarian concerns. She does not say, for example, where the Sabbath school she attended was located or with which church it was affiliated. She tells us her husband's name[55] but not those of her parents or of the clergyman whose family raised her after she was left an orphan. At another point she prays, "Bless the church to which I belong"[56] but neglects to give its name or location. Indeed, almost all of the specific

54. Although other New Testament verses incorporate the phrase, I believe that here Stewart is probably referring to 1 Timothy 2:4, "Who will have all men to be saved, and *to come unto the knowledge of the truth*," because this verse mentions salvation, and Stewart appends "as it is in Jesus," thereby clarifying her intention to wed this knowledge/truth to a saving faith in Jesus.

55. As a widow, Stewart would have enjoyed a social cachet unavailable to other women of her time. She had the respectability of having once been a married woman but without the present encumbrances of a husband who might have hindered her ministry. Therefore Stewart is careful to name her husband, because of the legitimation his name and status provided, while choosing not to give the names of other significant relations such as her parents.

56. Stewart, "Productions of Maria Stewart," 27.

information that we have about Stewart is derived from sources such as public records or extant letters rather than from her speeches as published in 1835.

Perhaps in omitting certain sectarian and personal details, Stewart hoped to universalize her message. By deemphasizing the specifics of her own life, Stewart may have intended, in minimizing the details of her role as messenger, to foreground the essence of her message. Indeed, Stewart tries to intrude on the narrative as little as possible. Stewart seems to be protesting that "all is to the glory of God, and none is to my own glory" by eliminating all specifics about herself except those that would validate her calling, identify her with her community, or reference her as a Christian woman of good character.

Stewart erases herself from within her writings, as when she "studiously effaces its author by referring to her[self] in the third person rather than the first" and when she repeatedly uses passive grammatical constructions to describe the events of her life.[57] Stewart does not intend to be autobiographical in her speeches except to the extent necessary to "establish her narrative credibility."[58] I believe that Stewart also uses the Bible, and her performance of the Bible, as a means to further hide herself.

In her constant quoting of the Bible, Stewart assumes the Bible as her own voice and also its authority as her own. Scripture legitimated Stewart, and so she apparently believed that few biographical details were needed. By hiding herself in the Bible and speaking only of and through it (but almost never of herself), Stewart may have thought to make of herself a smaller target for those who would attack her for having been so presumptuous as to have taken to the public stage as a woman, speaking to men and to women, on political and theological themes as she did. Stewart's words made people—black and white, male and female—angry.

In her speeches, Stewart advocates not violence, but self-determination for blacks. Nevertheless, she is clear that God's judgment against America for the sin of slavery is certain. Stewart argues that America is not the "city set upon a hill" of Pilgrim proclamation. Instead, taking images from the book of Revelation, Stewart charges that the United States is less like some New Jerusalem descending from heaven and more like Babylon, the scriptural icon of all that stood in opposition to the will of God.

57. Moody, *Sentimental Confessions*, 45.
58. Ibid., 28.

However, by using the Bible to bring this charge against America, Stewart also documents her own facility with the Bible. Even as she brings her own charges against the United States, she does so in a way—by using the Bible—that presents her as a virtuous woman. She is virtuous because she has read and studied the Bible so carefully that she has even committed such large portions of it to memory so that she can perform it in public. Indeed, she has not brought a charge against the United States; she has only read the charge that God has already brought, because she has read this charge from the pages of the Bible.

By her skillful use of biblical allusions and quotations, Stewart manages to efface herself (or most of the personal details of her life) from her writing while simultaneously revealing herself as an evangelical woman utterly committed to the authority of the Bible. She harmonizes texts across the Old and New Testaments as though the Bible were a unified whole, rather than many books written at different times and in different locations, because she sees the entire Bible as the work of the one God. She carefully draws her listeners into the semiotic webs surrounding the scriptures she quotes so that these texts add layers and textures to their uses in her speeches.

⚔ ✳ CHAPTER 3 ✳

Maria Stewart's
Defenses of Women

*N*INETEENTH-CENTURY African American evangelical women like Maria Stewart shaped a convergence of theological and cultural forces in their efforts to redefine black womanhood in terms that were not constrained by those that circumscribed the lives of nineteenth-century white women. In a myriad of ways, they redesigned, or rejected, the "Cult of True Womanhood," which had emerged as the Victorian-era ideal of femininity, but which stubbornly excluded them. Instead, African American women used the urgency of the struggle against slavery, the liminal nature of their own status as women, and evangelical arguments for human equality before God as means of crafting new roles for themselves in the public sphere. The authority of scripture—that central, unifying tenet of evangelicalism—was an essential tool for women like Stewart, who, having put on the whole armor of God, and having taken up the Bible like a sword[1] against the injustices they abhorred, had sheathed themselves in biblical authority as well.

In the eighteenth and nineteenth centuries, evangelical Christianity began to provide American women (both black and white) with theologically

---

1. Ephesians 6:11, 17: "Put on *the whole armour of God*, that ye may be able to stand against the wiles of the devil . . . and the *sword* of the Spirit, *which is the word of God*."

legitimated but limited access to the public sphere.[2] In evangelicalism's emphasis upon a personal experience of salvation, it provided points of liminality, which are experiences that pull people out of their own time and space and create new social orders and relationships. Women began to outnumber men in many Protestant churches in New England.[3] Noticing by the early nineteenth century that women outnumbered men in their churches, New England ministers began arguing that women's more sensitive natures made them more innately attuned to religion.[4] It was in this historical context and geographical region that Maria Stewart received her call to enter the public arena.

2. Evangelicalism both undermined white male privilege and empowered disenfranchised blacks, women, and others because it challenged the social status quo in the antebellum South. Christine Leigh Heyrman, *Southern Cross: The Beginnings of the Bible Belt*, 1st ed. (New York: A. A. Knopf, 1997, distributed by Random House), 26. Susan Juster argues that as Baptist churches emerged in Connecticut and Rhode Island in the 1740s and 1750s, there was what she calls a "feminine drift" to their revival spirituality and that these churches modeled a less patriarchal order than the established Puritan churches from which they differentiated themselves. According to Juster, by the 1770s, those upstart Baptist churches had responded to Puritan persecution by forcing women out of decision-making roles. It was not until the 1820s and 1830s—some fifty years later—she argues, that those churches again provided women with significant access to the public sphere or decision-making power. Susan Juster, *Disorderly Women: Sexual Politics and Evangelicalism in Revolutionary New England* (Ithaca, NY: Cornell University Press, 1994).

3. According to Nancy F. Cott, female membership growth in New England Protestant churches outpaced that of male membership growth "by three to two""between 1798 and 1826." Nancy F. Cott, *The Bonds of Womanhood: "Woman's Sphere" in New England, 1780–1835* (New Haven, CT: Yale University Press, 1977), 132. Other sources document the proliferation of female evangelicals in New England between the late eighteenth and early nineteenth centuries. See, for example, Richard D. Shiels, "The Feminization of American Congregationalism, 1730–1835," in *History of Women in the United States: Historical Articles on Women's Lives and Activities*, ed. Nancy F. Cott (Munich: K. G. Saur, 1993), 3–19; Nancy F. Cott, "Young Women in the Second Great Awakening in New England," in Cott, *History of Women*, 20–34; and Cott, "'Female Laborers in the Church': Women Preachers in the Northeastern United States, 1790–1840," in Cott, *History of Women*, 166–91. See also Barbara Welter, "The Feminization of American Religion: 1800–1860," in *Dimity Convictions: The American Woman in the Nineteenth Century*, ed. Barbara Welter (Athens: Ohio University Press, 1976), 83–102.

4. Cott, *Bonds of Womanhood*, 128–29.

During the period between 1740 and 1845, several black and white women preachers sought to establish themselves across New England.[5] Although these women were often attacked or belittled, they nonetheless insisted that they had been sent by God. Nineteenth-century white women itinerant ministers like Harriet Livermore and Nancy Towle and nineteenth-century black women itinerants like Jarena Lee, Sojourner Truth, Zilpha Elaw, Rebecca Jackson, and Julia Foote were "part of a larger evangelical culture—both black and white—that sanctioned women's religious leadership."[6] Such women were "'biblical' rather than secular feminists," and they made "claims to female equality on the grounds of scriptural revelation, not natural rights."[7]

Particularly for black women, as evidenced in a number of biographies and autobiographies of the period, evangelical conversion had the ability to create powerful, new, and often liberating social relationships. These women understood conversion to bestow a kind of "democracy of saved souls" where all "were on an equal spiritual standing before the Lord."[8] While the "presence of large numbers of white and black women in the pulpit [between 1740 and 1845] seems to offer evidence of the democratization of American Christianity," it also suggests the power of the experience of salvation to diminish the importance of distinctions of race, class, and sex.[9] Indeed, more than twenty female evangelists' stories were

5. "Between 1740, when the revivals of the First Great Awakening began in New England, and 1845, when a second wave of revivals ended with the collapse of the Millerite movement, several generations of women struggled to invent an enduring tradition of female religious leadership." Catherine A. Brekus, *Strangers and Pilgrims: Female Preaching in America, 1740–1845* (Chapel Hill: University of North Carolina Press, 1998), 3.

6. Ibid., 5.

7. Ibid., 6–7.

8. Nellie McKay, "Nineteenth-Century Black Women's Spiritual Autobiographies: Religious Faith and Self-Empowerment," in *Interpreting Women's Lives: Feminist Theory and Personal Narratives*, ed. Joy Webster Barbre and Personal Narratives Group (Bloomington: Indiana University Press, 1989), 139–54, as quoted in Kimberly Rae Connor, *Conversions and Visions in the Writings of African-American Women* (Knoxville: University of Tennessee Press, 1994), 48.

9. Brekus, *Strangers and Pilgrims*, 11. However, Brekus notes that this "evangelical democratization" that seemed to permit women to preach was most visible among northern evangelicals and least visible among those in the South, 16.

published in the early part of the nineteenth century.[10] Central to many of these narratives was a description of the woman's salvation experience or calling to ministry as a sovereign and irresistible act of God to which the only appropriate and proper response was obedience.[11]

For Maria Stewart, her salvation experience, which occurred just at the end of the Second Great Awakening, marked the beginning of her crusade for the rights of African Americans. She writes, "I . . . was, as I humbly hope and trust, brought to the knowledge of the truth, as it is in Jesus, in 1830; in 1831, made a public profession of my faith in Christ. From the moment I experienced the change [of salvation], I felt a strong desire, with the help and assistance of God, to devote the remainder of my days to piety and virtue, and now possess that spirit of independence, that, were I called upon, I would willingly sacrifice my life for the cause of God and my brethren."[12]

Stewart asserts that it was the experience of salvation that gave her both the "desire" and the "spirit of independence" required to undertake her mission. Salvation provided a new theological focus for her public career: her highest obligation was not that she, as a woman, remain silent and at home, as the prevailing social order might have seemed to insist. Instead, she was being obedient to God by taking to the public sphere with her God-given message and the independent spirit required to proclaim that message. Having recast her mission as divine imperative, and having said that she "would willingly sacrifice [her] life for the cause," she could not be expected to shrink back because of anything as insignificant as social constraints.

Stewart categorizes her work as a divine mission to which she has been called. Her topics include political advancement and divine approbation and judgment. While some characterize her speeches as political, there is frequently very little difference between them and others' sermons. Did Maria Stewart understand what she was doing as preaching? She never calls it that.[13] Nevertheless, the line between simply giving a speech and preaching the Gospel is one that she frequently transgresses.

10. Ibid., 167.

11. Ibid., 162–93.

12. Stewart, "Productions of Maria Stewart," 3–4.

13. Although Stewart never claimed the ecclesial authority of the preacher, I believe that what she was doing qualified as preaching. She was proclaiming what she believed to be God's truth to God's people.

"Ar'n't I a Woman?"

The Cult of True Womanhood was the standard by which women were judged in the early nineteenth century. The feminine ideal, as presented in popular and religious publications of the nineteenth century, made women "the hostage in the home."[14] As the stock metaphor of sentimental fiction (the most popular literary genre of the period),[15] it encouraged men to go out to tame the wilderness and manipulate the marketplace, while women were supposed to find their highest satisfaction in "piety, purity, submissiveness and domesticity."[16] Men were to be the protectors; women were to be protected. According to this paradigm, women achieved the full flower of their humanity (and their greatest satisfaction) in the realm of the home, where their gentler, more sensitive natures might be spared the insults of a rough-and-tumble "man's world."

However, as many slave narratives point out, the home was not necessarily a safe place for black women. Additionally, as slaves, black men had the freedom neither to go out into the marketplace themselves nor to protect their wives, mothers, or daughters. Involuntary servitude complicated the African American woman's place in the antebellum home. It is just that

14. Barbara Welter, "The Cult of True Womanhood: 1820–1860," in *Dimity Convictions: The American Woman in the Nineteenth Century*, (Athens: Ohio University Press, 1976), 21.

15. Sentimentalism as a literary genre of the nineteenth century "emphasized the cultivation of sensibility, the glorification of virtue, the preservation of family life, the revival of religion, and the achievement of a utopian society." Foster, *Witnessing Slavery*, 64. Sentimentalism in nineteenth-century popular literature in the United States and England tended toward stock tropes of melodrama and undeserved suffering, such as lingering illness, separation from loved ones, poverty born bravely, and wrenching deathbed scenes, as well as stock tropes of innocence lost and deserved suffering, like the "bad death"—a death filled with torments and foreboding about coming judgment. It is frequently during a "bad death" scene that a character realizes, too late, the error of his or her ways. Perhaps the best-known example of nineteenth-century American sentimental literature is *Uncle Tom's Cabin* by Harriet Beecher Stowe, which, in its depictions of noble African Americans (like Uncle Tom) and wicked whites (like Simon Legree), fueled the growing abolition movement in the antebellum United States by graphically depicting the cruelty of slavery. The power of Stowe's novel was that it wedded the well-known images of sentimentality to the institution of slavery in a way that humanized African Americans as they had not been previously in the popular press.

16. Welter, "Cult of True Womanhood," 21.

juxtaposition between the supposed safety of the home and the real peril that the slavocracy posed for black women upon which many slave narratives turn. When the slave narrator depicted herself as a vulnerable servant and her master or mistress as a brutal tyrant, she was able to draw upon the well-established tropes of sentimental fiction (such as undeserved suffering) in order to establish herself as the more worthy character in her own life's drama.[17]

However, nearly every woman's slave narrative ends with an account of the former slave's improved family relations or social connections as a result of her having fled the coercive private sphere that enclosed her captivity in slavery. In so doing, the narrators transgressed the conventions of the Cult of True Womanhood. Home was not the safest place for them. Clearly, it was in escape from domestic captivity that, many slave narratives argued, African American women found greater safety and security.

Implicit in the Cult of True Womanhood was the supposition that white women were its fullest, highest expression. Behind it stood a hierarchy of race, class, and gender that consistently placed black women at or near the bottom—if they were seen at all. The cult "was a fearful obligation, a solemn responsibility, the nineteenth-century American woman had—to uphold the pillars of the Temple with her frail white hand."[18] The Cult of True Womanhood was just one part of a larger system of romanticized racial, gender, and class hierarchies that were intended to offer explanations for Western economic and social domination of slaves, local populations, and far-flung colonial holdings. This Victorian reasoning argued that whites were superior to other races, that women ought to be submissive to men, and that the West, by virtue of its moral, intellectual, and technological superiority, ought, by (divine) right, to rule the world.

Black women subverted these idealized race and gender roles of the Cult of True Womanhood even as they appropriated them in their efforts to create and project alternative identities for themselves. For example, when Sojourner Truth depicts a scene from the domestic sphere, she casts herself as the suffering (and therefore virtuous and pitiable) servant, a common and easily recognizable character in sentimental drama, while both

17. Raymond Hedin, "Strategies of Form in the American Slave Narrative," in *The Art of Slave Narrative: Original Essays in Criticism and Theory*, ed. John Sekora and Darwin T. Turner (Macomb: Western Illinois University, 1982), 27.
18. Welter, "Cult of True Womanhood," 21.

her white mistress and a hired white servant girl are shown as calculating and cruel. In the incident Truth retells, she is falsely accused of cooking poorly when in reality her hard work has been sabotaged by the vengeful white hireling. In this way, Truth shows herself to be more human and possessed of more godly character than the two white women. Moreover, Truth portrays herself as a harder worker than either the white woman who owns everything or the white woman who is being paid for her services, while Truth is working for nothing. Even though the episode took place in the home, the very sphere of womanhood, the two white women could not approach the Cult of True Womanhood's feminine ideal.[19]

That the Cult of True Womanhood excluded black women is not surprising, given the prevailing racial and social hierarchies of the nineteenth century. African American women were at the time barely considered to be human and were never to be treated as ladies. Terms like *lady* and even *woman* were so encumbered by the prevailing racial hierarchies of the day that they were not regarded as applicable to African American women.[20]

In a brutal example of the ways the law exempted black women from the protections afforded other women, a slave woman named Celia was convicted of murdering her master, who had regularly forced her to have sex and even impregnated her. In *State of Missouri v. Celia*, the case turned on whether or not Celia, a black woman and a slave, was covered under Missouri law, which prohibited rape against "any woman." The defense tried to prove that Celia had killed her owner in self-defense, since his ownership rights could not have extended to include rape. In convicting and ultimately executing Celia in 1855, just after she gave birth to a child probably fathered by her owner, the court upheld the owner's right to unimpeded sexual access to his property. As a slave, she had no right to protections afforded to "any woman."[21] For purposes of Missouri case law, "any woman" did not include any women of color like Celia.

This case points to a more disturbing perception about African American women that obtained in courtrooms and in the wider society: the unfortunate belief that black women could not be raped or otherwise sexually

19. Olive Gilbert and Sojourner Truth, *Narrative of Sojourner Truth, a Bondswoman of Olden Time: With a History of Her Labors and Correspondence Drawn from Her "Book of Life,"* Schomburg Library of Nineteenth-Century Black Women Writers (New York: Oxford University Press, 1991), 31–32.

20. Higginbotham, "African-American Women's History," 3–24.

21. Ibid., 7.

abused.[22] African American women of the antebellum period inhabited a kind of netherworld between the protections and restraints of the "Cult of True Womanhood," which put white women on a pedestal, and the denigrations and assaults of a society that viewed African American women as near savages. In the words of Elsa Barkley Brown, "Throughout U.S. history black women have been sexually stereotyped as immoral, insatiable, perverse; the initiators in all sexual contacts—abusive or otherwise."[23] This is particularly ironic, given that the dirty little secret of slavery turns out to be the impunity with which white owners, overseers, and others raped, sexually assaulted, and forced or coerced slaves into sexual liaisons. The threat and reality of rape is present in almost every nineteenth-century woman's slave narrative, as is the woman's efforts to resist or escape this abuse.[24]

Evangelicalism sometimes provided women with unusual but nonetheless limited access to the public sphere. Nevertheless, the restrictive ideals of the Cult of True Womanhood, which suggested that women reached their highest potential only through their work in the home, limited the social tolerance for their public works.[25] However, African American

22. Brown, "'What Has Happened Here,'" 47. Although Brown's comment here refers to black women throughout the course of US history and into the present, it also describes general perceptions toward black women of the nineteenth century.

23. Ibid.

24. Darlene Clark Hine, "Rape and the Inner Lives of Black Women in the Middle West: Preliminary Thoughts on the Culture of Dissemblance," in *Unequal Sisters: A Multicultural Reader in U.S. Women's History*, ed. Ellen Carol DuBois and Vicki Ruiz (New York: Routledge, 1990), 292. As examples of women's fight to control their own bodies, Hine cites Harriet A. Jacobs, *Incidents in the Life of a Slave Girl*, Schomburg Library of Nineteenth-Century Black Women Writers (New York: Oxford University Press, 1988); and Keckley, *Behind the Scenes*. Hine also refers to Rennie Simpson, "The Afro-American Female: The Historical Construction of Sexual Identity," in *Powers of Desire: The Politics of Sexuality*, New Feminist Library, ed. Ann Barr Snitow, Christine Stansell, and Sharon Thompson (New York: Monthly Review Press, 1983), 229–35.

25. Brekus writes, "At a time when popular authors proclaimed that home was women's 'appropriate sphere of action,' itinerant woman preachers were practically homeless in their constant travels, and were frequently unmarried." Catherine A. Brekus, *Strangers and Pilgrims: Female Preaching in America, 1740–1845* (Chapel Hill: University of North Carolina Press, 1998), 221. Some, like Jarena Lee, left children behind or, like Zilpha Elaw, ignored their husband's orders to stop their work. Ibid., 222. Such behavior was considered shocking by many people at the time.

women of the same period, motivated and empowered by the exigencies of their own personal battles for freedom and the broader struggle to end slavery for all blacks, frequently were less hesitant in their attempts to enter public discourse.

Black women were doubly stigmatized because of their race and their gender and had to endure the opposition not only of whites but also of black men, especially black clergymen. As a result of this opposition, "Even more than white women, black female preachers insisted that their authority to preach had come directly from the Holy Spirit."[26] Once African American women like Maria Stewart had taken to the public stage, they had to recast themselves against two competing perceptions: that of white women as pinnacle of a hierarchical ideal for all women and that of black women as sexually profligate savages who somehow deserved all of the mistreatment they received. They had to construct public personas while demonstrating that they were neither white women nor savages but black women who ought to be heard.

Why Sit Here and Die?

Female preachers were speaking publicly as early as the 1740s. By the 1830s, when Maria Stewart delivered her speeches, women such as Jarena Lee, Abigail Roberts, Sarah Hedges, and Ann Rexford had already been preaching for more than a decade.[27] As a woman political speaker, Stewart was a pioneer, but as a woman preacher in the evangelical tradition, she was part of a line—a long line, stretching back to the 1740s—when she took the stage with her message in the 1830s.

Like David Walker before her, Stewart protested the injustice of slavery, although she herself had never been a slave. However, where Walker seemed intent on provoking armed resistance with his writing against the slavocracy, Stewart's speeches are more subtle in their attack, although arguably no less incendiary. Indeed, Stewart's courage is evident in the fact that she began her public writing and speaking career a year after Walker had died, just after his radical text advocating slave insurrection had reached the South and raised the ire of the slavocracy. Though she

26. Ibid., 183.
27. Ibid., 197.

took up Walker's abolitionist work just after he died,[28] her writing shows that she was aware that such work might also cost her own life. Stewart wrote: "Many will suffer for pleading the cause of oppressed Africa, and I shall glory in being one of her martyrs; for I am firmly persuaded, that the God in whom I trust is able to protect me from the rage and malice of mine enemies, and from them that will rise up against me; and if there is no other way for me to escape, he is able to take me to himself, as he did the most noble, fearless, and undaunted David Walker."[29] Clearly, Stewart was well aware of the possibility that she would be hated and perhaps even attacked by some because she had dared speak out so boldly against slavery. Stewart's speaking career ended when she was hounded from Boston because of the controversy arising from the fact that she was a woman who had criticized men in her public speeches.[30]

Stewart's speeches were also unusual for a woman at the time because they were both explicitly theological and explicitly political. In addition to her nearly three-year public writing and speaking career (1831–33) and the later publication of her speeches (first collected in 1835), Stewart wrote for William Lloyd Garrison's abolitionist paper, *The Liberator*.[31] Stewart also penned a letter to the editor of the first African American newspaper, *Freedom's Journal*, in 1827.[32] After the Civil War, she was active in the nascent Freedman's Bureau, serving as matron of Freedman's Hospital (now Howard University Hospital) in Washington, DC.[33] In her public political speech and in the publication of her speeches, Stewart was a forerunner.

28. There is some controversy among scholars as to the cause of Walker's death. The timing of his death, coming just as his writings were beginning to evoke the slavocracy's protests, has caused some to speculate that Walker's death was not accidental. Although subsequent evidence has indicated that Walker died of "consumption," the way Stewart refers to Walker's death (as martyrdom, for example) suggests to me that she believed that his death was not accidental but rather a direct result of his efforts to end slavery. Of the controversy on this point, see Peter P. Hinks, *To Awaken My Afflicted Brethren: David Walker and the Problem of Antebellum Slave Resistance* (University Park: Pennsylvania State University Press, 1997), 269–70; and Hinks, introduction to Walker, *Appeal to the Coloured Citizens*, xliv.

29. Stewart, "Productions of Maria Stewart," 5.

30. James Oliver Horton, *Free People of Color: Inside the African American Community* (Washington, DC: Smithsonian Institution Press, 1993), 109–10.

31. Richardson, *Maria W. Stewart*, 10.

32. Moody, *Sentimental Confessions*, 26.

33. Richardson, *Maria W. Stewart*, 84–85.

Although she began virtually alone, many women, particularly African American women, were emboldened in the years leading up to and immediately following the Civil War, some perhaps even influenced by her example, to produce a flood of memoirs, journals, and quasi-political commentaries on the state of women's lives and the evils of slavery.[34]

The records that remain to us suggest that Stewart was a tenacious and persistent woman who advocated that others follow her example. When white businessmen attempted to take her husband's estate from her, she fought their spurious claims in court for more than two years. The Boston courts habitually provided so little protection for the property of free blacks that David Walker wrote "that in this very city, when a man of colour dies, if he owned any real estate it most generally falls into the hands of some white person. The wife and children of the deceased may weep and lament if they please, but the estate will be kept snug by its white possessor."[35] Sadly, the argument of Stewart's legitimate right to the estate did not carry the day; her husband's profitable business was taken from her control.[36] Still, Stewart did not give up her fight to win the pension that her husband had earned for her by fighting in the War of 1812. Indeed, when she finally did receive the pension money in 1878, she used it to republish her speeches in an 1879 volume entitled *Meditations from the Pen of Mrs. Maria W. Stewart.*[37] Despite the obvious disappointments and delays she experienced when seeking justice for herself, Stewart nonetheless urges, "Sue for your rights and privileges."[38] Later, and more insistently, she proclaims, "AND WE CLAIM OUR RIGHTS."[39] However, she says nothing specifically about her own personal legal battles, defeats, and disappointments.

More pragmatically, Stewart argues that African Americans have nothing to lose in forcefully presenting their case before whites. "Come let us

34. For example, during this period women like Jarena Lee published multiple versions of their memoirs, in which apologia for their public ministries are central themes. Compare, for example, Jarena Lee, "The Life and Religious Experience of Jarena Lee," in *Sisters of the Spirit: Three Black Women's Autobiographies of the Nineteenth Century,* ed. William L. Andrews Press (Bloomington: Indiana University Press, 1986), 25–48; and J. Lee, "Religious Experience and Journal."

35. Walker, *Appeal to the Coloured Citizens,* 12.

36. Richardson, *Maria W. Stewart,* 7.

37. Ibid., 79.

38. Stewart, "Productions of Maria Stewart," 17.

39. Ibid., 20. Emphasis in the original 1835 text.

plead our cause before the whites," she reasons, "if they save us alive, we shall live—and if they kill us, we shall but die."[40] Stewart reasons that since death is the inevitable end for all living beings, it ought not to be feared. We may die if we stay; we may die if we go. "Why sit ye here and die?" she asks.[41] Here Stewart quotes the words attributed to four lepers in 2 Kings 7:3: "And there were four leprous men at the entering in of the gate: and they said one to another, Why sit we here until we die?" Although they were despised because of the contagiousness of their diseased skin, the men go on to discover that the battle has already been won on their behalf, because God has intervened. Perhaps Stewart selected this particular text to argue that despite the oppression that African Americans experienced because of the color of their skin, they will arise to discover that God has intervened on their behalf in the battle for freedom. It is also interesting that Stewart chose to use the pronoun "ye"—that is, you—rather than "we" as it appears in 2 Kings 7:3. In choosing that pronoun, Stewart excludes herself because she has already made her decision. She is not going to just sit there and die. Here as elsewhere, Stewart speaks with a voice she has appropriated from the Bible, but she also reveals something about herself in the words she chooses.

Truth or Fiction? The Power of Depiction

While nineteenth-century African American women were less constrained than white women by Victorian ideals of womanhood, they were also less protected by them. In her excellent analysis of the life of Sojourner Truth, whose public advocacy in the latter part of the nineteenth century was much more widely known than Maria Stewart's in the earlier part of that century, Nell Painter uncovers the ways that others (particularly white women) manipulated Sojourner Truth's image, conjuring up a being who was depicted as unfeminine, exotic, simple, and coarse.[42] As Painter ably shows, Sojourner Truth was, like many African American women of her day, struggling against the proscriptions and prejudices that delimited the

40. Ibid., 51.
41. Ibid.
42. Nell Irvin Painter, *Sojourner Truth: A Life, a Symbol*, 1st ed. (New York: W. W. Norton, 1996).

lives of black women in the United States. Painter does an excellent job of pointing out the inaccuracies of others in reporting the particulars of Sojourner Truth's life. Uncovering the real Sojourner Truth is a task made all the more difficult by the fact that her words were recorded by others; even her famous *Narrative of Sojourner Truth* is in fact the work of an amanuensis. The life of Sojourner Truth offers several clear examples of the manipulation of her public image. On the one hand, whites tried to produce one type of image and understanding of Truth. On the other hand, Truth cleverly manipulated her own image, at times powerfully using photography to express her self-understanding and shape her public persona.

Painter has a field day pointing out the ways in which Harriet Beecher Stowe crafted a completely African, completely exotic, completely other "Libyan Sibyl" out of Truth, a creation that seem to have suited Stowe's hierarchical and elitist conceptions of race much better than they suited reality.[43] In describing Truth as a "Libyan Sibyl"—even to the point of misrepresenting Truth's posture and appearance—Stowe in fact misrepresents Truth.

But Stowe was not the only author who produced an enduring misrepresentation of Sojourner Truth. Perhaps it is for her dismantling of the myth that Frances Dana Gage erected around Truth and the famous "Ar'n't I a Woman?" speech that Painter's biography is best known. Meticulously, Painter shows that over time, Truth's words are coated with thicker and thicker layers of dialect more appropriate to a southern slave than to a northern-born woman whose first language was Dutch, as Truth's was. That generations of Americans would prefer Gage's racist misconstruction of "Ar'n't I a Woman?" to Marius Robinson's less histrionic, more contemporaneous account of Truth's words, buttresses Painter's argument that the symbol that others created of Truth had a compelling power and better suited popular conceptions of African American women than it did the truth about Truth.[44]

43. Ibid., 151–63.

44. Indeed, in the question-and-answer period following a lecture on Sojourner Truth, Painter suggested that had Truth been literate, and her image less malleable by others, she might also be less well known. As a dark-complexioned, illiterate former slave, Truth (like Harriet Tubman) suited the majority culture's popular, nineteenth-century conceptions of black women. Painter notes that other black women of the

Sojourner Truth provides an excellent example of the ways some nineteenth-century African American women were contrasted, and contrasted themselves, with the white feminine ideal in their work in the public arena. As Painter shows, Truth's public image was manipulated by those who wanted to define her as a kind of "Libyan Sibyl"—as an exotic who was different in almost every respect from the ideal white woman. Nevertheless, Truth fought back with her use of cartes de visite—calling cards with her picture on them. In the photos, she was obviously a woman, yet neither was she the exotic African "Libyan Sibyl" nor the white feminine ideal. She was, as a consequence of the negative construction of her identity, perhaps more intentional, and less limited, in constructing an alternative public persona.

That Sojourner Truth understood the power of her own symbolism is evidenced by her use of cartes de visite sporting her image, taking advantage of the latest technology of the age, photography. As she put it, she sold "the shadow to support the substance,"[45] shrewdly merchandising both the cartes and her *Narrative* to support and further her public ministry. Although she was illiterate, Truth carefully constructed an image of herself that reflected nineteenth-century norms for women's deportment and behavior, while giving the impression of literacy. On one such carte, she is seen with knitting in her hands, reading glasses on her face, and an open book nearby. She is dressed demurely, in a simple black frock with a white cap on her head and a white shawl across her shoulders. Surely, the spectacles and the book give the impression that Truth could read, while the knitting and the restrained dress were meant to demonstrate both Truth's respectability and her femininity. No doubt this presentation was meant to contradict others' representations of Sojourner Truth. She is no Libyan Sibyl in her cartes de visite; instead, she is an African American woman whose very bearing is intended to refute popular misconceptions about her. (See figure 1.)

The troubled times that shaped Truth's life also produced the Civil War, the emancipation of four million blacks from involuntary chattel slavery, the emergence of the nascent women's rights movement, and a host of

day who were either lighter complexioned or literate were nowhere to be seen on the public stage. Nell Painter, paper presented at the Du Bois Institute of the African American Studies Department, Harvard University, October 16, 1996.

45. Gilbert and Truth, *Narrative of Sojourner Truth*, iv.

Fig. 1. Sojourner Truth carte de visite, unidentified photographer, 1864. The caption below the photo reads, "I sell the shadow to support the substance. Sojourner Truth." (Library of Congress)

other social and political movements. Painter suggests that Truth came to represent not only an individual life but also an ideological symbol in the hands of others—she became the objectification of all former slaves, all black women, and all true believers. From evidence of the conflation of Truth's life story with that of other, mainly southern slaves, her construction as an entirely other African, as in Harriet Beecher Stowe's "Libyan Sibyl" essay, or suffragette, as in Frances Dana Gage's construction of a broken-dialect "Ar'n't I a Woman?" speech a decade after it was ostensibly given, Painter concludes that others of Truth's time did not hesitate to ascribe to her a mythic history and identity that fit their needs better than they fit her real life story. Painter accuses others of a scurrilous or at best careless disregard for either Truth's real life or her real words, as when they construct for her a dialect unlikely to have reflected her true speech. Again and again, according to Painter, the truth of who Sojourner Truth was, was sublimated to the contemporary, pragmatic purposes to which others sought to put her image.

Sojourner Truth was not the only nineteenth-century African American woman to carefully present herself to the world by word and image. Jarena Lee produced an autobiography in 1849 that included an illustration of her in a pose strikingly similar to that which Truth would later adopt. She is dressed modestly, again with a white cap and shawl covering her head and shoulders. Two books and several sheets of paper are tucked under the books, and she has a writing quill in her hand. (See figure 2.)

Like Maria Stewart, Jarena Lee was a freeborn African American woman. In the course of her itinerant ministry, Lee traveled from New York to Maryland and as far west as Ohio. In one year, 1835, she "traveled over 700 miles and gave almost the same number of sermons."[46] Her preaching was groundbreaking not only because of her gender but also because of her race. It is clear from her narrative that her practice of addressing mixed-race audiences was quite unusual for the time and frequently contested.

Resistance from whites on account of her race was not the sum of the opposition Lee faced. Among African Americans and within her own African Methodist Episcopal (AME) denomination, Lee endured hindrances especially from her own ecclesial authorities who felt her unqualified for ministry because of her gender. To those who resisted her ministry because

46. Andrews, introduction to *Sisters of the Spirit*, 6.

Fig. 2. Jarena Lee frontispiece illustration from the 1849 edition of her autobiography. The caption below the illustration reads, "Mrs. Jarena Lee. Preacher of the A.M.E. Church. Aged 60 years on the 11th day of the 2nd month 1844. Philadelphia 1844." (Library of Congress)

of either her race or her gender, Lee presented the compelling testimony of the fruit of her ministry and the evidence of her person (as documented by the illustration that prefaced her autobiography).

Disappearing Act

Unlike Sojourner Truth and Jarena Lee, who sought to control how they were perceived by selecting and distributing images of themselves, Maria Stewart seems to have taken an opposite approach. Rather than representing herself, Stewart seems intent upon effacing herself from her narrative.[47] The 1835 edition of her speeches includes no visual representation of her; in it she tells us little of a personal nature about herself.[48] Although she tells us the year, we do not learn the date of her birth, nor does she even mention her parents' names. She tells us that when her parents died, she was raised by a "clergyman's family" but gives us no more detail about him than that—we are not told the clergyman's name, his family's location, or even his denominational affiliation. We are told that she attended "Sabbath School" but no more than that about her education. This is precious little information.[49]

However, regarding her salvation experience and calling to ministry, Stewart waxes eloquent: "[I] was, as I humbly hope and trust, brought to the knowledge of the truth, as it is in Jesus, in 1830. . . . From the moment I experienced the change, I felt a strong desire, with the help and assistance of God, to devote the remainder of my days to piety and virtue, and . . . were I called upon, I would willingly sacrifice my life for the cause of God and my brethren."[50]

47. Moody, *Sentimental Confessions*, 26–50.

48. When Maria Stewart republished her speeches in 1879, in *Meditations from the Pen of Maria Stewart*, she included more autobiographical information, much of which was in the form of letters of attestation from others who knew her, like abolitionist and publisher William Lloyd Garrison and Episcopal pastor Alexander Crummell. Richardson, *Maria W. Stewart*, 87–109. For a comparison of the increased autobiographical detail of Maria Stewart's second volume, *Meditations from the Pen of Maria Stewart*, published in 1879, relative to her first volume, *Productions of Mrs. Maria W. Stewart*, published in 1835, see Moody, *Sentimental Confessions*, 26–50. Stewart's second volume was essentially a reprint of her 1835 volume with expanded autobiographical information.

49. Stewart, "Productions of Maria Stewart," 3–4.

50. Ibid., 4.

Of the difficulties she has faced in life, she says little: only that she "has, as it were, upon one hand, basked in the sunshine of prosperity; and, on the other, she has drunk deep in the cup of sorrow."[51] However, rather than dwell upon those difficulties, she turns the discussion away from her personal struggles and again toward her personal sense of mission:

> Never did I realize, till I was forced to, that it was from God I derived every earthly blessing, and that it was God who had a right to take them away. I found it almost impossible to say "Thy will be done."[52] It is now one year since Christ first spoke peace to my troubled soul. Soon after I presented myself before the Lord in the holy ordinance of baptism, my soul became filled with holy meditations and sublime ideas; and my ardent wish and desire have ever been, that I might become a humble instrument in the hands of God, of winning some poor souls to Christ.[53]

As always, Stewart references scripture. The words "Thy will be done" recall Matthew 6:10, the words of the Lord's Prayer: "Thy kingdom come. Thy will be done in earth, as it is in heaven." They also recall Jesus's words in the Garden of Gethsemane as he wrestled with God's will that he go to the Cross. The image of Jesus in Gethsemane is one of him at his lowest point; he is small before the will of God, and he is alone—even his disciples are asleep or about to betray him. In this very personal moment of prayer, Jesus seems to decrease, that God's will might increase. By presenting this particular image, Stewart focuses our attention again upon God, while deflecting it from herself.

Unlike Jarena Lee and Sojourner Truth, who presented their persons (in photographs, illustrations, and rich autobiographical detail) as evidence against the prejudices and pejoratives that society held about African American women, Maria Stewart only, always, answered with the Word of God. It was not personal; it was not about her. Her legitimation was not to be based upon the evidence of her life experiences—except her experience of God's salvation. At every moment—even at her most self-revelatory—the words are not hers but God's, as found in the Bible.

51. Ibid., 23.

52. Matthew 26:42: "He went away again the second time, and prayed, saying, O my Father, if this cup may not pass away from me, except I drink it, *thy will be done*." Similarly, Luke 22:24: "Saying, Father, if thou be willing, remove this cup from me: nevertheless *not my will, but thine, be done*."

53. Stewart, "Productions of Maria Stewart," 23–24.

She is not Maria Stewart; she is Deborah, warrior prophetess, ready to do battle with words as her weapons. She is Queen Esther, interceding on behalf of her people. She is Word, re-membered and incarnate. These are her credentials: they are the only credentials she gives us. They are the only credentials she seems to believe she needs.

In many ways, Stewart's reticence to reveal herself resembles what historian Darlene Clark Hine calls the culture of dissemblance: "the behavior and attitudes of Black women that created the appearance of openness and disclosure but actually shielded the truth of their inner lives and selves from their oppressors." Postbellum African American women responded to the pressures exerted by wider society to "control their productive and reproductive capacities and their sexuality"[54] by shielding their private lives from others.[55] That is, some black women shielded their private lives because of their concerns that others' hostile gaze would distort their images. While such women seemed to be self-revealing, in actuality, they disclosed little about themselves. Although the "culture of dissemblance" developed in response to observations of African American women following the Civil War, Hine's characterization of it also seems to describe Stewart's tactics in her 1835 volume. She tells us little about herself; therefore, there is little about her that can be attacked or belittled. Rather than present us with an image, as Jarena Lee or Sojourner Truth chose to do, she presents us with the Bible. The Bible is the only visible target because Stewart has hidden herself within its pages.

I Am Black, but Comely

Freer of the constraints of the Cult of True Womanhood, black women also found in the abolitionist movement powerful theological motivations for their social action and public engagement. Energized by the fight against slavery, they pioneered social engagement that would echo later Pentecostal women's preaching and teaching ministries, which were fueled by a similar eschatological urgency. Black women wrestled against the vague

54. Hine, "Rape and the Inner Lives of Black Women," 292.

55. Hine further explains, "Because of the interplay of racial animosity, class tensions, gender role differentiation, and regional economic variations, Black women, as a rule, developed and adhered to a cult of secrecy, a culture of dissemblance, to protect the sanctity of inner aspects of their lives." Ibid., 293–94.

and degraded place that society accorded them, and in battling racial oppression and slavery, they also fought the gender oppression that sought to lock them out of public discourse.

However, rather than accept this nebulous social space, some black women of the nineteenth century went on to create an alternative social identity, emerging more trangressively than contemporaneous white women into the public sphere. In many ways, it was precisely the low regard in which American society held black women that allowed those same women greater freedom to recast themselves not as ladies in the Victorian sense but as public figures: as ministers, as orators, and as activists. They were not constrained, as white women were, by a restrictive ideal to be upheld.

What Maria Stewart makes of questions of gender is complicated—even conflicted. On one hand, she advocates very traditional roles for women, as mothers and wives, for example. She espouses feminine virtues that echo those of the Victorian Cult of True Womanhood, as well as the *Haustafeln*, or subordination codes of scripture.[56] However, Stewart is careful to draw distinctions between the lives of African American women and their white counterparts. She delineates these differences subtly in some cases and with the occasional broadside in others. Ultimately, Stewart's rhetoric on questions of gender works to undermine white women's positions of privilege, as she hopes to provoke African American women to take the places of privilege and honor that they have earned. Finally, and perhaps most interestingly, Stewart clings to protestations of ladylike modesty even as she argues, with increasing boldness, that she, as a woman, has every right to a place in public discourse—a place that American women had not occupied before.

Biblical texts like 1 Timothy 2:11–12,[57] are known as *Haustafeln* or "household codes." These texts recommend that women be subject to men's authority in all things. The genre also includes texts like Colossians 3:22,[58] which directs servants to obey their masters. Taken together, the texts seem to reinforce social hierarchies that place men above all other

56. Biblical texts like 1 Timothy 2:11–12 and Colossians 3:22 are known as *Haustafeln*, or "household codes."

57. 1 Timothy 2:11–12: "Let the woman learn in silence with all subjection. But I suffer not a woman to teach, nor to usurp authority over the man, but to be in silence."

58. Colossians 3:22: "Servants, obey in all things your masters according to the flesh; not with eyeservice, as menpleasers; but in singleness of heart, fearing God."

creatures; women, children, and servants all take lower places in the social schema the *Haustafeln* intend to dictate.

As an African American woman fighting slavery and racial and gender prejudice, Stewart had to articulate her abolitionist and equalitarian views in such a way as to negate the power of the *Haustafeln*. As an evangelical woman, Stewart had to construct her argument in such a way as not to offend the sensibilities of other biblically literate and Bible-loving colleagues and friends.

Didn't Mary Preach?

Maria Stewart begins her nearly three-year public oratorical career with protestations of modesty that were almost *de rigueur* for a woman of the period. Never mind that her rhetoric soon turned fiery; she begins with a skillfully written disclaimer: "Feeling a deep solemnity of soul, in view of our wretched and degraded situation ... I have thought thus publicly to express my sentiments before you. I hope my friends will not scrutinize these pages with too severe an eye, as I have not calculated to display either elegance or taste in their composition, but have merely written the meditations of my heart as far as my imagination led."[59]

For a short while, she continues to decry her skills as almost unequal to the task toward which her heart and piety compel her: "My Respected Friends, I feel almost unable to address you; almost incompetent to perform the task; and, at times, I have felt ready to exclaim, O that my head were waters, and mine eyes a fountain of tears,[60] that I might weep day and night, for the transgressions of the daughters of my people. Truly, my heart's desire and prayer is that Ethiopia might stretch forth her hands unto God.[61] But we have a great work to do."[62]

It is not surprising that Stewart laces this partial disclaimer with biblical text, nor is it surprising that she has chosen the words of the Weeping Prophet, Jeremiah, to express her feelings. In some ways, this reference to

59. Stewart, "Productions of Maria Stewart," 3.

60. Jeremiah 9:1: "*Oh that my head were waters, and mine eyes a fountain of tears, that I might weep day and night for the slain of the daughter of my people!*"

61. Psalms 68:31: "Princes shall come out of Egypt; *Ethiopia shall soon stretch out her hands unto God.*"

62. Stewart, "Productions of Maria Stewart," 6.

Jeremiah is a way of wrapping herself in the prophet's mantle and tear-stained persona.

However, her next biblical reference is one to which Stewart returns again and again. She quotes Psalms 68:31:"Princes shall come out of Egypt; Ethiopia *shall soon* stretch out her hands unto God." That is, she nearly quotes it. In writing that"Ethiopia *might* stretch forth her hands," Stewart turns the Ethiopian prophecy into a heartfelt hope, a whispered prayer.

Stewart's protests of her own inadequacy fit a pattern that would have been well known to her audiences. Sentimental literature was full of such formulaic reticence, which would have been unnecessary had the nineteenth-century woman writer in question not eventually overcome her qualms and gone on to write the book that featured her polite pro-testations of inadequacy on page one or two. So it was with Stewart, that her polite attempts to apologize for her lack of skill are soon followed by passionate declarations of her charge.

Stewart's discussion of David Walker is very revealing."If there is no other way for me to escape," she writes, then God "is able to take me to himself, as he did the most noble, fearless, and undaunted David Walker."[63] David Walker, whom Stewart claimed as mentor and friend, died in 1830; in 1831, Stewart wrote "Religion and the Pure Principles of Morality, the Sure Foundation on Which We Must Build." The circumstances of Walk-er's death were regarded by some as mysterious,[64] but it occurred at about the same time that his radical abolitionist publication, *David Walker's Appeal to the Coloured Citizens of the World*, reached the South. That Stewart considered her calling similar to Walker's is important. She certainly be-lieved that such a career cost Walker dearly, yet she states that she is willing to follow him in this career. Moreover, she does not hesitate to state that she is following in the footsteps of a man.

How does Stewart explain such courage? How does she justify such forthrightness in an age when women are expected to remain at home, quietly knitting—at least if the sentimental fiction of the time is to be believed? At times she is coy, blaming men for the necessity of her public crusade:"Had those men among us, who have had an opportunity, turned their attention as assiduously to mental and moral improvements as they

63. Ibid., 5.
64. Richardson, *Maria W. Stewart*, 8.

have to gambling and dancing, I might have remained quietly at home, and they stood contending in my place."[65]

This explanation seems quite threadbare. There is nothing more unlikely than that a woman like Stewart would have been content to have "remained quietly at home" even if there had been men willing to stand "contending" in her place. "Our situation is grim," Stewart seems to be arguing, and she must intervene because of the seriousness of the situation. Stewart reasons that someone had to do something, even if that someone were a woman.

It was not until her farewell address to the city of Boston in September 1833 that Stewart gave a fuller accounting of her right, as a woman, to undertake so groundbreaking a position on the public stage. As she does elsewhere, so here again she uses scripture references to bolster her case: "What if I am a woman; is not the God of ancient times the God of these modern days? Did he not raise up Deborah, to be a mother, and a judge in Israel? Did not queen Esther save the lives of the Jews?"[66]

In making her case for her own work, Stewart points to two unusual women from the Bible: Deborah, the warrior prophetess who ruled Israel during the period of loose tribal confederacy that preceded the Davidic monarchy,[67] and Esther, the queen whose intercession on behalf of her people was made possible by her marriage to a foreign king.[68] Both were leaders; both were instrumental in protecting their people; both were women of whom little (of a political nature) might normally be expected.

Stewart continues: "What if I am a woman? . . . And [did not] Mary Magdalene first declare the resurrection of Christ from the dead?"[69] This "didn't Mary Magdalene preach?" line of reasoning is a far cry from Stewart's original argument that she became an abolitionist writer and speaker only because there were no men to do it, so that she "might have remained quietly at home, and they stood contending in [her] place."[70]

The difficulty that Stewart faced was a difficulty that evangelical women often face—even today. If they seek to justify their work or ministry by recourse to the Bible, then they must first provide a refutation of the Bible's

65. Stewart, "Productions of Maria Stewart," 67.
66. Ibid., 75.
67. Judges 4 and 5.
68. The book of Esther.
69. Stewart, "Productions of Maria Stewart," 75.
70. Ibid., 67.

codes of submission, which many evangelicals read as prohibitions against women's autonomous leadership. Interestingly, Stewart's recourse to biblical women such as Mary Magdalene was not uncommon; several of her contemporaries made similar arguments.

Jarena Lee was an African American itinerant minister of the nascent AME denomination who published an account of her work in 1836. She sought, but never received, ordination from the denomination's founder, Richard Allen, and frequently had to give an account of her calling to ministry in the face of those who thought public ministry an inappropriate occupation for a woman. Although she clashed frequently with AME founder and first bishop Allen, her relationship with him appears to have remained cordial. Interestingly, while Allen sought independence from the predominantly white Methodist Church in matters of finance and polity, he deferred to Methodism in his resistance to women preachers, arguing that it simply "did not allow for women preachers."[71]

Jarena Lee's rhetorical strategy[72] against Pauline[73] proscriptions prohibiting women's ministry is to undermine Paul with his own writings. First, Lee argues that Paul himself recognizes the importance of a woman's preaching ministry when he records that Mary Magdalene was the first to report that Jesus's tomb was empty.[74] "Did not Mary first preach the

71. Andrews, introduction to *Sisters of the Spirit*, 5.

72. Lee uses other strategies, such as quoting texts that exemplify the liberating standards she wishes to highlight. (She begins by quoting Joel 2:28, which foretells gender equality in the receipt of heavenly charisma and is repeated in Acts 2.) Elsewhere, Lee writes that God wiped her mind of concerns for her sick child, to no ill effect, to suggest that responsibilities to the kingdom of God outweighed the domestic chores many of the time regarded as women's only legitimate concern. This episode serves to reinscribe the hierarchy of concerns Lee outlines—a hierarchy that places gender concerns far below "spiritual" matters like preaching or doing ministry. However, I will limit my discussion here to focus on Lee's rhetorical strategies with regard to Paul.

73. Although modern biblical scholarship disputes the origins of many parts of the New Testament traditionally ascribed to the Apostle Paul, within the nineteenth-century black church, traditional attributions of Pauline authorship were rarely questioned. For the purposes of this chapter, I will speak as Lee believed—that is, I will speak as though none of the epistles traditionally ascribed to Paul were, or ought to be, contested as such.

74. In the Synoptic Gospels (Matthew, Mark, and Luke), Mary Magdalene is the first to report that Jesus's tomb is empty. In the Gospel of John, she is the first to report the resurrection of Jesus. Here Lee conflates the four canonical gospels in describing Mary Magdalene's role.

risen Saviour," she asks, "and is not the doctrine of the resurrection the very climax of Christianity—hangs not all our hope on this, as argued by St. Paul?"[75] Indeed, while Paul does argue for the centrality of the resurrection to the proclamation of the Gospel, he makes no special claims to Mary Magdalene's role in that proclamation.[76] Here Lee in fact argues for privileging some of Paul's writings over others, with a clear appeal to the centrality of Jesus's life as paradigm for weighing relative importance. Why does Lee mention Paul, when narratives that describe Mary's role as reporter of the empty tomb are written in the Gospels? Most certainly, Lee's argument here is not with the Gospels but with the texts mandating women's submission to men that are found in Paul's writings. Her purpose is to elevate questions of resurrection and preaching over those of gender and to place the argument in the mouth of the New Testament writer regarded as responsible for having outlined the most blatantly gender-based limitations.[77] In other words, if the resurrection is of central importance and its preaching essential to Christian faith (as even Paul agrees, as she has pointed out), then the sex of the messenger can only be, at best, of secondary import.

Another contemporary of Maria Stewart was evangelist Julia Foote. Foote sought and received ordination in the African Methodist Episcopal Zion denomination. Like Stewart and Lee, Foote was also a widow. In her autobiography, *A Brand Plucked from the Fire*, Foote details the process by which she converted to the view that women had as much right to preach as men did. "I had always been opposed to the preaching of women, and had spoken against it, though, I acknowledge, without foundation," Foote admits.[78] Eventually, Foote's mind began to change with regard to the question of women preachers, motivated, at least in part, by her own experience of a calling to ministry.

75. J. Lee, "The Life and Religious Experience of Jarena Lee," 36. Here Lee seems to refer to 1 Corinthians 15:12–19, which argues the centrality of the doctrine of the resurrection to Christian belief.

76. As Paul lists those who have seen the resurrected Jesus, he mentions Peter (Cephas)—while seeming to omit Mary Magdalene from the list—but he includes himself. See 1 Corinthians 15:3–9.

77. Examples of the type of scriptures against which Lee was arguing include 1 Timothy 2:11–12 and 1 Corinthians 11:3 and 14:34–35. These texts recommend that women be subject to men's authority in all things and remain silent in the church.

78. Foote, "A Brand Plucked from the Fire," 67.

From the New Testament, Foote notes that the same Greek word[79] is translated as "servant of the church" when referring to a woman, Phoebe, but "minister" when referring to a man, Tychicus. (Compare Romans 16:1 and Ephesians 6:21.)[80] Convinced that the New Testament modeled women's active participation in ministry, she writes, "When Paul said, 'Help those women who labor with me in the Gospel,'[81] he certainly meant that they did more than to pour out tea."[82]

Julia Foote, Jarena Lee, and Maria Stewart all seemed intent upon answering questions about their own pioneering ministries with irrefutable biblical images of other pioneering women: Deborah, Esther, Phoebe, and of course, Mary Magdalene, whose role as first to declare the empty tomb is documented in each of the four canonical gospels. By using scripture to argue against other scripture—in this case, the restrictions of the *Haustafeln*—these women do as evangelical women have done before and since: they make a biblically sensitive case for their own rights.

By at least the middle of the nineteenth century, such arguments in favor of women preachers had been made in several places. One example is Rev. Luther Lee's published sermon preached on the occasion of the ordination of a "Rev. Miss Antoinette L. Brown." The sermon contains a Greek exegesis of Romans 16:1, of Phoebe as deacon/minister[83] that is similar to Foote's, and of Deborah as a prophetess[84] that is similar to Stewart's. Luther Lee's sermon also contains historical arguments making reference, for example, to Pliny the Younger's letters to Trajan and their discussion of the roles of women in the early church.[85] Like Lee, Stewart

---

79. The Greek word is transliterated as *diakonon* in Romans 16:1 and *diakonos* in Ephesians 6:21. From this Greek word the English "deacon" is derived.

80. Foote, "A Brand Plucked from the Fire," 79. In the text of her narrative, Foote mistakenly lists Romans 19:1; this should be Romans 16:1. This suggests that she had not done the Greek translation herself but had learned of it from others and perhaps had recorded the reference incorrectly.

81. Philippians 4:3: "And I intreat thee also, true yokefellow, *help those women which laboured with me in the gospel*, with Clement also, and with other my fellowlabourers, whose names are in the book of life."

82. Foote, "A Brand Plucked from the Fire," 79.

83. Rev. Luther Lee, "Woman's Right to Preach the Gospel," in *Holiness Tracts Defending the Ministry of Women*, ed. Donald W. Dayton (New York: Garland, 1985), 11–15.

84. Ibid., 7.

85. Ibid., 14.

includes historical as well as theological arguments for women's rights in her speeches.

What If I Am a Woman?

Like Julia Foote, Maria Stewart seems to have undergone a change of heart regarding the role of women in ministry. She had always called for women to do their duty to their families: to train their children to be virtuous, for example. "O woman, woman! Upon you I call; for upon your exertions almost entirely depends whether the rising generation shall be any thing more than we have been or not. O woman, woman! Your example is powerful, your influence great; it extends over your husbands and over your children, and throughout the circle of your acquaintance. Then let me exhort you to cultivate among yourselves a spirit of Christian love and unity, having charity one for another, without which all our goodness is as sounding brass, and as a tinkling cymbal."[86] Here Stewart expresses sentiments quite in keeping with the Cult of True Womanhood, which credited women with disproportionate powers and responsibilities to inspire others to virtue and goodness.

However, Stewart also understood that the situation was much more complicated for African American women, who also suffered the consequences of racial prejudice over and above the expectations society placed on them because of their gender. She explains that she had asked women "who transact business for themselves" if they would hire black girls who presented "satisfactory references."[87] All she is asking for black women is "equal opportunity with others" for employment. She does not explain, but presumably the businesswomen of whom she had inquired were white. They respond that "for their part they have no objection" but fear to hire African American workers because it would put them "in danger of losing the public patronage."[88] "And such is the powerful force of prejudice," Stewart laments. "Let our girls possess what amiable qualities of soul they may; let their characters be fair and spotless as innocence itself; let their

---

86. 1 Corinthians 13:1: "Though I speak with the tongues of men and of angels, and have not charity, I am become *as sounding brass, or a tinkling cymbal.*" Stewart, "Productions of Maria Stewart," 62–63.

87. Ibid., 52.

88. Ibid.

natural taste and ingenuity be what they may; it is impossible for scarce an individual of them to rise above the condition of servants."[89]

Stewart realizes that even though black women may possess all of the qualities extolled in the Cult of True Womanhood, color prejudice still stands as an unreasonable impediment to their progress in society. "Ah!" she exclaims. "Why is this cruel and unfeeling distinction? Is it merely because God has made our complexion to vary? If it be, O shame to soft, relenting humanity!"[90]

Still, Stewart doesn't let blacks off the hook, even though color prejudice continues to stigmatize them. She argues that if the free people of color behaved more virtuously, both slavery and color prejudice would disappear. In this, Stewart seems unaware that by blaming the victims of the slavocracy for the abuses of the slavocracy, she is little different from those who defended slavery as an institution necessary for the containment and training of ignorant, savage blacks. Both the slavocracy and, here, Stewart argue that at least part of the oppression of blacks is caused by the blacks' lack of virtue: "Yet, after all, methinks were the American free people of color to turn their attention more assiduously to moral worth and intellectual improvement, this would be the result: prejudice would gradually diminish, and the whites would be compelled to say, unloose those fetters!"[91]

For Stewart, the answer to prejudice is self-sufficiency and a kind of nascent Black Nationalism. She argues that "it is no use to murmur nor to repine; but let us promote ourselves and improve our own talents."[92] Moreover, as she views education as a key to the improvement of the condition of African Americans, she enjoins black women to build schools themselves if necessary:

> Why cannot we do something to distinguish ourselves, and contribute some of our hard earnings that would reflect honor upon our memories, and cause our children to arise and call us blessed?[93] Shall it any longer be said of the daughters of Africa, they have no ambition, they have no force? By no means. Let every female heart become united, and let us

89. Ibid.
90. Ibid.
91. Ibid.
92. Ibid., 12.
93. Proverbs 31:28: "*Her children arise up, and call her blessed; her husband also, and he praiseth her.*"

raise a fund ourselves; and at the end of one year and a half, we might be able to lay the corner-stone for the building of a High School, that the higher branches of knowledge might be enjoyed by us; and God would raise us up, and enough to aid us in our laudable designs.[94]

Not surprisingly, Stewart quotes the passage from Proverbs 31 that describes the "virtuous woman"—a biblical picture of household management and good business sense. She goes on to encourage her listeners to prudent household management as the key to her school-building scheme. "Let each one strive to excel in good housewifery, knowing that prudence and economy are the road to wealth."[95] "It is of no use," Stewart opines, "for us to sit with our hands folded, hanging our heads like bulrushes, lamenting our wretched condition; but let us make a mighty effort, and arise; and if no one will promote or respect us, let us promote and respect ourselves."[96]

"Daughters of Africa" is a phrase that Stewart uses throughout her text. For Stewart, it signifies the special, even covenantal relationship between people of African descent and God, and it grows out of interpretations of Psalms 68:31, the so-called Ethiopian prophecy. Nevertheless, it cannot be overlooked that when she refers to "Americans" she means whites and that "sons and daughters of Africa" are so called to distinguish African Americans from white Americans. For example, in one use of this distinction, Stewart ruefully notes that it is the work of the sons and daughters of Africa that has enriched the white Americans: "The [white] Americans have practised nothing but head-work these 200 years, and we [African Americans] have done their drudgery. And is it not high time for us to imitate their examples, and practise head-work too, and keep what we have got, and get what we can?"[97]

Moreover, she is aware that as a consequence of the combination of gender and racial prejudice, the ease of the whites, particularly white women, has been purchased at the price of the hard labor of the daughters of Africa. "How long shall a mean set of men flatter us with their smiles, and enrich themselves with our hard earnings; their wives' fingers sparkling with rings, and they themselves laughing at our folly?"[98] Clearly, here Stewart is de-

94. Stewart, "Productions of Maria Stewart," 16.
95. Ibid.
96. Ibid., 15.
97. Ibid., 17.
98. Ibid., 16.

nouncing as "mean" white men who "enrich themselves" at blacks' expense, so that their wives, twice removed (by race and gender) from the actual work, might enjoy the proceeds of it as their fingers "sparkl[e] with rings."[99]

By the end of her speaking career, Maria Stewart has come far from the demure protestations she made at the outset. No longer does she argue that she became an abolitionist writer and speaker only because there were no men to do it, so that she "might have remained quietly at home, and they stood contending in [her] place."[100] Instead, she is ready to argue that women have a God-given place in public life and that she has a God-given place in public life.

It is in her "Farewell Address to Her Friends in the City of Boston," delivered on September 21, 1833, that Stewart is the most forthright in her declarations on gender. Gone are the coy facades; in their place, she makes a bold case for the rights of women. In this final address, Stewart again describes her calling to public ministry, but her terminology is, if possible, even more dramatic than in previous speeches. She describes a scene she says she imagined after her salvation: "After these convictions, in imagination I found myself sitting at the feet of Jesus, clothed in my right mind.[101] For I before had been like a ship tossed to and fro, in a storm at sea. Then was I glad when I realized the dangers I had escaped; and then I consecrated my soul and body, and all the powers of my mind to his service, from that time, henceforth; yea, even for evermore, amen."[102]

Stewart has previously stated that she has felt a calling to a ministry

99. Ibid.

100. Ibid., 67.

101. Luke 8:35–36: "Then they went out to see what was done; and came to Jesus, and found the man, out of whom the devils were departed, sitting at the feet of Jesus, clothed, and in his right mind: and they were afraid. They also which saw it told them by what means he that was possessed of the devils was healed." (See also Mark 5:15.) Stewart has condensed the text, combining "clothed," and "in his right mind" to become "clothed in my right mind"—a figure of speech that remains common in African American church life today. That is, from a story about demon possession and deliverance, Stewart derives a statement about a return to sanity and clear thinking through the power of Christ. She declares herself to be "clothed in her right mind"—able to see clearly through the dangers at hand.

102. "Henceforth and forever" occurs in several places in the Bible: Psalms 125:2, Psalms 131:3, Isaiah 9:7, Isaiah 59:21, Micah 4:7. Each time, it is a statement about enduring reality and suggests that which is both preexistent and eternal. Stewart, "Productions of Maria Stewart," 73.

that might cost her life. In her first statement of this sense of calling, she invokes her mentor, David Walker, whose death had cast a long shadow over her own work. However, here she has intensified the scene, invoking not Walker but Jesus, so that this coming to consciousness about her own vocation has not been accompanied by fallen human heroes like Walker but has taken place in the very presence of God. Stewart further suggests that, although imagined, this encounter has taken place somehow outside of *kronos*[103] time, by her use of the phrase "from that time, henceforth; yea, even for evermore, amen,"[104] which places the scene in the realm of the divine and eternal *kairos*.[105]

Then Stewart intensifies the scene even further, continuing her identification with Jesus by likening herself to one of his disciples: "I found that religion was full of benevolence; I found that there was joy and peace in believing,[106] and I felt as though I was commanded to come out of from the world and be separate;[107] to go forward and be baptized. Methought I heard a spiritual interrogation, are you able to drink of that cup that I have drank of? And to be baptized with the baptism that I have been baptized with? And my heart made this reply: Yea, Lord, I am able."[108]

Recalling when Jesus asked his disciples if they were able "to drink of the cup that [he would] drink"[109] invokes images of communion and cov-

103. *Kronos*, transliterated from the Greek New Testament, meaning ordinary "time."

104. Stewart, "Productions of Maria Stewart," 73.

105. *Kairos*, transliterated from the Greek New Testament, meaning "a fitting season, or time of opportunity."

106. Romans 15:13: "Now the God of hope fill you with all *joy and peace in believing,* that ye may abound in hope, through the power of the Holy Ghost."

107. 2 Corinthians 6:16–18: "Wherefore *come out* from among them, and *be ye separate,* saith the Lord, and touch not the unclean thing; and I will receive you, And will be a Father unto you, and ye shall be my sons and daughters, saith the Lord Almighty."

108. Matthew 20:22–23: "But Jesus answered and said, Ye know not what ye ask. *Are ye able to drink of the cup that I shall drink of, and to be baptized with the baptism that I am baptized with?* They say unto him, *We are able.* And he saith unto them, Ye shall drink indeed of my cup, and be baptized with the baptism that I am baptized with: but to sit on my right hand, and on my left, is not mine to give, but it shall be given to them for whom it is prepared of my Father." Stewart, "Productions of Maria Stewart," 73.

109. Matthew 20:22.

enant.[110] In the Gospel of Matthew, it foreshadows Jesus's passion and the suffering that those gathered disciples would experience as they sought to continue the Jesus movement after Jesus's death and resurrection. The cup is also a multivalent image, invoking as it does Jesus's final prayers in the Garden of Gethsemane and his final wrestling with the will of God that he go to the Cross.[111] It is this cup—a cup of communion, of covenant, of sacrifice, and of suffering—that Stewart describes in the context of her acceptance of calling to public ministry. Yet it is not an easy cup for her to drink.

"O how bitter was that cup," she remembers:

> Yet I drank it to its very dregs. It was hard for me to say, thy will be done;[112] yet I was made to bend and kiss the rod. I was at last made willing to be any thing or nothing, for my Redeemer's sake. Like many, I was anxious to retain the world in one hand, and religion in the other. "Ye cannot serve God and mammon,"[113] sounded in my ear, and with giant-strength, I cut off my right hand, as it were, and plucked out my right eye, and cast them from me, thinking it better to enter life halt and maimed, rather than having two hands or eyes to be cast into hell.[114] Thus ended

110. See, for example, Matthew 26:27–28: "And he took the cup, and gave thanks, and gave it to them, saying, Drink ye all of it; For this is my blood of the new testament, which is shed for many for the remission of sins." In this text describing the Last Supper, Jesus institutes what is commemorated in churches throughout the world as Christian communion.

111. Matthew 26:39–42: "And he went a little farther, and fell on his face, and prayed, saying, O my Father, if it be possible, let this cup pass from me: nevertheless not as I will, but as thou wilt. And he cometh unto the disciples, and findeth them asleep, and saith unto Peter, What, could ye not watch with me one hour? Watch and pray, that ye enter not into temptation: the spirit indeed is willing, but the flesh is weak. He went away again the second time, and prayed, saying, O my Father, *if this cup may not pass away from me, except I drink it, thy will be done.*"

112. Matthew 26:42: "He went away again the second time, and prayed, saying, O my Father, if this cup may not pass away from me, except I drink it, *thy will be done.*" This allusion continues Stewart's extended metaphor of "drinking the cup" as a symbol of doing God's will rather than her own.

113. Matthew 6:24; Luke 16:13.

114. Matthew 5:29–30: "And if thy right eye offend thee, pluck it out, and cast it from thee: for it is profitable for thee that one of thy members should perish, and not that thy whole body should be cast into hell. And if thy right hand offend thee, cut it off, and cast it from thee: for it is profitable for thee that one of thy members

these mighty conflicts, and I received this heart-cheering promise, "That neither death, nor life, nor principalities, nor powers, nor things present, nor things to come, should be able to separate me from the love of Christ Jesus, our Lord."[115]

Stewart explains that accepting this calling was both difficult and painful. When she writes, "It was from God I derived every earthly blessing, and that it was God who had a right to take them away,"[116] to what loss is she really referring? Is she obliquely acknowledging that she was having difficulty accepting that God had taken husband, mentor, and family from her, as she believed? She certainly suggests by the quotation "ye cannot serve God and mammon"[117] that she expects her course to be a financially difficult one. After all, she has chosen to serve God rather than to seek material wealth. She makes veiled references to personal sacrifices she likens to "pluck[ing] out my right eye" and "cut[ting] off my right hand" but adds "as it were" to remind us that she refers not to actual amputation but instead to her own determination to make all of herself and all of her own

---

should perish, and not that thy whole body should *be cast into hell*." Matthew 18:8–9: "Wherefore if thy hand or thy foot offend thee, cut them off, and cast them from thee: it is *better for thee to enter into life halt or maimed*, rather than having two hands or two feet to be cast into everlasting fire. And if thine eye offend thee, pluck it out, and cast it from thee: it is better for thee to enter into life with one eye, rather than having two eyes to *be cast into hell fire*." Matthew 9:43–47: "And if thy hand offend thee, cut it off: it is better for thee to enter into life maimed, than having two hands to go into hell, into the fire that never shall be quenched: Where their worm dieth not, and the fire is not quenched. And if thy foot offend thee, cut it off: it is better for thee *to enter halt into life*, than having two feet *to be cast into hell*, into the fire that never shall be quenched: Where their worm dieth not, and the fire is not quenched. And if thine eye offend thee, pluck it out: it is better for thee to enter into the kingdom of God with one eye, than having two eyes to be *cast into hell fire*." Each example from Matthew relates to a different offense, although all suggest an identically radical remedy. The sin in question is not the point of Stewart's usage but rather her willingness to "pluck out [her own] eye" or "cut off [her own] hand" if those body parts posed an impediment to fulfilling the will of God. Indeed, Stewart indicates that by some Herculean effort of "giant-strength" she has already done away with those members in her pursuit of the kingdom. Undoubtedly, she means this metaphorically, perhaps to describe having given up something quite dear to herself in her desire to please God.

115. Stewart, "Productions of Maria Stewart," 73.

116. Ibid., 23.

117. "Mammon" here refers to money or wealth.

desires subordinated to the will of God. Stewart ends these thoughts with the affirmation of Romans 8:38: having demonstrated her willingness to spare nothing of herself in her pursuit of God, she notes a text that seems to proclaim God's unfailing and unending love for her, which is more powerful even than life, death, angels, the present or the future.[118]

We can only speculate as to what personal sacrifice Stewart was referring. However, we do know that she was a relatively young woman when left widowed and childless and that she did not remarry. Certainly, she may have longed for a husband and children; however, it was nearly impossible for a married woman of that day to carry out the sort of public activism that Stewart performed. Of the other women mentioned in this chapter—Jarena Lee, Julia Foote, and Sojourner Truth—all were unmarried or widowed at the time of their public speaking or preaching careers. Marriage and children might have been something Stewart was aware that she had to sacrifice for the sake of her public career. Certainly, the imagery that Stewart chose to describe that sacrifice, imagery of plucked-out eyes and cut-off hands, is that of wrenchingly painful personal loss.

Stewart continues in her description of the divine charge she bears:

> And truly, I can say with St. Paul, that at my conversion, I came to the people in the fullness of the gospel of grace.[119] Having spent a few months in the city of ____, previous, I saw the flourishing condition of their churches, and the progress that they were making in their Sabbath Schools. I visited their Bible Classes, and heart of the union that existed in their Female Associations. On my arrival here, not finding scarce an individual who felt interested in these subjects, and but few of the whites, except Mr. Garrison . . . and hearing that those gentlemen had observed that female influence was powerful, my soul became fired with a holy zeal for your cause;[120] every nerve and muscle in me was engaged in your

118. Romans 8:38–39: "For I am persuaded, that neither *death*, nor *life*, nor *angels*, nor principalities, nor powers, nor *things present*, nor *things to come*, Nor height, nor depth, nor any other creature, *shall be able to separate us from the love of God, which is in Christ Jesus our Lord.*" Notice that Stewart personalizes the text, changing "us" to "me."

119. Romans 15:29: "And I am sure that, when I come unto you, I shall come in *the fulness of the blessing of the gospel* of Christ."

120. Stewart's use of the phrase "your cause" and later "your behalf" suggests that she is speaking about the concerns of her audience: that is, the concerns of African Americans.

behalf. I felt that I had a great work to perform; and was in haste to make a profession of my faith in Christ, that I might be about my Father's business.[121]

Here she likens her salvation experience to that of Paul, who was traditionally regarded as the author of most of the New Testament, and therefore, was also author of many of the *Haustafeln*, or household codes of submission. Although higher biblical criticism calls into question many of the traditional suppositions of Pauline authorship, Stewart nevertheless gives no indication of having been influenced by those studies. She names Paul, supposed author of the texts that demand that slaves obey their masters[122] and that wives submit themselves to their husbands.[123] However, it is this same Paul whose transcendent encounter with Jesus on the Damascus road[124] led not only to a dramatic salvation and healing but also to a dramatic social transformation requiring even a name change. (Although he was previously called Saul, after his Damascus road experience he is known as Paul.) Finally, it is this same Paul whose pen produced one of the most amazing statements of equality the Bible offers, when he wrote, "There is neither Jew nor Greek, there is neither bond nor free, there is neither male nor female: for ye are all one in Christ Jesus."[125]

Which of the many "Pauls" did Stewart mean to invoke when she compared her experiences to his, as reported in the Bible? Was she comparing herself to the Paul whose salvation knocked him out of his social order and into a new relationship with the world around him (including his Jewish roots, the Roman world, and the growing church)? Was she appropriating his stature as apostle, teacher, and evangelist and attempting to liken herself to him in his many whirlwind preaching visits to "the city of ____" or "the city of ____" in the book of Acts? Was she using Paul to refute Paul—laying her own powerful salvation narrative, so like his, against the

121. Stewart, "Productions of Maria Stewart," 74.

122. Colossians 3:22–23: "Servants, obey in all things your masters according to the flesh; not with eyeservice, as menpleasers; but in singleness of heart, fearing God. And whatsoever ye do, do it heartily, as to the Lord, and not unto men."

123. Ephesians 5:22–24: "Wives, submit yourselves unto your own husbands, as unto the Lord. For the husband is the head of the wife, even as Christ is the head of the church: and he is the saviour of the body. Therefore as the church is subject unto Christ, so let the wives be to their own husbands in every thing."

124. Acts 9:1–22.

125. Galatians 3:28.

Haustafeln? Perhaps Stewart simply meant that, like Paul, she was coming to bring the Gospel, as she understood it.[126] All are possibilities. However, later in the same speech, she adds, "Did St. Paul but know of our wrongs and deprivations, I presume he would make no objections to our pleading in public for our rights."[127] This can be none other than an abrogation of the *Haustafeln* as having no legitimacy during the crisis in which Stewart found herself.

Not long after this, Stewart reports that she began speaking publicly. She assures us that this groundbreaking behavior came at the instigation of God:

> Soon after I made this profession, the Spirit of God came before me, and I spake[128] before many. When going home, reflecting on what I had said, I felt ashamed, and knew not where I should hide myself. A something said within my breast, "press forward, I will be with thee." And my heart made this reply, Lord, if thou wilt be with me, then will I speak for thee so long as I live. And thus far I have every reason to believe that it is the divine influence of the Holy Spirit operating upon my heart that could possibly induce me to make the feeble and unworthy efforts that I have.[129]

When she falters, she believes that God has urged her onward. God encourages her. So it is, Stewart explains, that she began her work. God told her to speak, and Maria Stewart spoke:

> And thus for wise and holy purposes, best known to himself, he has raised me in the midst of my enemies,[130] to vindicate my wrongs before

126. This reading is closest to the scripture to which her text has alluded, Romans 15:29: "And I am sure that, when I come unto you, I shall come in the fulness of the blessing of the gospel of Christ."

127. Stewart, "Productions of Maria Stewart," 75.

128. "Spake" is an arcane form of *spoke*. In using this archaic variant, Stewart reproduces one of the grammatical forms found frequently in the King James Version of the Bible.

129. Stewart, "Productions of Maria Stewart," 74.

130. Psalms 110:1–2: "The LORD said unto my Lord, Sit thou at my right hand, until I make thine enemies thy footstool. The LORD shall send the rod of thy strength out of Zion: rule thou *in the midst of thine enemies*." In this very theologically complex passage, "the LORD" speaks to "my Lord." One possible explanation that some Christian theologians have offered is that this conversation takes place between persons of

this people; and to reprove them for sin, as I have reasoned to them of righteousness and judgment to come.[131] "For as the heavens are higher than the earth, so are his ways above our ways, and his thoughts above our thoughts."[132] I believe, that for wise and holy purposes, best known to himself, he hath unloosed my tongue[133] and put his word in my mouth,[134] in order to confound and put all those to shame that have rose up against me.[135] For he hath clothed my face with steel, and lined my forehead with

---

the Triune Godhead. However, this does not appear to be an allusion to Psalms 23:5, where "presence" replaces "midst": "Thou preparest a table before me *in the* presence *of mine enemies:* thou anointest my head with oil; my cup runneth over."

131. John 16:8: "And when he is come, he will *reprove* the world *of sin,* and of *righteousness, and of judgment.*"

132. For anyone who was still wondering why God might have chosen so unusual a candidate for ministry as Stewart, she throws this in, as God speaks in Isaiah 55:9: "For as the heavens are higher than the earth, so are my ways higher than your ways, and my thoughts than your thoughts." If her audience still can't understand why God might have chosen her to bring the word, Stewart suggests that they consider the fact that God's reasoning is sometimes as unfathomable as the heavens are high.

133. Here the priest Zacharias, who was Elisabeth's husband, is healed after having been made mute. His first comments are to praise God for the son, John the Baptist, that he is miraculously to be given. Luke 1:64: "And his mouth was opened immediately, and his *tongue loosed,* and he spake, and praised God." Zacharias was not able to speak until he stopped doubting and proclaimed the praises of God.

134. In each of the following cases, God is anointing a prophet by putting the words of God into the mouth of a human being: Deuteronomy 18:18: "I will raise them up a Prophet from among their brethren, like unto thee, and will put my words in his mouth; and he shall speak unto them all that I shall command him." Numbers 22:38: "And Balaam said unto Balak, Lo, I am come unto thee: have I now any power at all to say any thing? *the word* that God *putteth in my mouth,* that shall I speak." Isaiah 51:16: "And I have *put* my *words in thy mouth,* and I have covered thee in the shadow of mine hand, that I may plant the heavens, and lay the foundations of the earth, and say unto Zion, Thou art my people." Isaiah 59:21: "As for me, this is my covenant with them, saith the LORD; My spirit that is upon thee, and my *words* which I *have put in thy mouth,* shall not depart out of thy mouth, nor out of the mouth of thy seed, nor out of the mouth of thy seed's seed, saith the LORD, from henceforth and for ever." Jeremiah 1:9: "Then the LORD put forth his hand, and touched my mouth. And the LORD said unto me, Behold, I have *put my words in thy mouth.*" Jeremiah 5:14: "Wherefore thus saith the LORD God of hosts, Because ye speak this word, behold, I will make *my words in thy mouth* fire, and this people wood, and it shall devour them."

135. Psalms 35:4: "Let them be *confounded and put to shame* that seek after my soul: let them be turned back and brought to confusion that devise my hurt."

brass. He hath put his testimony within me, and engraven his seal on my forhead.[136] And with these weapons I have indeed set the fiends of earth and hell at defiance. . . . What if I am a woman?[137]

In many of the biblical allusions here, Stewart invokes images of prophets and priests being prepared by God to do ministry. Even more strikingly, she quotes a conversation within the Triune Godhead to suggest that she is doing the work of the Holy Spirit by preparing the world for the rule of God. These are very significant claims but can best be understood when one takes Stewart's scriptural choices seriously.

Thus emboldened, thus sanctified, thus prepared, thus armed, Maria Stewart went out to perform her mission. It is a prophetic mission of personal vindication and national reproof; moreover, equipped as she is with holy armor, she is ready to do battle not only against human powers, but spirits, demons, and "fiends of earth and hell" as she calls them. She went out to address the injustices that African Americans experienced at the hands of their countrymen and women. Having cast this call as a holy mission from God and feeling thus equipped, Stewart sweeps away any qualms that her sex might disqualify her. "What if I am a woman?" she asks dismissively. She is, she suggests, the woman God has sent to do the job. Anyone who stood in her way stood against the purposes of God.

In an earlier address, Stewart had answered her own question. What if she were a woman? "Methinks I heard a spiritual interrogation—'Who shall go forward, and take off the reproach that is cast upon the people of color? Shall it be a woman?' And my heart made this reply—'If it is thy will, be it even so, Lord Jesus!'"[138] And what if she were a woman? She was the woman God had sent to do the job.

Sketches of the Fair Sex

Maria Stewart's husband, James, shared her admiration of the work of David Walker. James Stewart may have helped distribute Walker's *Appeal to the Coloured Citizens of the World* by sewing copies of it into the pockets of

136. Revelation 9:4: "And it was commanded them that they should not hurt the grass of the earth, neither any green thing, neither any tree; but only those men which have not *the seal of God in their foreheads*."
137. Stewart, "Productions of Maria Stewart," 74–75.
138. Ibid., 51.

used clothing he sold to sailors who arrived in the port of Boston.[139] Maria Stewart regarded Walker as a mentor and identified him as a martyr to the cause of African Americans' rights in her first public essay, "Religion and the Pure Principles of Morality."[140]

In his *Appeal*, David Walker called upon people of color to resist American chattel slavery, which he regarded as the most sinful in his supposedly Christian nation. In fact, Walker argued that slavery in the United States was also the most inhumane of all of the slave regimes of history. In his effort to show slavery as incompatible with either Christianity or civilization, Walker devoted much of his text to responding to Thomas Jefferson's *Notes on the State of Virginia*. In particular, Walker sought to refute Jefferson's racist supposition that "blacks, whether originally a distinct race, or made distinct by time and circumstances, are inferior to the whites in the endowments both of body and mind."[141]

Walker specifically chose to respond to Thomas Jefferson's comments about blacks not only because of the calumny of Jefferson's remarks but also because of Jefferson's fame and renown. Walker reminded his readers, "Do you know that Mr. Jefferson was one of as great characters as ever lived among the whites? See his writings for the world, and public labours for the United States of America. Do you believe that the assertions of such a man, will pass away into oblivion unobserved by this people and the world? If you do you are much mistaken.... I say that unless we try to refute Mr. Jefferson's arguments respecting us, we will only establish them."[142] Walker knew that the words of a man of Thomas Jefferson's stature, as a former president of the United States, author of the Declaration of Independence, and founder of the University of Virginia, would carry enormous weight. For a black man to logically and persuasively dispute

139. Marilyn Richardson repeats Charles M. Wiltse's thesis that James Stewart sewed Walker's text into the pockets of clothing he sold to southern-bound sailors in an effort to circulate the book. Richardson, *Maria W. Stewart*, 6–7. Charles Maurice Wiltse, introduction to *David Walker's Appeal, in Four Articles, Together with a Preamble, to the Coloured Citizens of the World, but in Particular, and Very Expressly, to Those of the United States of America*, by David Walker, edited by Wiltse (New York: Hill and Wang, 1965), viii–ix.

140. Stewart, "Productions of Maria Stewart," 5.

141. Jefferson, *Notes on the State of Virginia*, 143.

142. Walker, *Appeal to the Coloured Citizens*, 17–18.

such a man's words would go far, in Walker's estimation, to prove the rational abilities of blacks and thus disprove Jefferson's thesis of blacks' inherent inferiority.

Like her mentor David Walker, Maria Stewart chose a historical document to which she might address some of her thoughts. However, unlike Walker, Stewart chose an author with whom she, in the main, agreed. In her "Farewell Address to Her Friends in the City of Boston," Maria Stewart chose to respond to John Adams's *Sketches of the History, Genius, Disposition, Accomplishments, Employments, Customs and Importance of the Fair Sex, in All Parts of the World*,[143] the title of which Stewart mercifully reduced to *Sketches of the Fair Sex*.

David Walker disparaged Thomas Jefferson; Maria Stewart appreciated John Adams. However, the author of *Sketches of the Fair Sex* was not the second president of the United States but rather a Rev. John Adams (1750?–1814), who compiled children's books.[144] It is not clear whether Stewart understood that the John Adams who authored *Sketches of the Fair Sex* was not the John Adams who authored the Massachusetts state constitution or served as the second president of the United States. Nevertheless, there is a certain poetic parallelism to it: Walker had his Jefferson, and Stewart had her Adams.

John Adams's treatise attempted to argue in favor of women, the "fair sex," by selecting historical examples of their talents and naming the enlightened societies that permitted them free exercise of those talents. While modern historians might question the historical accuracy of some of his examples, Adams's intent suited Stewart well. She makes reference to Adams's examples of the heroic and sagacious exploits of women throughout time, arguing that, according to Adams, "Northern nations"

143. John Adams, *Sketches of the History, Genius, Disposition, Accomplishments, Employments, Customs, Virtues and Vices, of the Fair Sex, in All Parts of the World* (Boston: printed for Joseph Bumstead, 1807). The book was initially published in 1796 in Philadelphia. Marilyn Richardson agrees with this identification, which I had made independently of her work. Richardson, *Maria W. Stewart*, 24.

144. According to *The Dictionary of National Biography*, John Adams (1750?–1814) was a "compiler of books for young readers." However, unlike the Adamses (John and John Quincy) who formed the first political dynasty of US presidential politics, this John Adams was British. George Smith and Sidney Lee, *The Dictionary of National Biography* (Oxford: Oxford University Press, 1920), 6.

(that is, northern European nations) "imagined that women . . . had about them, an inconceivable something, approaching divinity."[145]

Stewart argues by way of *Sketches of the Fair Sex* that "a belief . . . that the Deity more readily communicates himself to women, has at one time or other, prevailed in every quarter of the earth," including Germany, Britain, Greece, Rome, and Egypt, and among the Jews.[146] Stewart goes on to argue that if such prophetic women once existed, it should not be surprising that they still exist. I believe that she speaks of herself (and perhaps others like her) when she writes, "If such women as are here described have once existed, be no longer astonished then, my brethren and friends, that God at this eventful period should raise up your own females to strive, by their example both in public and private, to assist those who are endeavoring to stop the strong current of prejudice that flows so profusely against us at present. No longer ridicule their efforts, it will be counted for sin."[147]

It is sin, Stewart declares, to oppose a woman who is speaking at the behest of God. In other words, get out of her way: Stewart is a woman on a mission. As she has used scripture to argue her right to speak, so Stewart also uses Adams's history for validation. Her overall argument remains constant: what if she is a woman? Her gender should pose no bar—political, theological, or even historical—to her public activism.

145. Stewart, "Productions of Maria Stewart," 76.

146. Ibid.

147. Genesis 15:6: "And he believed in the LORD; and *he counted it to him for righteousness.*" Psalm 106:31: "And that was *counted unto him for righteousness* unto all generations for evermore." Proverbs 27:14: "He that blesseth his friend with a loud voice, rising early in the morning, it shall be *counted a curse to him.*" Romans 4:3: "For what saith the scripture? Abraham believed God, and it was *counted unto him for righteousness.*" Stewart, "Productions of Maria Stewart," 76–77.

* CHAPTER 4 *

Maria Stewart's Attitudes
toward Race and Nation

*M*ANY HAVE NOTED African Americans' fondness for appropriations of the story of the Exodus. The biblical tale of God's deliverance of Israel from bondage in Egypt is one that has found expression in the spirituals, African American folklore, and innumerable sermons. Blacks identified not only with the role of Israel in the biblical narrative but also with the indictment of America as Israel's historic foe, the slaveholding nation of Egypt. This interpretation differed from that of white Americans, who saw their republic as the biblical ideal of Israel rather than as the slavocracy of Egypt. As Albert J. Raboteau has observed, "Exodus functioned as an archetypal event for the slaves."[1]

In his *Appeal,* David Walker wrote, "Though our cruel oppressors and murders, may (if possible) treat us more cruel, as Pharaoh did the Children of Israel, yet the God of the Ethiopians, has been pleased to hear our moans in consequence of oppression, and the day of our redemption from abject wretchedness draweth near, when we shall be enabled, in the most extended sense of the word, to stretch forth our hand to the Lord our

---

1. Raboteau, *Slave Religion,* 311; Raboteau, "African-Americans, Exodus and the American Israel," in *African-American Christianity: Essays in History,* ed. Paul E. Johnson (Berkeley: University of California Press, 1994), 1–17.

God."[2] The text is noteworthy for its references to the Exodus: to Pharaoh and the children of Israel but also to Ethiopia and even to the God of the Ethiopians. In this, Walker identifies the God of the Ethiopians and of the children of Israel to have been one and the same God. As Theophus Smith notes, "reciprocally with the invocation of the God of the Ethiopians, the writer intends to remake Afro-Americans in the image of Hebrew slaves crying out under Egyptian bondage."[3]

Such is the power of this narrative that its author has chosen for himself the power of naming; this basic right was routinely denied to slaves. Specifically, Walker chooses a heroic appellation for African Americans, identifying them spiritually and rhetorically with the mighty and salvific Ethiopia of Psalms 68:31.[4] But the text goes further. Not only does Walker name black people specifically (Ethiopian), but he also invokes God by a name that specifically links the divine to an African people: "the God of the Ethiopians." The words evoke both a redemptive identity for black people and a redemptive identification with the God of black people. They also combine allusions to the Exodus and to Ethiopians—people of African descent.

The Exodus Motif and the Ethiopian Prophecy

Following in her mentor's footsteps, Maria Stewart invokes both the Exodus and the Ethiopians in her indictment of the slavocracy. However, while Stewart does occasionally reference the story of the Exodus, she turns more frequently to the Ethiopians of Psalms 68:31 as descriptive of God's relationship with people of African descent.

"Ethiopianism," as it was called, was a religious version of the "romantic racialism" that gained currency during the nineteenth century.[5] Psalms 68:31

2. Walker, *Appeal to the Coloured Citizens*, 2.
3. T. Smith, *Conjuring Culture*, 59.
4. Psalms 68:31: "Princes shall come out of Egypt; Ethiopia shall soon stretch out her hands unto God."
5. "Romantic racialism," refers to the belief in a kind of simplistic, hierarchical, and romantic reification of racial characteristics that was pervasive in the United States of the nineteenth century. According to this paradigm, all of the races had specific characteristics: blacks were believed to be particularly sensitive and spiritual by nature. (Interestingly, women were credited with many of these same characteristics according to the Cult of True Womanhood; the description served as a rationale for racial and gender hierarchies based upon the qualities presumed to be inherent in the differ-

was the central text for the Ethiopianists, who argued a type of romantic racialism that insisted upon a special and inherent spiritual sensitivity for people of African descent. From this rationale flowed several back-to-Africa schemes (both evangelistic and political) as well as eschatologies predicting the eventual ascent of black people. The theory reached its greatest popularity in the late nineteenth century among African American reformers like Edward Wilmot Blyden, Martin Delaney, and Alexander Crummell. However, in its conflation of Ethiopia with all of Africa and its insistence upon viewing Africans as God's chosen people, particularly, the theory has resonances ranging from the words of Prince Hall in the late eighteenth century[6] to those of Marcus Garvey in the twentieth. From Ethiopianism flow streams that become both Pan-Africanism and Black Nationalism.

According to the Ethiopianist school of thought, African peoples possessed a special spirituality and receptivity to the preaching of the Gospel and conflated Ethiopia with all of Africa, invoking a noble African past and predicting a bright future for black people. "For antebellum black Christians," George Frederickson explains, "the Ethiopian prophecy had two clear meanings: that black people throughout the world would soon be converted to Christianity and that God would deliver New World Africans from slavery."[7]

In *The Talking Book*, Allen Callahan traces American and African American biblical appropriations of the Ethiopian prophecy from Cotton Mather's use of the text in his 1706 catechism through Marcus Garvey's pan-Africanism and into the art of Dizzy Gillespie and Romare Bearden and beyond. Callahan notes the text's use as a means of identifying African Americans with Africa for the purposes of doing missions, constructing Black Nationalist thought, and predicting African advancement. Although he does not mention Maria Stewart specifically in this regard, Callahan does examine her mentor,

---

ent races and sexes.) George M. Frederickson, *Black Liberation: A Comparative History of Black Ideologies in the United States and South Africa* (New York: Oxford University Press, 1995), 57–93.

6. In July of 1826, David Walker, Maria Stewart's mentor, joined the Prince Hall Masonic Lodge #459. Prince Hall had founded the black Masonic movement when white Masons prohibited blacks from joining their lodge. Hinks, introduction to Walker, *Appeal to the Coloured Citizens*, xxiii. Given this connection, it seems likely that Stewart also learned of Hall's teachings—on the Ethiopian prophecy, as well as on black self-sufficiency—from Walker.

7. Frederickson, *Black Liberation*, 63.

David Walker, and his use of the text of Psalms 68:31. In Walker's use, "the God of the Bible, the God of justice, is 'the God of the Ethiopians.'"[8]

A generation before Maria Stewart, Prince Hall, father of the black Masonic movement, used the verse in a speech given just outside of Boston, the city where Stewart made most of her public orations. Indeed, Stewart would later make one of her speeches in a Masonic hall. Prince Hall's use of Psalms 68:31 foreshadowed later Ethiopianist interpretations of scripture and history when he said, "Thus doth Ethiopia begin to stretch forth her hand, from a sink of slavery to freedom and equality."[9] In his rewriting of the verse, Ethiopia reaches out not to God but to freedom: in other words, to reach to God *is* to reach to freedom.

By the end of the nineteenth century, the text was in frequent use among various African American intellectuals. When Edward Wilmot Blyden, who, along with other influential and educated Victorian-era blacks like Martin Delaney and Alexander Crummell,[10] advocated the repatriation and evangelization of Africa by African Americans, he demonstrated typical Ethiopianist representations of Africa, and Africans, as beautiful and worthwhile: they are "courteous . . . confiding, unsuspicious, childlike, hospitable, honest, peaceable, and anxious to learn."[11]

However, although Stewart valorizes Africa, she has no desire to go there. Instead, she questions the motives of the American Colonization Society and all others who were trying to repatriate blacks to Africa rather than to incorporate them fully into the United States. She writes, "If the colonizationists are real friends to Africa, let them spend the money which

8. Callahan, *The Talking Book*, 143.

9. Prince Hall, "Pray God Give Us the Strength to Bear Up under All Our Troubles," in *Lift Every Voice: African American Oratory, 1787–1900*, ed. Philip S. Foner and Robert James Branham (Tuscaloosa: University of Alabama Press, 1998), 49.

10. W. E. B. Du Bois extols Crummell in a chapter of his groundbreaking classic text, *The Souls of Black Folk*.

11. Edward Wilmot Blyden, *Christianity, Islam and the Negro Race* (Chesapeake, VA: ECA Associates, 1990), 187. Interestingly, this romanticized view of racial difference derives as much from Victorian cultural norms like the Cult of True Womanhood as it does from the text of the Ethiopian prophecy, which, while suggesting that Ethiopians will stretch their hands to God, does not indicate that they will do so because they are innately more spiritual or sensitive. Many of the descriptors of blacks used here were often also used to describe women's gentler nature as depicted in popular literature of the time. In the hands of men, such rhetoric explained why women needed to be protected by men. In Blyden's hands, it is used to describe why African Americans had a responsibility to evangelize Africa's heathen hordes.

they collect, in erecting a college to educate her injured sons in this land of gospel light and liberty."[12]

Stewart protests that those who would send free blacks to Africa would "drive us to a strange land."[13] Like many African Americans of the period, Stewart had been born in America and had no recollection or direct knowledge of Africa. America was her home. Behind efforts to evict free blacks from the United States to Africa, she perceived that the Americans' motives were not altruistic but racist. Fearing that blacks could "never rise to respectability in this country," the whites instead strove to remove them from North America. So, even for this self-avowed "daughter of Africa," repatriation would only happen over her dead body. "But before I go," Stewart wrote, "the bayonet shall pierce me through."[14]

For Blyden, the Ethiopian prophecy was the starting point of a broader effort at rehabilitating the image of Africa and Africans. He goes on to ask: "Tell me, now, ye descendants of Africa, tell me whether there is anything in the ancient history of your African ancestors, in their relation to other races, of which you need to be ashamed. Tell me, if there is anything in the modern history of your people, in their dealings with foreign races, whether at home or in exile, of which you need to be ashamed?"[15] For Blyden and others, Africans and African Americans had nothing of which to be ashamed and much for which they could justifiably be proud. The Ethiopian prophecy was taken to indicate the place of Africa and Africans in the providential plans of God.

Maria Stewart makes frequent mention of the Ethiopian prophecy. She refers to it twice in her first speech, "Religion and the Pure Principles of Morality,"[16] once in the "Lecture Delivered at the Franklin Hall,"[17] again

12. Stewart, "Productions of Maria Stewart," 69.

13. Ibid., 72.

14. Ibid.

15. Blyden, *Christianity, Islam and the Negro Race*, 186.

16. Both allusions to Psalms 68:31 here occur in the context of prayer. Stewart writes, "Truly, my heart's desire and prayer is, that *Ethiopia might stretch forth her hands unto God*" and then, later, "Grant that every daughter of Africa may consecrate her sons to thee from birth. And do thou, Lord, bestow upon them wise and understanding hearts. Clothe us with humility of soul, and give us a becoming dignity of manners: may we imitate the character of the meek and lowly Jesus; and *do grant that Ethiopia may soon stretch forth her hands unto thee*." Stewart, "Productions of Maria Stewart," 5, 11.

17. "And were it not that the King eternal has declared that *Ethiopia shall stretch forth her hands unto God*, I should indeed despair." Stewart, "Productions of Maria Stewart," 54.

in "An Address Delivered before the Afric-American Female Intelligence Society of America,"[18] and finally, once in "An Address Delivered at the African Masonic Hall."[19]

Only Stewart's final, farewell address lacks any explicit mention of the Ethiopian prophecy.[20] However, that speech concludes with what must be regarded as a poetic version of the text of Psalms 68:31. The poem is called "The Negro's Complaint." Although Stewart is not believed to have been the author of the poem, it is significant because she chose to include it in her speech, where it functions as an explication of the Ethiopian prophecy that she has so often quoted:

> "The Negro's Complaint"[21]
> FORC'D from home and all its pleasures,
>   Afric's coast I left forlorn;
> To increase a stranger's treasures,
>   O'er the ranging billows borne.
> Men from England[22] bought and sold me,
>   Paid my price in paltry gold;
> But though slave they have enroll'd me,
>   Minds are never to be sold.

18. "But God has said, that *Ethiopia shall stretch forth her hands unto him.*" Stewart, "Productions of Maria Stewart," 60.

19. Stewart writes, "Sin and prodigality have caused the downfall of nations, kings and emperors; and were it not that God in wrath remembers mercy; we might indeed despair; but a promise is left us; *'Ethiopia shall again stretch forth her hands unto God.'*" Stewart, "Productions of Maria Stewart," 65.

20. Stewart's last address contains her most vehement defenses of women, including protracted allusions to John Adams's *Notes on the Fair Sex.* Stewart regarded this text as historical evidence of women's active participation in civil society from antiquity onward.

21. Marilyn Richardson writes that this poem "appeared, in part and without attribution, in the 19 March 1831 issue of *The Liberator,* p. 46, where it was suggested that it might in fact be a hymn." Richardson does not believe it likely that Stewart authored the poem, however. Richardson, *Maria W. Stewart,* 75.

22. Stewart inserted a note here in the poem: "England had 800,000 Slaves, and she has made them FREE! AMERICA has 2,250,000! And she HOLDS THEM FAST!!!" By this comment, she notes that England (which is charged in the poem with enslaving Africans) has ended slavery, while the United States has allowed its "peculiar institution" to continue and even to grow.

Still in thought as free as ever,
  What are England's rights,(I ask;)
Me from my delights to sever,
  Me to torture, me to task?
Fleecy locks and black complexion,
  Cannot forfeit Nature's claim;
Skins may differ, but affection
  Dwells in white and black the same.[23]

Why did all-creating Nature,
  Make the plant for which we toil?
Sighs must fan it, tears must water,
  Sweat of ours must dress the soil.
Think, ye masters iron-hearted,
  Lolling at your jovial boards:[24]
Think how many backs have smarted
  For the sweets your cane affords.[25]

Is there, as ye sometimes tell us,
  Is there ONE who reigns on high?
Has He bid you buy and sell us,
  Speaking from His throne, the sky?
Ask Him if your knotted scourges,
  Fetters, blood-extorting screws,
Are the means which duty urges,
  Agents of his will to use?

Hark! He answers—wild tornadoes,
  Strewing yonder sea with wrecks:

23. This part of the poem is interesting in that it suggests the text of Jeremiah 13:23: "Can the Ethiopian change his skin, or the leopard his spots?" Just as the Ethiopian prophecy (Psalms 68:31) specifically mentions Ethiopians, so does this verse from Jeremiah. Like the poem, it mentions the Ethiopian in the context of unchangeable skin color.

24. The poem indicts those who, benefiting from the work of others, may "loll" or relax at the table ("boards"), which groans under the weight of food purchased with the "sighs . . . tears" and "sweat" of the slave. Others benefit from, and even eat, the sugarcane (and other foods) that African slaves have produced.

25. This line is an obvious reference to trade in sugarcane, which was particularly profitable for the English during the period of its slave trade.

Wasting towns, plantations, meadows,
    Are the voice with which He speaks.
He, foreseeing what vexation
    Afric's sons would undergo,
Fix'd their tyrant's habitation
    Where has whirlwind answers—"No!"

By our blood in Afric wasted,
    Ere our necks receiv'd the chain;
By the miseries which we tasted,
    Crossing in your barks the main.[26]
By our sufferings, since ye brought us
    To the man-degrading mart;[27]
All sustained with patience, taught us
    Only by a broken heart.

Deem our nation brutes no longer,
    Till some reason ye shall find
Worthier to regard and stronger
    Than the color of our kind!
Slaves of gold! whose sordid dealings
    Tarnish all your boasted powers;
Prove that ye have human feelings,
    Ere ye proudly question ours!

One stanza of the poem suggests an expectation that God will not deal kindly with those who enslave others. The stanza asks if it is God's will that the slavocracy use such brutal methods (like "scourges, fetters [and] screws" that draw the victim's blood as they restrain him) as were in common usage. "Is there, as ye sometimes tell us, / Is there ONE who reigns on high? / Has He bid you buy and sell us, / Speaking from His throne, the sky? / Ask Him if your knotted scourges, / Fetters, blood-extorting screws, / Are the means which duty urges, / Agents of his will to use?" Does God approve of the slavocracy and its behavior toward the Africans in its midst? The poet answers this question resoundingly in the negative in the next stanza. It is the poet's belief that natural disasters like "wild

26. That is, crossing the ocean in your (slave) ships.
27. That is, to the slave markets, where humans were bought and sold like livestock.

tornadoes" are signs of God's displeasure over the slave trade, even as they are harbingers of an even more deadly coming judgment.

The poet points to the irrationality of judging people by the color of their skin rather than, for example, "the content of their character" (as Martin Luther King Jr. suggested) and advises the listening audience to find a "worthier" reason than "the color of our kind" by which to judge people of African descent. Then, in a line of reasoning similar to David Walker's rejection of Jefferson's *Notes on the State of Virginia*, the poem turns the tables on slaveholders, questioning their reason and humanity and calling *them* slaves: "slaves of gold" enslaved by their own desire for wealth. Since the "sordid dealings" of slavery "tarnish" the slavocracy's image, the author ends, "Prove that ye have human feelings / Ere ye proudly question ours!" Rather than question blacks' capacity for civilization, the poet suggests, the slavocracy should prove that *it* is capable of civilized behavior—by eliminating the scourge of slavery in its midst.

Ultimately, the Ethiopian prophecy identified Africans as people with a special relationship to God, and as such, a people of promise. The biblical text came to be used as a part of broader themes reaffirming Africa's place among the civilized world and Africans' place within humanity. The flip side of nineteenth-century African Americans' interpretation of the Ethiopian prophecy was an expectation that God's elevating Africans to their rightful place of honor would correspond to a reversal of European power. The expected "political, industrial and economic renaissance"[28] for African Americans believed to have been predicted by Psalms 68:31 would be accompanied by the decline of Europe. The "Rising Africa" theme (as the text was generally interpreted by African Americans of the nineteenth century) was only one side of Ethiopianism. "The balancing theme looks to the decline of the West," explains William J. Moses. "The rise in the fortunes of Africa and all her scattered children would be accompanied by God's judgment upon the Europeans."[29] Maria Stewart and David Walker clearly subscribed to both sides of the Ethiopian prophecy in its predictions of the rise of Africa and the fall of the West.

It should not be surprising that the change in Africa's fortunes should be expressed in mercantile terms like "economic" or "industrial." Much of

28. Wilson Jeremiah Moses, "The Poetics of Ethiopianism: W. E. B. Du Bois and Literary Black Nationalism," *American Literature* 47, no. 3 (1975): 412.

29. Ibid., 414.

the Ethiopianist censure of the West had to do with the wealth that the West was reaping at its slaves' expense. Surely, Stewart, Walker, and others mused, the judgment coming upon the West and the blessings coming to Africa would be expressed in the same sorts of material terms. That is, the West's economic and industrial success would be repaid to Africa as, in a complete reversal of the current injustice, the Africans and the African diaspora profited while Europe and the United States withered away.

Note the increasingly apocalyptic tone of Stewart's use of the Ethiopian prophecy. In her first speech, "Religion and the Pure Principles of Morality," she writes, "Truly, my heart's desire and prayer is, that Ethiopia might stretch forth her hands unto God,"[30] and then, later, "Grant that every daughter of Africa may consecrate her sons to thee from birth. And do thou, Lord, bestow upon them wise and understanding hearts. Clothe us with humility of soul, and give us a becoming dignity of manners: may we imitate the character of the meek and lowly Jesus; and do grant that Ethiopia may soon stretch forth her hands unto thee."[31]

The pleading tone of her first speech is quickly replaced by encouragement in her second: "And were it not that the King eternal has declared that Ethiopia shall stretch forth her hands unto God, I should indeed despair."[32] Stewart's belief in the coming ascendance of Africa and of her scattered children is then stated more emphatically in her third speech: "But God has said, that Ethiopia shall stretch forth her hands unto him."[33]

In her fourth of five speeches, "An Address Delivered at the African Masonic Hall," Stewart finally allows her audience to glimpse the flip side of the Ethiopian prophecy's theme of African ascendance when she hints at a coming collapse elsewhere. With a clearly growing confidence in her reading of the text, Stewart writes, "Sin and prodigality have caused the downfall of nations, kings and emperors; and were it not that God in wrath remembers mercy; we might indeed despair; but a promise is left us; 'Ethiopia shall again stretch forth her hands unto God.'"[34] She does not tell us

30. Stewart, "Productions of Maria Stewart," 5–6.

31. Ibid., 11.

32. Ibid., 54. Stewart's second speech is titled "Lecture Delivered at the Franklin Hall, Boston, September 21, 1832."

33. Ibid., 60. Stewart's third speech was "An Address Delivered Before the Afric-American Female Intelligence Society of Boston."

34. Ibid., 65.

which "nations, kings and emperors" she expects to receive God's wrath as a result of their "sin and prodigality"[35] as Africa and the African diaspora experience the mercy predicted in Psalms 68:31, but in the context of her universal disapprobation of the slave regime, there can be little doubt who she believes will be the recipient of God's wrath. Those who hold slaves, those who profit from slavery, and those who protect the slavocracy are all in danger of swiftly approaching punishment for those sins. Certainly, the United States was included in this sweeping indictment. As Stewart notes in a gloss on "The Negro's Complaint," which ends her final speech, "England had 800,000 Slaves, and she has made them FREE! AMERICA has 2,250,000! And she HOLDS THEM FAST!!!" While this comment suggests that it might be possible for England to escape the coming judgment, she makes it clear that unless America repents, it will not.

American Jeremiad

The jeremiad is perhaps the earliest genre of American literature. A prophetic denunciation of present conduct and forewarning of coming apocalypse, the American jeremiad was forged of bits of the Bible and other "sacred scriptures" of democratic myth, like the Declaration of Independence and the US Constitution. As a "national ritual not only of self-condemnation, but also an appeal to the most optimistic aspect of the American mythology of mission," the earliest jeremiads preached coming judgment for the congregation's breach of its sacred covenant with God—that errand in the wilderness that had first brought pilgrims to the shores of North

35. I am persuaded that Stewart uses the term "prodigality" to suggest the slavocracy's reckless extravagance. It is certainly also a reference to the parable of the prodigal son of Luke 15:13–32 and to the son's foolishness—his reckless extravagance—in squandering his inheritance. As such, the reference suggests the loss of a birthright. However, Stewart's use here may be multivalent. Just as in the parable of the prodigal son, forgiveness was available once he had returned to his father, so Stewart may mean to suggest the possibility of repentance for prodigal nations. Still, Stewart's choice of "prodigality" clearly suggests the United States. Proponents of American Exceptionalism believed that the United States was founded to be a nation with a special relationship with God—a birthright, if you will—to be the New Jerusalem. In attacking "prodigality," Stewart may intend to point her audience toward the United States not as a New Jerusalem but as a nation that had, like a prodigal son, wandered far from its birthright, squandering all as it went.

America—while ever holding out the hope that repentance would forestall destruction.[36]

In exploring the jeremiad as a genre, scholars have traced it from Puritan preachers' sermonic exhortations against declination (from the covenant between the Christian colonizers of the New World and their God) to its development as a kind of "theological rationale for the sufferings of a chosen people."[37] The jeremiad assumes that there is indeed a group of people chosen by God, whose responsibility it is to live up to this covenantal relationship lest there be dire consequences. It both offers up the chilling prospect of coming judgment for continued disobedience and balances this threat against the hopeful promise of reconciliation if God's people will only repent and return to the standards that their covenantal relationship requires of them. In the hands of Puritan preachers, the people of promise were those who had settled New England and had what they believed was a God-given charge to build a godly nation. Ultimately, however, the jeremiad also suggests the possibility of a catastrophic reversal: the people of the covenant would be reduced from children of promise to outcasts from the grace of God.

The jeremiad takes its name from the biblical prophet Jeremiah, who predicted the destruction of the temple of Jerusalem and the conquest of Judah by the Babylonians, which he saw as "punishments for departing from the Mosaic covenant."[38] Jeremiah, the "Weeping Prophet," also believed to have been responsible for the book of Lamentations, warned his Judean compatriots of the dangers of continued disobedience to God: the loss of the temple, and even the loss of the land of promise in a catastrophic exile.

The jeremiad was and is the ultimate expression of American civil religion. As David W. Blight notes, "The contours of America's civil religion were forged by the actions and rhetoric of the Founding Fathers during

36. David W. Blight, *Frederick Douglass' Civil War: Keeping Faith in Jubilee* (Baton Rouge: Louisiana State University Press, 1989), 105.

37. James H. Moorhead, *American Apocalypse: Yankee Protestants and the Civil War, 1860–1869* (New Haven, CT: Yale University Press, 1978), 44. See also Perry Miller, *The New England Mind: From Colony to Province* (Cambridge, MA: Harvard University Press, 1953).

38. Wilson Jeremiah Moses, *Black Messiahs and Uncle Toms: Social and Literary Manipulations of a Religious Myth* (University Park: Pennsylvania State University Press, 1982), 30.

the Revolutionary era. America's mission as a chosen people formed the core idea of a national faith; indeed, this concept of mission became the central unifying myth of nineteenth-century America. . . . In the Revolution, Americans experienced their 'exodus'; in the Declaration of Independence, they possessed their 'sacred scriptures'; in Washington they found a Moses, and in Jefferson, a high priest. But like the children of Israel, the Americans had to be tested."[39] In this context, jeremiads frequently combine the words of biblical scripture with those of civic religion and social contract, blurring the lines between American government and the souls of its people.

African Americans transformed the jeremiad, perhaps raising it to its greatest rhetorical heights during their two great struggles for that which democracy tantalizingly promised but society intransigently denied them. First in the years preceding the Civil War and then in the years of the civil rights movement, two men—Frederick Douglass and Martin Luther King Jr.—prophesied deliverance for African Americans and trouble for those who didn't work to swiftly dismantle the mechanisms of oppression holding blacks in check. Behind the visionary references to the watchwords of liberty and democratic process, the African American jeremiad was stained with blood drawn by the overseer's lash and lynching rope and shadowed by the threat of violence. Hopeful in its appeal to American conscience, the jeremiad in the hands of blacks nevertheless also played upon whites' long-held fears of chaos, of riot, of violent uprisings against them. The dark side of the jeremiad promised a righting of things, a righting both sudden and furious, and a great and terrible day of the Lord.

Martin Luther King Jr. gave what is perhaps the best-known example of a modern-day jeremiad in his "I Have a Dream" speech, which he delivered on August 28, 1963, from the steps of the Lincoln Memorial in Washington, DC. Although it is the habit of contemporary commentators to note only the hopeful climax of the speech, including King's vision of an America where his "four children will one day live in a nation where they will not be judged by the color of their skin but by the content of their character," the speech begins with warning rather than hope. In the less frequently repeated opening lines of the speech, King laments that the United States has failed to live up to the promises of its own founding documents. Even as he stood in the "symbolic shadow" of the Great

39. Blight, *Frederick Douglass' Civil War*, 104–5.

Emancipator, Abraham Lincoln, and in the figurative shadow of a century of frustration, King knew that the promise of emancipation had yet to be enjoyed by all African Americans. King declared:

> Fivescore years ago, a great American, in whose symbolic shadow we stand today, signed the Emancipation Proclamation. This momentous decree came as a great beacon light of hope to millions of Negro slaves who had been seared in the flames of withering injustice. It came as a joyous daybreak to end the long night of their captivity.
>
> But one hundred years later, the Negro still is not free; one hundred years later, the life of the Negro is still sadly crippled by the manacles of segregation and the chains of discrimination; one hundred years later, the Negro lives on a lonely island of poverty in the midst of a vast ocean of material prosperity; one hundred years later, the Negro is still languished in the corners of American society and finds himself an exile in his own land.
>
> So we've come here today to dramatize a shameful condition. In a sense we've come to our nation's capital to cash a check. When the architects of our republic wrote the magnificent words of the Constitution and the Declaration of Independence, they were signing a promissory note to which every American was to fall heir. This note was a promise that all men, yes, black men as well as white men, would be guaranteed the unalienable rights of life, liberty, and the pursuit of happiness.
>
> It is obvious today that America has defaulted on this promissory note in so far as her citizens of color are concerned. Instead of honoring this sacred obligation, America has given the Negro people a bad check; a check which has come back marked "insufficient funds."

As is typical of the jeremiad, the promise of redemption here is counterbalanced against the threat of judgment, of riot, and of destruction. Although King only hints at the possibility of violence, the hint is nonetheless present. What, for example, does he expect will happen if blacks "refuse to believe that the bank of justice is bankrupt"? King goes on, developing the idea of coming judgment:

> We refuse to believe that there are insufficient funds in the great vaults of opportunity of this nation. And so we've come to cash this check, a check that will give us upon demand the riches of freedom and the security of justice.

We have also come to this hallowed spot to remind America of the fierce urgency of now. This is no time to engage in the luxury of cooling off or to take the tranquilizing drug of gradualism. Now is the time to make real the promises of democracy; now is the time to rise from the dark and desolate valley of segregation to the sunlit path of racial justice; now is the time to lift our nation from the quicksands of racial injustice to the solid rock of brotherhood; now is the time to make justice a reality for all of God's children. It would be fatal for the nation to overlook the urgency of the moment. This sweltering summer of the Negro's legitimate discontent will not pass until there is an invigorating autumn of freedom and equality.

Nineteen sixty-three is not an end, but a beginning. And those who hope that the Negro needed to blow off steam and will now be content, will have a rude awakening if the nation returns to business as usual.

There will be neither rest nor tranquility in America until the Negro is granted his citizenship rights. The whirlwinds of revolt will continue to shake the foundations of our nation until the bright day of justice emerges.[40]

Again, although subtly, King hints at the danger the nation faces if it continues to deny blacks their basic rights. What is the "rude awakening" to which he alludes if not the possibility of increasing social unrest? "It would be fatal for the nation to overlook the urgency of the moment," he notes. "The whirlwinds of revolt will continue to shake the foundations of our nation until the bright day of justice emerges." Although in the next sentences he warns his listening audience not to engage in violence, he has nonetheless raised the specter of violence and judgment as a threat if justice continues to be delayed.

While the speech holds out the possibility of violence, it suggests that redemption is also possible if the nation lives up to the promise of its founding documents. King notes that the covenantal relationship typified by the promise that "all men . . . would be guaranteed the 'unalienable Rights' of 'Life, Liberty and the pursuit of Happiness'" has instead resulted in a "bad check, . . . which has come back marked 'insufficient funds.'" Here as elsewhere, the speech is rife with the terms of American civil religion, including references to the Declaration of Independence and, later, to the words of the patriotic hymn "My Country, 'Tis of Thee."

40. King, "I Have a Dream," 102–3.

Although King and Douglass are perhaps the best-known proponents of the genre of African American jeremiad, the folklore, songs, and writings of blacks in the United States are filled with similarly apocalyptic musings. Frequently, even Jesus is portrayed as an avenger.

As one scholar has noted, "Although Jesus was ubiquitous in the spirituals, it was not invariably the Jesus of the New Testament of whom the slaves sang, but frequently a Jesus transformed into an Old Testament warrior whose victories were temporal as well as spiritual: 'Mass Jesus' who engaged in personal combat with the Devil; 'King Jesus' seated on a milk-white horse with sword and shield in hand." Again and again, when the slaves sang about Jesus, he was not advocating that they turn the other cheek but was instead as angry as they were, and coming to bring judgment. Evident here is that the slaves exercised selectivity, preferring some parts of the Bible to others.[41]

However, this transformation of Jesus into warrior is also found in the New Testament. As Theophus Smith notes, "The sword-wielding Jesus riding a white horse is a terrifying figure portrayed in the most explicit terms in Revelation 19:11–13."[42] Such images of the once gentle Jesus, now filled with angry zeal similar to that with which he cleared the temple of its cheating moneychangers, populate African American folklore and song of the antebellum period.

While slaveholders were preaching the submission of slaves to their masters as the biblical ideal,[43] the slaves themselves were teasing a different standard of conduct from the text—one that envisioned an apocalyptic judgment visited by God upon the slavocracy. Their grandchildren and great-grandchildren would continue this prophetic tradition. This African American appropriation lifted up as its models figures like Gideon, who, outnumbered and scared, nevertheless routed the Midianites,[44] and

41. Levine, *Black Culture and Black Consciousness*, 43.

42. T. Smith, *Conjuring Culture*, 223.

43. See, for example, Ephesians 6:5–7: "Servants, be obedient to them that are your masters according to the flesh, with fear and trembling, in singleness of your heart, as unto Christ; Not with eyeservice, as menpleasers; but as the servants of Christ, doing the will of God from the heart." Such texts were frequently cited in the hopes that they would elicit obedience from those slaves who feared not only their master's but Christ's displeasure.

44. See Judges 6–8. Gideon's small, ragtag force frightened and then overwhelmed the Midianites after suffering under their cruelty for seven years.

Joshua, whose assault against the seemingly impregnable fortress of Jericho was low-tech, high-faith, simple, and successful.[45]

The appeal for oppressed people of such figures of biblical vengeance is clear. Since continued peace would only result in continued oppression, African Americans began to call "not to send peace, but a sword";[46] in their popular imagination, even Jesus was holding a blade.

Violence begets violence. It should therefore have come as no surprise to those who captured and held Africans in bondage by means of physical, emotional, and spiritual tyranny that the very slave system they had built would precipitate violent resistance on the part of the enslaved. In a significant move from proclaiming judgment to bringing it, some blacks not only pictured Jesus with a sword of vengeance but also took up the sword themselves. The fury of the uprisings plotted by the likes of Denmark Vesey or Nat Turner is not unprecedented, given the brutality that blacks suffered because of the "peculiar institution." Indeed, evidence exists to suggest that many slaveholders were understandably fearful of the possibility of slave insurrection. What may have been quite unanticipated by the slavocracy, however, was the extent to which slaves would find justification for revolt in the pages of the Bible, or in the person of the Lamb of God.

However, unlike Vesey, Turner, or even her mentor, David Walker, Maria Stewart called for a divine judgment rather than a human uprising. At one point, in anticipation of a violent reaction to the oppression they receive, Stewart writes to African Americans, "Then, my brethren, sheath your swords, and calm your angry passions. Stand still, and know that the Lord he is God.[47] Vengeance is his, and he will repay."[48] At another time, she writes, "Far be it from me to recommend to you, either to kill, burn or destroy. But I would strongly recommend to you, to improve your talents."[49]

45. See Joshua 6. The people circled the city performing rituals prescribed by God, and the city walls fell. Such stories as this and that of Gideon must have been endlessly encouraging to an African American minority locked in conflict with the heavily armed white majority.

46. Matthew 10:34.

47. Psalms 46:10: "*Be still, and know that I am God:* I will be exalted among the heathen, I will be exalted in the earth."

48. Romans 12:19: "Dearly beloved, avenge not yourselves, but rather give place unto wrath: for it is written, *Vengeance is mine; I will repay,* saith the Lord."

49. Stewart, "Productions of Maria Stewart," 4.

In this near allusion to John 10:10,[50] Stewart advocates a gentle revolution rather than a bloody one. If her recommendation here is read through John 10:10, then to "kill, burn or destroy" would be to act in opposition to Christ, who has come "that they might have life, and that they might have it more abundantly." She calls for African Americans to rise up to their true potential rather than to stage a violent uprising as Walker and others had done or desired.

Interestingly, while Stewart advises her audience not to "kill, burn or destroy," all common practices in slave revolts, she does not include an admonition against stealing, as it is present in John 10:10. As Frederick Douglass noted, for a slave to escape bondage was to steal from his master—even if it was his own body that he had stolen. Theft was quite common among slaves, who were always in want of food, clothing, and other necessities. In recognition of theft as a continuing problem, the slave Jupiter Hammon even advised his fellow slaves not to steal from their masters in his "Address to the Negroes in the State of New York" in 1786.[51] So by omitting "steal" from her list of prohibitions, Stewart carefully warns her audience against the violence of slave revolts but not necessarily against slave escapes.

African American jeremiads also operate on multiple levels, troping as they do both the common culture, history, and experience of Americans (as heteroglossia), even as they invoke the particular experiences of black people in ways hidden from other listeners (as glossolalia).[52] Maria Stewart demonstrates this gift for code shifting in her public speeches. Stewart's speeches point to divine approbation toward blacks as evidence of the coming judgment of whites. In her speeches, blacks, not whites, are the children of God's promise, as her frequent use of terms like "daughters of Africa" attests. Stewart uses the phrase "daughters of Africa" seven times in her first speech alone. She occasionally varies it as "daughters of my people" or "daughters of our land," which also serve as identifiers of African American women. In "daughters of Africa," Stewart echoes the biblical "daughters of Zion,"[53] "daughters of Israel,"[54] or "daughters of Judah,"[55] which are

50. John 10:10: "The thief cometh not, but for to steal, and to kill, and to destroy: I am come that they might have life, and that they might have it more abundantly."

51. Milton C. Sernett, Afro-American Religious History: A Documentary Witness (Durham, NC: Duke University Press, 1985), 35.

52. From Henderson's metaphor of "speaking in tongues."

53. Song of Solomon 3:11; Isaiah 3:16–17; Isaiah 4:4.

54. Deuteronomy 23:17; Judges 11:40; 2 Samuel 1:24.

55. Psalms 48:11; Psalms 97:8.

found in the Bible as identifiers of the women of the Mosaic covenant or Davidic covenants.

Stewart is prophesying a radical reversal: a comeuppance for the wealthy West and a vindication for suffering Africa, out of whose spilled blood Western wealth has flowed. Yet she must say it in ways that encode her meanings so that she is not killed because of such incendiary words. For example, she writes simply, "you ... fare sumptuously every day,"[56] quoting Luke 16:19–31, the parable of Lazarus and the rich man. The parable describes a rich man in hell and a poor man in heaven, but in the context of Stewart's usage, it predicts the ultimate Ethiopianist upending as the result of the slavocracy's failure to heed Jeremiah's many warnings: blacks will be blessed and whites will be punished—by God.

Did Stewart really mean to eschew physical violence as a means of destroying the slave regime? This is not at all clear. Her texts are full of violence promised, but it is the violence of God's coming judgment rather than of the eruptions of blacks' righteous anger. Whether this was a rhetorical strategy Stewart employed so that she might avoid what she believed to have been David Walker's fate (martyrdom) or because she really did not advocate violence is not clear. However, although her rhetorical purpose is unclear, the wisdom of her rhetorical method is unmistakable. Stewart, unlike Walker, lived to speak and write another day.

Stewart's words, and those of every Jeremiah before or since, operate on many levels. On one level, they call white America, generally, and its slaveholding and segregationist strains, particularly, to repentance. This call, made in the commonly held language of the Declaration of Independence and the like, resounds in ways that all can understand—like heteroglossia. On another level, they call African Americans to arms and to action in ways that may or may not be comprehensible to others—like glossolalia—because they undermine the foundations of hegemony and assert a new paradigm where black life is the interpretive key. They flip the established order upside down, calling that which is accepted in society unacceptable before God.

Reading the Handwriting on the Wall

In the convoluted conundrum that became the "peculiar institution" in the United States, human beings became chattel to sell or breed. While

56. Stewart, "Productions of Maria Stewart," 20.

it was illegal to teach one's slave to read in many jurisdictions, an owner could rape that same slave with impunity. Underpinning the lucrative commerce in human bodies and forced labor was a contorted ideological and theological system of signs and meaning that understood peoples of African descent to have been cursed to be a perpetual servant class, destined by God to be "hewers of wood and drawers of water"[57]—servants to others—only, forever. As slaveholders interpreted the Bible, Africans were eternally cursed to be servants, but when Africans interpreted it, they saw for themselves a noble past and a destiny of divine favor and blessing. Among African American exegetes, two strategies emerged to undermine the ideological foundations of slavery and racial prejudice and as essential first steps toward their liberation: their hermeneutics write whites out of positions of privilege within the biblical text, or they write blacks into positions of privilege within the text.

Central to the system of signs and meaning used to justify the oppression of African Americans was an understanding of physical blackness to be the result of the so-called curse of Ham[58] or the mark of Cain.[59] Indeed, it is the theological equation of blackness with cursing by the slavocracy that many black writers and orators most forcefully refute in their work. So powerful and pervasive was the prevailing religious understanding of the rightness of slavery in the minds of many slaveholders that Frederick Douglass remarked: "Were I to be again reduced to the chains of slavery, next to that enslavement, I should regard being the slave of a religious master the greatest calamity that could befall me. For of all slaveholders with whom I have ever met, religious slaveholders are the worst. I have

57. Joshua 9:23.

58. Genesis 9:18–27. For a further discussion of the use of this and other scriptures to suggest that physical blackness was a mark of God's disfavor, and of African American exegetes' responses to such interpretation, see, for example, Felder, *Troubling Biblical Waters*; Felder, *Stony the Road We Trod*, 127–45; Charles B. Copher, "The Black Presence in the Old Testament," in Felder, *Stony the Road We Trod*, 146–64; and Katie Geneva Cannon, "Slave Ideology and Biblical Interpretation," in *The Recovery of Black Presence: An Interdisciplinary Exploration*, ed. Randall C. Bailey and Jacquelyn Grant (Nashville: Abingdon, 1995), 119–28. See also Stacy Davis, "Nineteenth Century Exegesis of the Curse of Canaan in the U.S. South," in *This Strange Story: Jewish and Christian Interpretation of the Curse of Canaan from Antiquity to 1865* (Lanham, MD: University Press of America, 2008), 129–45; and Sylvester A. Johnson, *The Myth of Ham in Nineteenth-Century American Christianity: Race, Heathens, and the People of God* (New York: Palgrave Macmillan, 2004).

59. Genesis 4:8, 11, 15.

ever found them the meanest and basest, the most cruel and cowardly, of all others."[60]

The implications of Douglass's observations are clear: religious slaveholders, believing their mastery over others to be the exercise of a divine right, were more cruel than the nonreligious in their domination of their slaves. Later, in an appendix to his autobiography, Douglass differentiated between true Christianity and the religion of the slaveholders, likening the latter to the "ancient scribes and Pharisees"[61] whom Jesus derided for their hypocrisy.

In a typical jeremiad, Douglass predicts God's judgment upon the sort of religion that could justify the evils of slavery, even as he points out its hypocrisy in the light of its own rhetoric (especially American rhetoric of democratic equality). This approach might be understood as an attempt to write the slavocracy out of its position of privilege with regard to the biblical text.

Maria Stewart demonstrates a similar metaphorical magic in her public speeches. In an early example of African American jeremiad, Stewart tropes on the rhetoric of the American Revolution and the book of Revelation. By bringing these two contexts into relief, she suggests that despite its high-minded talk of "equal rights," America is less like a free nation and more like Babylon, a wicked city about to be judged by God:[62]

> Did every gentleman in America realize, as one, that they had got to become bondmen, and their wives, their sons, and their daughters servants forever, to Great Britain . . . their hearts would die within them, and death would be far more preferable. Then why have not Afric's sons a right to feel the same? Are not their wives, their sons, and their daughters, as dear to them as those of the white man's? Certainly, God has not deprived them of the divine influences of his Holy Spirit, which is the greatest of all blessings, if they ask him. Then why should man any longer deprive his fellow-man of equal rights and privileges? Oh, America, America,

60. Frederick Douglass, "Slaveholding Religion and the Christianity of Christ," in *African American Religious History: A Documentary Witness*, 2nd ed., ed. Milton C. Sernett (Durham, NC: Duke University Press, 1999), 103.

61. Ibid., 107.

62. Possibly, Stewart is alluding to Revelation 17 and 18, with its descriptions of Babylon's sins: merciless mercantilism and oppression of God's faithful ones. Here her criticism of the United States as Babylon must also be an indictment of the riches the United States has extorted from the work of enslaved Africans.

foul and indelible is thy stain! Dark and dismal is the cloud that hangs over thee, for thy cruel wrongs and injuries to the fallen sons of Africa. The blood of her murdered ones cries to heaven for vengeance against thee. Thou art almost become drunken with the blood of her slain; thou hast enriched thyself through her toils and labors; and now thou refuseth to make even a small return. . . . Our souls are fired with the same love of liberty and independence with which your souls are fired.[63]

The text notes divine approbation toward blacks as evidence of the coming judgment of whites. If America denies blacks the very "liberty and independence" it demanded from the British, how can it be a free nation? If God gives black people the gift of the Holy Spirit, "the greatest of all blessings," how can judgment be avoided by whites who do not even give blacks the fair wages of their labors? Stewart invokes judgment as the only fitting punishment for the oppressors her words and worldview have indicted. Moreover, she has employed the high worship words of democracy, "liberty and independence" in contradistinction to the lowest biblical image of sin and judgment, Babylon, to make her case for a reconstructed social order where "many of the sable-skinned Africans you now despise, will shine in the kingdom of heaven as the stars forever and ever."[64] To Maria Stewart's way of thinking, the United States is not the Israel of God's deliverance, as some New Englanders preached, but rather the Egypt of Israel's enslavement. The United States is not the shining city on hill of Puritan rhetoric; instead, it is Babylon, city of sin whose judgment is sure.

As a hermeneutic scheme, Ethiopianism writes blacks into positions of privilege, envisioning for them a bright future and a special relationship with God. The African American jeremiad, on the other hand, represents a strategy of writing whites out of positions of privilege with regard to biblical hermeneutics, and even with regard to the founding documents and images of American democratic myth. Maria Stewart did both in her speeches. Again and again she cast America not as an Israel but as Babylon. The sins of the United States were legion in her view, but chief among them were not only Americans' failure to notice that they were not the chosen ones but their compounding that error by persecuting and even enslaving those African children of promise in their midst.

63. Stewart, "Productions of Maria Stewart," 18–19.
64. Ibid., 19.

Conclusion

*J*OYCELYN MOODY wrestles with the angst she first experienced when a couple of young white men in her classes on nineteenth-century black women's autobiography simply didn't "get it" and as she later considered the incidents when they continued to haunt her.[1] The incidents highlight the linguistic and experiential divide that can separate black women's texts from nonblack and/or nonfemale audiences. As Moody describes the mission of her classes, her intention to traverse the divide was an appropriate, forward-thinking, liberationist project: teaching ethnic texts in a multiethnic classroom as a means of decoding and demystifying the experiences of ethnic others.

That nineteenth-century manuscripts would need to be decoded and that such efforts would occasionally fail are important points that emphasize the chasm that separates the linguistic and symbolic worlds of blacks and whites, of men and women. That the subversive task of the past was to *encode* language (as when an illiterate former slave woman like Sojourner Truth slips zingers past her white, female amanuensis) and the subversive task of the present is to *decode* language (as when Moody then explains those same zingers to her predominantly white, female students) is also evidence of how much times have changed.

---

1. Joycelyn Moody, "'By Any Other Name': Theoretical Issues in the Teaching of Nineteenth-Century Black Women's Autobiography," in *Bridging the Gap: Literary Theory in the Classroom*, ed. J. M. Q. Davies, Locust Hill Literary Studies, no. 17 (West Cornwall, CT: Locust Hill, 1994), 129–43.

Yet the worldview and rhetoric of nineteenth-century African American writers represents a linguistic and semiotic world conjured out of black people's experiences—especially their experiences of oppression. The stories are hewn out of words that must at times pour forth over others' ears in a sound like tongues: by turns glossolalic and heteroglossic, the words at once strange and yet strangely familiar. Encoded in the biblical hermeneutics they produced, the words of these black mystics may sometimes require decoding for others to truly understand them. Yet clear understanding is crucial.

Maria Stewart used the Bible in ways that were subtle (as when she argued, with increasing urgency, for her rights as a woman speaker) and not so subtle (as when she preached a coming judgment upon the United States for its sins). It is important to note the ways in which she forged and reinforced her own personal philosophy and ideology of race and gender from those sacred texts, even as she alternatively disappeared into them or draped them around her like a protective cloak. Maria Stewart's use of the Bible is part of a long and continuing evangelical tradition. In any one of a number of evangelical churches today, one will hear similar uses of prooftexts that draw upon scripture across the lines of specific books or even whole testaments of the Bible to reinforce the user's authority in the minds of a Bible-believing congregation.

Finding Stewart in Her Bible

And what does Stewart's use of the Bible teach us about her? It tells us that her objection to violence was thoroughgoing and stood in opposition to the teachings of her mentor, David Walker. She frequently changed words or phrases from Bible verses she was quoting to deemphasize the violence in them. It tells us that Stewart also came, gradually, to differ with Walker on the role of women in public life. After a while, Stewart became convinced that women had a place in public; the carefully delineated gender roles she advocates in her first speech have disappeared by her last. Although Stewart's use of the Bible tells us that, like Walker, she expected God to judge the slavocracy, Stewart also blamed black people for the delay in this judgment. While Walker placed most of the blame on the slavocracy for the deplorable state of Africans in America, Stewart felt that blacks were also somewhat responsible because of their failure to resist oppression and their failure to recognize their true stature and covenantal relationship with God.

Stewart's use of the Bible also tells us that she was making arguments for female empowerment that were very similar to those of later evangelical women. She likened her spiritual vocation to the call stories of biblical prophets and leaders, sprinkling her speech with texts intended to bolster her authority before biblically literate audiences.

Stewart's biblical appropriations also lay bare her theology. She was expecting God to judge the slavocracy for its sins against God and black people. (For Stewart, to sin against black people was to sin against God.) This coming apocalypse of judgment was hindered by black people themselves: their ignorance and disunity stayed God's hand. Stewart's call to African Americans was to get ready so that judgment could come to those who oppressed them.

I am not suggesting here that listeners to Stewart's speeches caught all of her many allusions to scripture. I do believe, however, that many did recognize the familiar cadences and poetic phrases of the King James Version of the Bible. Just as in black churches today preachers move toward the "celebration"—or more emotive ending of the sermon—by quoting other familiar sermons, hymns, or religious ideas—so Stewart sought acceptance for her message in its many familiar phrases and themes. Because the phrases and ideas are familiar and deeply connected to other contexts of worship, they tend to elicit immediate and emotive responses from the listening congregation.

A black Christian pastor may begin, "He is the King of Kings. He is the Lily of the Valley. He is the bright and morning star." His listeners may not be able to place those scripture references, but they will surely identify the texts the pastor is quoting with messianic prophecy and, thus, with Jesus. With each further phrase, the pastor is able to build upon the congregation's previous experiences of those phrases and so build the sermon to an ecstatic and emotive climax. Stewart may have similarly moved her audiences by using phrases and ideas richly steeped in scripture. Those who heard and recognized her allusions would then be able to bring to their engagement with her words some of the emotional power of their previous encounters with those same biblical texts. Further, as music or culture commented on those texts (as the Negro spiritual "No Hidin' Place" commented on Revelation 6:16), that would add layers of meaning to Stewart's words.

I believe that Stewart's use of the Hebrew Bible tends to underscore her conception of African Americans as people of a special covenant with God. They are not Gentiles grafted into the people of God (as some Christians of the biblical period were described by the Apostle Paul),[2] but rather they are people of a more ancient claim to God's favor. From the Ethiopian prophecy (Psalms 68:31), Stewart (and many other African Americans) chose to argue an African ascendancy or ancient origin in the heart of God.

Moreover, Stewart argues, it is a new day for women as well. Perhaps her initial reasoning (that she had to act because the men wouldn't) is a bit threadbare. Nevertheless, Stewart comes increasingly into a sense of herself as called by God and thus empowered by God. Although she occasionally fell into the snare that the Cult of True Womanhood had set for nineteenth-century women—as in her teachings that blamed women for the failings of the entire society—she nonetheless demonstrates real movement in her understanding of the role of women (as independent and autonomous beings) in the wider society.

Finally, Stewart sought to speak a new reality into being—in effect to prophesy deliverance for her people—using that most powerful of shared texts, the Bible. In it she saw the possibility of covenantal relationship with God for a people as yet denied even the full rights of citizenship or full acknowledgment of their humanity. From it she spoke of full equality—if not in this life, then before the "awful bar of God"[3] on Judgment Day. And as is the way of prophets, she had to speak of the vision before others could apprehend it.

As Stewart did, so others do. Yet these practices have been little studied because they violate so many tenets of historical-critical biblical exegesis. In studying the biblical appropriations of women like Maria Stewart, we unlock a continuing folk tradition that thrives far from the halls of academia, in thousands and thousands of evangelical churches, Bible studies, and prayer meetings. In identifying the theological work Stewart was doing, and by calling her a "preacher" despite her lack of clerical claims or credentials, we open the door to recognizing the wider range of theological

2. Romans 11.

3. Of Thomas Jefferson's death, David Walker notes that "he is gone to answer at the bar of God, for the deeds done in his body while living." Walker, *Appeal to the Coloured Citizens*, 16.

thought and discussion that shapes churches and faith communities, even though it is untouched and unexamined by the academy.

Further, in studying Maria Stewart, we remember a fierce and tenacious woman whose words still vibrate with truth and power today. She was doing something different from black men like David Walker (although she followed in his tradition); she was also doing something different from the majority of white women of her age. (Indeed, she was quite unique among African American women of her day.) Her work therefore deserves the attention that such uniqueness merits.

From Stewart to Obama?

Maria Stewart predicted an age of African ascension: that the "daughters of Africa" would one day rise to take their rightful places of leadership. In these days, which have seen the election of the first African American president of the United States, Barack Hussein Obama, we have perhaps lost some sense of the miraculousness of Stewart's words. None in history had ever risen from a people held in race-based chattel slavery to lead a multiethnic nation in which they were not the majority. Yet Stewart was saying that such a day would come. In the context of the fulfillment of some of Stewart's prophetic vision, it is utterly appropriate that we should return to her prescient words and read them afresh today.

Barack Obama also represents a return to an art that Stewart pioneered: the use of the Bible in the construction of progressive political thought. Barack Obama's speeches have been filled with biblical references and liberal theology.[4] For a long time in American political discourse, the Bible was the exclusive refuge of the religious right. Obama has made it safe for Democrats to go back into the Bible, so to speak. In fact, at least some part of Obama's electoral victory should be credited to his facility with the

4. John B. Judis, "Obama, Niebuhr, and U.S. Politics," *New Republic*, December 13, 2009, http://www.tnr.com/blog/the-plank/obama-niebuhr-and-us-politics; Mark Tooley, "Niebuhr and Obama," *The American Spectator*, January 20, 2009, http://spectator.org/archives/2009/01/20/niebuhr-and-obama; David Gibson, "Of Niebuhr and Nobels: Divining Obama's Theology," *Politics Daily*, December 12, 2009, http://www.politicsdaily.com/2009/12/12/of-niebuhr-and-nobels-divining-obamas-theology/.

5. John W. Kennedy, "Preach and Reach," *Christianity Today*, October 6, 2008, http://www.christianitytoday.com/ct/2008/october/18.26.html; Jonathan Weisman, "Obama to Deliver Values Speech at St. Louis Church Conference," *Wash-

Bible, his comfort with evangelical culture, and his ability to invoke the culture and spirit of black churches while on the stump for votes.[5] I believe that Stewart would have been pleased.

What If?

African American biblical scholar Brian Blount reminds us that hermeneutics has a cultural component.[6] The way a text is understood can disenfranchise, or it can empower. M. M. Bakhtin points out that even written communication has a social component in its interpretation that is not entirely under the control of the writer or speaker but also resident in the social locations and experiences of the readers or hearers.[7]

What I am suggesting is that there is are distinctly African American biblical hermeneutics: it is the possibility posited by Vincent Wimbush early on in this project. Wimbush asks, "What might happen if . . . African American experience . . . were the starting and focal point for reading, for interpretation? What if the reading of and thinking about the Bible . . . were problematized and [the Bible] read through and in connection with African American experience?"[8]

ington Post, July 5, 2008, http://voices.washingtonpost.com/44/2008/07/obama-to-deliver-values-speech.html. Photos of Obama standing behind the pulpit of Ebenezer powerfully linked the politician with the legacy of Martin Luther King Jr. and the broader struggle for civil rights in the United States. Zimbio, January 20, 2008, http://www.zimbio.com/pictures/XCFw9vzySta/Barack+Obama+Speaks +Ebenezer+Baptist+Church; "The Ebenezer Sermon," *Atlantic*, January 20, 2008, http://andrewsullivan.theatlantic.com/the_daily_dish/2008/01/the-ebenezer-se.html; Lynn Sweet, "Obama at Ebenezer Baptist in Atlanta. Clinton at Abyssinian Baptist in Harlem. Pictures," *Chicago Sun-Times*, January 20, 2008, http://blogs.suntimes.com/sweet/2008/01/sweet_obama_at_ebenerzer_bapti.html. Long before he was a candidate for public office, Barack Obama had described his salvation experience in his autobiography in terms any evangelical would recognize. Obama wrote, "But kneeling beneath that cross on the South Side of Chicago, I felt God's spirit beckoning me. I submitted myself to His will and dedicated myself to discovering His truth." Barack Obama, *The Audacity of Hope: Thoughts on Reclaiming the American Dream* (New York: Three Rivers, 2006), 208.

6. Blount, *Cultural Interpretation*.

7. Bakhtin, *The Dialogic Imagination*.

8. Wimbush, "Reading Darkness, Reading Scriptures," 9–10.

Indeed, I asked. What if? What if there is another layer of meaning to be deciphered that resides in the life experiences of speaker and of hearer? What if we reject the myth of scientific objectivity that has so long defended historical-critical biblical scholarship from just charges that it is not value-neutral but rather serves to reinscribe the values and sensibilities of the majority culture? What if we let those cultural critics, historians, and literary and biblical scholars free to examine African American hermeneutics within its own context and without reference to the majority culture as standard, as so many of them are itching to do? What if—rather than excluding those at the margins—we accept them as legitimate arbiters of meaning, and as legitimate loci of context, subtext, and interpretation?

If the African American experience is the starting and focal point for Bible reading and interpretation in many African American communities and for many African Americans, then much work remains to be done in examining the interpretations thus produced. Like a Möbius strip that moves eternally upon the axes of reader, hearer, speaker, and meaning-maker or performer, script, stage, and audience, never revealing its beginning or end, so African American biblical hermeneutics can elaborate on the Bible even as it illuminates the African American experience. Each continually influences the other.

Were Maria Stewart here today, she would probably ask where are the generations who have taken up the gauntlet she had thrown down. She would most certainly ask us what use had we made of her words, her warnings, and her admonitions and how we had heeded them, given the lengths to which she went to preserve them for us. Where are the Maria Stewarts of this day—those who are crafting and explaining, teaching and interpreting, out of their own experiences and those of their people? They are waiting out there, waiting to be discovered and explored. And we are waiting, waiting to hear words we do not yet know we need to hear. And we are waiting to hear words spoken in others' tongues—in languages we do not yet understand—but nevertheless long to hear.

Bibliography

Abbington, James. "Biblical Themes in the R. Nathaniel Dett Collection: Religious Folk-Songs of the Negro." In *African Americans and the Bible: Sacred Texts and Social Textures*, edited by Vincent L. Wimbush and Rosamond C. Rodman, 281–96. New York: Continuum, 2000.

Adams, John. *Sketches of the History, Genius, Disposition, Accomplishments, Employments, Customs, Virtues and Vices, of the Fair Sex, in All Parts of the World.* Boston: printed for Joseph Bumstead, 1807.

Andrews, William L., ed. *Classic African American Women's Narratives.* Oxford: Oxford University Press, 2003.

———. Introduction. *Sisters of the Spirit: Three Black Women's Autobiographies of the Nineteenth Century*, ed. William L. Andrews, 1–22. Religion in North America. Bloomington: Indiana University Press, 1986.

Angier, Natalie. "Do Races Differ? Not Really, Genes Show." *New York Times*, August 22 2000.

———. "Race No More Than Skin Deep, DNA Indicates." *Cleveland Plain Dealer*, August 22 2000.

Bakhtin, M. M. *The Dialogic Imagination: Four Essays by M. M. Bakhtin.* Translated by Caryl Emerson and Michael Holquist. Edited by Michael Holquist. Austin: University of Texas Press, 1981.

Balmer, Randall Herbert. *Mine Eyes Have Seen the Glory: A Journey into the Evangelical Subculture in America.* New York: Oxford University Press, 1993.

Bebbington, D. W. *Evangelicalism in Modern Britain: A History from the 1730s to the 1980s.* London: Unwin Hyman, 1989.

Blight, David W. *Frederick Douglass' Civil War: Keeping Faith in Jubilee.* Baton Rouge: Louisiana State University Press, 1989.

Blount, Brian K. *Can I Get a Witness? Reading Revelation through African American Culture.* 1st ed. Louisville, KY: Westminster John Knox, 2005.

———. *Cultural Interpretation: Reorienting New Testament Criticism.* Minneapolis: Fortress, 1995.

———. *Go Preach! Mark's Kingdom Message and the Black Church Today.* The Bible and Liberation. Maryknoll, NY: Orbis Books, 1998.

————. *Then the Whisper Put on Flesh: New Testament Ethics in an African American Context*. Nashville: Abingdon, 2001.

Blount, Brian K., et al., eds. *True to Our Native Land: An African American New Testament Commentary*. Minneapolis: Fortress, 2007.

Blyden, Edward Wilmot. *Christianity, Islam and the Negro Race*. Baltimore: Black Classic Press, 1994.

Boyer, Horace Clarence. "African American Gospel Music." In *African Americans and the Bible: Sacred Texts and Social Textures*, edited by Vincent L. Wimbush and Rosamond C. Rodman, 464–88. New York: Continuum, 2000.

Brekus, Catherine A. *Strangers and Pilgrims: Female Preaching in America, 1740–1845*. Chapel Hill: University of North Carolina Press, 1998.

Broughton, Virginia W. "Twenty Year's Experience of a Missionary." In *Spiritual Narratives*, 1–140. New York: Oxford, 1988.

Brown, Elsa Barkley. "'What Has Happened Here': The Politics of Difference in Women's History and Feminist Politics." In *"We Specialize in the Wholly Impossible": A Reader in Black Women's History*, edited by Darlene Clark Hine, Wilma King, and Linda Reed, 39–56. Brooklyn, NY: Carlson, 1995.

Burnim, Mellonee. "Biblical Inspiration, Cultural Affirmation: The African American Gift of Song." In *African Americans and the Bible: Sacred Texts and Social Textures*, edited by Vincent L. Wimbush, and Rosamond C. Rodman, 603–15. New York: Continuum, 2000.

Byron, Gay L. "Ancient Ethiopia and the New Testament: Ethnic (Con)Texts and Racialized (Sub)Texts." In *They Were All Together in One Place? Toward Minority Biblical Criticism*, edited by Randall C. Bailey, Tat-siong Benny Liew, and Fernando F. Segovia, 161–92. Atlanta: Society of Biblical Literature, 2009.

Callahan, Allen Dwight. *The Talking Book: African Americans and the Bible*. New Haven, CT: Yale University Press, 2006.

Cannon, Katie Geneva. "Slave Ideology and Biblical Interpretation." In *The Recovery of Black Presence: An Interdisciplinary Exploration*, edited by Randall C. Bailey and Jacquelyn Grant, 119–28. Nashville: Abingdon, 1995.

Cheney, Charise. "Representin' God: Masculinity and the Use of the Bible in Rap Music." In *African Americans and the Bible: Sacred Texts and Social Textures*, edited by Vincent L. Wimbush and Rosamond C. Rodman, 804–16. New York: Continuum, 2000.

Cone, James H. *The Spirituals and the Blues: An Interpretation*. Maryknoll, NY: Orbis Books, 1991.

Connor, Kimberly Rae. *Conversions and Visions in the Writings of African-American Women*. Knoxville: University of Tennessee Press, 1994.

Copher, Charles B. "The Black Presence in the Old Testament." In *Stony the Road We Trod: African American Biblical Interpretation*, edited by Cain Hope Felder, 146–64. Minneapolis: Fortress Press, 1991.

Cott, Nancy F. *The Bonds of Womanhood: "Woman's Sphere" in New England, 1780–1835*. New Haven, CT: Yale University Press, 1977.

————. "'Female Laborers in the Church': Women Preachers in the Northeastern United States, 1790–1840." In *History of Women in the United States: Historical Articles on Women's Lives and Activities*, edited by Nancy F. Cott, 166–91. Munich: K. G. Saur, 1993.

————. "Young Women in the Second Great Awakening in New England." In *History of Women in the United States: Historical Articles on Women's Lives and Activities*, edited by Nancy F. Cott, 20–34. Munich: K. G. Saur, 1993.

Davies, J. M. Q. *Bridging the Gap: Literary Theory in the Classroom*. Locust Hill Literary Studies, no. 17. West Cornwall, CT: Locust Hill, 1994.

Davis, Stacy. *This Strange Story: Jewish and Christian Interpretation of the Curse of Canaan from Antiquity to 1865*. Lanham, MD: University Press of America, 2008.

"A Dialogue between Christ, a Youth, and the Devil." In *The New England Primer*, 1777 ed., http://www.sacred-texts.com/chr/nep/1777/index.htm.

De Groot, Christiana, and Marion Ann Taylor, eds. *Recovering Nineteenth-Century Women Interpreters of the Bible*. Atlanta: Society of Biblical Literature, 2007.

Douglass, Frederick. *Narrative of the Life of Frederick Douglass, an American Slave*. Edited by David W. Blight. Bedford Books in American History. Boston: Bedford Books of St. Martin's Press, 1993.

————. "Slaveholding Religion and the Christianity of Christ." In *African American Religious History: A Documentary Witness*, 2nd ed., edited by Milton C. Sernett, 102–11. Durham, NC: Duke University Press, 1999.

Du Bois, W. E. B. *The Souls of Black Folk*. 1st Vintage Books/Library of America ed. New York: Vintage Books/Library of America, 1986.

Elrod, Eileen Razzaria, ed. *Piety and Dissent: Race, Gender, and Biblical Rhetoric in Early American Autobiography*. Amherst: University of Massachusetts Press, 2008.

Equiano, Olaudah. "The Interesting Narrative of the Life of Olaudah Equiano, or Gustavus Vassa, the African, Written by Himself." In *The Norton Anthology of African American Literature*, edited by Henry Louis Gates and Nellie Y. McKay, 138–64. New York: W. W. Norton, 1997.

Evans, James H. *We Have Been Believers: An African-American Systematic Theology*. Minneapolis: Fortress, 1992.

Exum, J. Cheryl. "Murder They Wrote: Ideology and the Manipulation of Female Presence in Biblical Narrative." *USQR* 43 (1989): 19–39.

Felder, Cain Hope. "Race, Racism, and the Biblical Narratives." In *Stony the Road We Trod: African American Biblical Interpretation*, edited by Cain Hope Felder, 127–45. Minneapolis: Fortress, 1991.

————, ed. *Stony the Road We Trod: African American Biblical Interpretation*. Minneapolis: Fortress Press, 1991.

————. *Troubling Biblical Waters: Race, Class, and Family*. Bishop Henry McNeal Turner Studies in North American Black Religion, vol. 3. Maryknoll, NY: Orbis Books, 1991.

Fineman, Howard. "Bush and God." *Newsweek*, March 10, 2003, 22–30.

Foote, Julia A. J. "A Brand Plucked from the Fire: An Autobiographical Sketch by Mrs. Julia A. J. Foote." In *Spiritual Narratives*, 1–124. New York: Oxford, 1988.

Foster, Frances Smith. *Witnessing Slavery: The Development of Ante-Bellum Slave Narratives*. Contributions in Afro-American and African Studies. Westport, CT: Greenwood, 1979.

Frederickson, George M. *Black Liberation: A Comparative History of Black Ideologies in the United States and South Africa*. New York: Oxford University Press, 1995.

Fulkerson, Mary McClintock. "Joyful Speaking for God: Pentecostal Women's Performances." In *Changing the Subject: Women's Discourses and Feminist Theology*, 239–98. Minneapolis: Fortress, 1994.

Gadamer, Hans-Georg. *Truth and Method*. Translated by Joel Weinsheimer and Donald G. Marshall. New York: Continuum, 1996.

Gates, Henry Louis. "The Trope of the Talking Book." In *The Signifying Monkey: A Theory of Afro-American Literary Criticism*, 127–69. New York: Oxford University Press, 1988.

Gates, Henry Louis, and Nellie Y. McKay. "Preface: Talking Books." In *The Norton Anthology of African American Literature*, edited by Henry Louis Gates and Nellie Y. McKay, xxvii–xli. New York: W. W. Norton, 1997.

Gibson, David. "Of Niebuhr and Nobels: Divining Obama's Theology." *Politics Daily*, December 12, 2009, http://www.politicsdaily.com/2009/12/12/of-niebuhr-and-nobels-divining-obamas-theology/.

Giddings, Paula. *When and Where I Enter: The Impact of Black Women on Race and Sex in America*. 1st ed. New York: W. Morrow, 1984.

Gilbert, Olive, and Sojourner Truth. *Narrative of Sojourner Truth, a Bondswoman of Olden Time: With a History of Her Labors and Correspondence Drawn from Her "Book of Life."* Schomburg Library of Nineteenth-Century Black Women Writers. New York: Oxford University Press, 1991.

Gilkes, Cheryl Townsend. "'Go and Tell Mary and Martha': The Spirituals, Biblical Options for Women, and Cultural Tensions in the African American Religious Experience." *Social Compass* 43, no. 4 (1996): 536–81.

———. *If It Wasn't for the Women—: Black Women's Experience and Womanist Culture in Church and Community*. Maryknoll, NY: Orbis Books, 2001.

Griffin, Farah J. "Adventures of a Black Child in Search of Her God: The Bible in the Works of Me'shell N'degeocello." In *African Americans and the Bible: Sacred Texts and Social Textures*, edited by Vincent L. Wimbush and Rosamond C. Rodman, 773–81. New York: Continuum, 2000.

Guy-Sheftall, Beverly, ed. *Words of Fire: An Anthology of African-American Feminist Thought*. New York: New Press, 1995. Distributed by W. W. Norton.

Haley, Alex. *Roots*. 1st ed. Garden City, NY: Doubleday, 1976.

Hall, Prince. "Pray God Give Us the Strength to Bear Up under All Our Troubles." In *Lift Every Voice: African American Oratory, 1787–1900*, ed. Philip S. Foner and Robert James Branham, 45–51. Tuscaloosa: University of Alabama Press, 1998.

Harlan, Louis R. "Booker T. Washington and the Politics of Accommodation." In *Black Leaders of the Twentieth Century*, edited by John Hope Franklin and August Meier, 1–18. Urbana: University of Illinois Press, 1982.

Hatch, Nathan O., and Mark A. Noll. Introduction to *The Bible in America: Essays in Cultural History*, edited by Nathan O. Hatch and Mark A. Noll. New York: Oxford University Press, 1982.

Haywood, Chanta M. *Prophesying Daughters: Black Women Preachers and the Word, 1823–1913*. Columbia: University of Missouri Press, 2003.

Hedin, Raymond. "Strategies of Form in the American Slave Narrative." In *The Art of Slave Narrative: Original Essays in Criticism and Theory*, edited by John Sekora and Darwin T. Turner. Macomb: Western Illinois University, 1982.

Henderson, Mae G. "Speaking in Tongues: Dialogics, Dialectics, and the Black Woman Writer's Literary Tradition." In *Changing Our Own Words: Essays on Criticism, Theory, and Writing by Black Women*, edited by Cheryl A. Wall, 16–37. New Brunswick, NJ: Rutgers University Press, 1989.

Heyrman, Christine Leigh. *Southern Cross: The Beginnings of the Bible Belt*. 1st ed. New York: A. A. Knopf, 1997. Distributed by Random House.

Higginbotham, Evelyn Brooks. "African-American Women's History and the Metalanguage of Race." In *"We Specialize in the Wholly Impossible": A Reader in Black Women's History*, edited by Darlene Clark Hine, Wilma King, and Linda Reed, 3–24. Brooklyn, NY: Carlson, 1995.

———. *Righteous Discontent: The Women's Movement in the Black Baptist Church, 1880–1920*. Cambridge, MA: Harvard University Press, 1993.

Hine, Darlene Clark. "Rape and the Inner Lives of Black Women in the Middle West: Preliminary Thoughts on the Culture of Dissemblance." In *Unequal Sisters: A Multicultural Reader in US Women's History*, edited by Ellen Carol DuBois and Vicki Ruiz, 292–97. New York: Routledge, 1990.

Hinks, Peter P. Introduction to *David Walker's Appeal to the Coloured Citizens of the World*, by David Walker, edited by Peter P. Hinks. University Park: Pennsylvania State University Press, 2000.

———. *To Awaken My Afflicted Brethren: David Walker and the Problem of Antebellum Slave Resistance*. University Park: Pennsylvania State University Press, 1997.

Horton, James Oliver. *Free People of Color: Inside the African American Community*. Washington, DC: Smithsonian Institution Press, 1993.

Houchins, Sue E. Introduction to *Spiritual Narratives*. Schomburg Library of Nineteenth-Century Black Women Writers. New York: Oxford University Press, 1988.

Irons, Charles. *The Origins of Proslavery Christianity: White and Black Evangelicals in Colonial and Antebellum Virginia*. Chapel Hill: University of North Carolina Press, 2008.

Israel, Adrienne M. *Amanda Berry Smith: From Washerwoman to Evangelist*. Studies in Evangelicalism, no. 16. Lanham, MD: Scarecrow, 1998.

Jacobs, Harriet A. *Incidents in the Life of a Slave Girl.* Schomburg Library of Nineteenth-Century Black Women Writers. New York: Oxford University Press, 1988.

Jefferson, Thomas. "Declaration of Independence." http://www.archives.gov/exhibit_hall/charters_of_freedom/declaration/declaration_transcription.html.

———. *Notes on the State of Virginia.* Edited by William Harwood Peden. Chapel Hill: University of North Carolina Press, 1955.

Johnson, Sylvester A. *The Myth of Ham in Nineteenth-Century American Christianity: Race, Heathens, and the People of God.* New York: Palgrave Macmillan, 2004.

Jones, Lewis E. "There Is Power in the Blood." In *African American Heritage Hymnal: 575 Hymns, Spirituals and Gospel Songs,* ed. Rev. Dr. Delores Carpenter and Rev. Nolan E. Williams Jr., 258. Chicago: GIA Publications, 2001.

Judis, John B. "Obama, Niebuhr, and U.S. Politics." *New Republic,* December 13, 2009, http://www.tnr.com/blog/the-plank/obama-niebuhr-and-us-politics.

Juster, Susan. *Disorderly Women: Sexual Politics and Evangelicalism in Revolutionary New England.* Ithaca, NY: Cornell University Press, 1994.

Keckley, Elizabeth. *Behind the Scenes.* New York: G. W. Carleton, 1868.

Kennedy, John W. "Preach and Reach." *Christianity Today,* October 6, 2008, http://www.christianitytoday.com/ct/2008/october/18.26.html.

King, Martin Luther, Jr. "I Have a Dream." In *I Have a Dream: Writings and Speeches that Changed the World,* edited by James Melvin Washington, 101–6. San Francisco: HarperSanFrancisco, 1992.

Kirk-Duggan, Cheryl. "Hot Buttered Soulful Tunes and Cold Icy Passionate Truths: The Hermeneutics of Biblical Interpolation in R & B (Rhythm & Blues)." In *African Americans and the Bible: Sacred Texts and Social Textures,* edited by Vincent L. Wimbush and Rosamond C. Rodman, 782–803. New York: Continuum, 2000.

Lash, Nicholas. *Theology on the Way to Emmaus.* London: SCM Press, 1986.

Ledgard, J. M. "We Are All African Now." *Intelligent Life,* Summer 2009, 66–71.

Lee, Jarena. "The Life and Religious Experience of Jarena Lee." In *Sisters of the Spirit: Three Black Women's Autobiographies of the Nineteenth Century,* ed. William L. Andrews, 25–38. Bloomington: Indiana University Press, 1986.

———. "Religious Experience and Journal of Mrs. Jarena Lee, Giving an Account of Her Call to Preach the Gospel." In *Spiritual Narratives,* 1–97. New York: Oxford University Press, 1988.

Lee, Rev. Luther. "Woman's Right to Preach the Gospel." In *Holiness Tracts Defending the Ministry of Women,* edited by Donald W. Dayton, 1–22. New York: Garland, 1985.

Levine, Lawrence W. *Black Culture and Black Consciousness.* New York: Oxford University Press, 1977.

Marable, Manning, and Leith Mullings, eds. *Let Nobody Turn Us Around: Voices of Resistance, Reform, and Renewal: An African American Anthology.* Lanham, MD: Rowman and Littlefield, 2000.

Martin, Clarice J. "The *Haustafeln* (Household Codes) in African American Biblical Interpretation: 'Free Slaves' and 'Subordinate Women.'" In *Stony the Road We Trod: African American Biblical Interpretation*, edited by Cain Hope Felder, 206–31. Minneapolis: Fortress, 1991.

McCarthy, Timothy Patrick, and John Campbell McMillian, eds. *The Radical Reader: A Documentary History of the American Radical Tradition*. New York: New Press, 2003.

McKay, Nellie. "Nineteenth-Century Black Women's Spiritual Autobiographies: Religious Faith and Self-Empowerment." In *Interpreting Women's Lives: Feminist Theory and Personal Narratives*, edited by Joy Webster Barbre and Personal Narratives Group, 139–54. Bloomington: Indiana University Press, 1989.

Miller, Keith D. "City Called Freedom: Biblical Metaphor in Spirituals, Gospel Lyrics, and the Civil Rights Movement." In *African Americans and the Bible: Sacred Texts and Social Textures*, edited by Vincent L. Wimbush and Rosamond C. Rodman, 546–57. New York: Continuum, 2000.

Miller, Perry. *The New England Mind: From Colony to Province*. Cambridge, MA: Harvard University Press, 1953.

Moody, Joycelyn. "'By Any Other Name': Theoretical Issues in the Teaching of Nineteenth-Century Black Women's Autobiography." In *Bridging the Gap: Literary Theory in the Classroom*, ed. J. M. Q. Davies, Locust Hill Literary Studies, no. 17 (West Cornwall, CT: Locust Hill, 1994), 129–43.

———. *Sentimental Confessions: Spiritual Narratives of Nineteenth-Century African American Women*. Athens: University of Georgia Press, 2001.

Moorhead, James H. *American Apocalypse: Yankee Protestants and the Civil War, 1860–1869*. New Haven, CT: Yale University Press, 1978.

Moses, Wilson Jeremiah. *Black Messiahs and Uncle Toms: Social and Literary Manipulations of a Religious Myth*. University Park: Pennsylvania State University Press, 1982.

———. "The Poetics of Ethiopianism: W. E. B. Du Bois and Literary Black Nationalism." *American Literature* 47, no. 3 (1975): 411–26.

Myers, William H. "The Hermeneutical Dilemma of the African American Biblical Student." In *Stony the Road We Trod: African American Biblical Interpretation*, edited by Cain Hope Felder, 40–56. Minneapolis: Fortress, 1991.

Nero, Charles I. "'Oh, What I Must Tell This World!' Oratory and Public Address of African-American Women." In *Black Women in America*, edited by Kim Marie Vaz, 261–75. Thousand Oaks, CA: Sage, 1994.

Newman, Richard, Patrick Rael, and Phillip Lapsansky, eds. *Pamphlets of Protest: An Anthology of Early African-American Protest Literature, 1790–1860*. New York: Routledge, 2001.

"No Hidin' Place." In *Songs of Zion*, edited by J. Jefferson Cleveland and Verolga Nix, 141. Nashville: Abingdon, 1981.

Noll, Mark A. *The Civil War as a Theological Crisis*. Chapel Hill: University of North Carolina Press, 2006.

———. *The Rise of Evangelicalism: The Age of Edwards, Whitefield, and the Wesleys.* A History of Evangelicalism, vol. 1. Downers Grove, IL: InterVarsity, 2003.

Obama, Barack. *The Audacity of Hope: Thoughts on Reclaiming the American Dream.* New York: Three Rivers, 2006.

Painter, Nell Irvin. Paper presented at the Du Bois Institute of the African American Studies Department, Harvard University, October 16, 1996.

———. *Sojourner Truth: A Life, a Symbol.* 1st ed. New York: Norton, 1996.

Phillips, Ulrich Bonnell. *American Negro Slavery: A Survey of the Supply, Employment and Control of Negro Labor as Determined by the Plantation Regime.* 1st paperback ed. Baton Rouge: Louisiana State University Press, 1966.

Quarles, Benjamin. *Black Abolitionists.* New York: Oxford University Press, 1969.

Raboteau, Albert J. "African-Americans, Exodus and the American Israel." In *African-American Christianity: Essays in History,* edited by Paul E. Johnson, 1–17. Berkeley: University of California Press, 1994.

———. *Slave Religion: The "Invisible Institution" in the Antebellum South.* New York: Oxford University Press, 1978.

Rael, Patrick. *Black Identity and Black Protest in the Antebellum North.* John Hope Franklin Series in African American History and Culture. Chapel Hill: University of North Carolina Press, 2002.

Richardson, Marilyn, ed. *Maria W. Stewart, America's First Black Woman Political Writer: Essays and Speeches.* Blacks in the Diaspora. Bloomington: Indiana University Press, 1987.

Ricoeur, Paul, and Mark I. Wallace. *Figuring the Sacred: Religion, Narrative, and Imagination.* Minneapolis: Fortress, 1995.

Romero, Lora. *Home Fronts: Domesticity and Its Critics in the Antebellum United States.* New Americanists. Durham, NC: Duke University Press, 1997.

Rudwick, Elliott. "W. E. B. Du Bois: Protagonist of the Afro-American Protest." In *Black Leaders of the Twentieth Century,* edited by John Hope Franklin and August Meier, Blacks in the New World, 63–83. Urbana: University of Illinois Press, 1982.

Saillant, John. "Origins of African American Biblical Hermeneutics in Eighteenth-Century Black Opposition to the Slave Trade and Slavery." In *African Americans and the Bible: Sacred Texts and Social Textures,* edited by Vincent L. Wimbush and Rosamond C. Rodman, 236–50. New York: Continuum, 2000.

Schüssler Fiorenza, Elisabeth. *Bread Not Stone: The Challenge of Feminist Biblical Interpretation.* 10th anniversary ed. Boston: Beacon, 1995.

———. "Transforming the Legacy of the Woman's Bible." In *Searching the Scriptures,* vol. 1, *A Feminist Introduction,* 1–24. New York: Crossroad, 1993–94.

Segovia, Fernando F. "'And They Began to Speak in Other Tongues': Competing Modes of Discourse in Contemporary Biblical Criticism." In *Reading from This Place,* edited by Fernando F. Segovia and Mary Ann Tolbert, 1–32. Minneapolis: Fortress, 1995.

Sernett, Milton C. *Afro-American Religious History: A Documentary Witness.* Durham, NC: Duke University Press, 1985.

Shiels, Richard D. "The Feminization of American Congregationalism, 1730–1835." In *History of Women in the United States: Historical Articles on Women's Lives and Activities*, edited by Nancy F. Cott, 3–19. Munich: K. G. Saur, 1993.

Simpson, Rennie. "The Afro-American Female: The Historical Construction of Sexual Identity." In *Powers of Desire: The Politics of Sexuality*, edited by Ann Barr Snitow, Christine Stansell, and Sharon Thompson, New Feminist Library, 229–35. New York: Monthly Review Press, 1983.

Smith, Abraham. "Toni Morrison's *Song of Solomon*: The Blues and the Bible." In *The Recovery of Black Presence: An Interdisciplinary Exploration: Essays in Honor of Dr. Charles B. Copher*, edited by Randall C. Bailey and Jacquelyn Grant, 107–15. Nashville: Abingdon, 1995.

Smith, George, and Sidney Lee. *The Dictionary of National Biography*. Oxford: Oxford University Press, 1920.

Smith, Theophus H. *Conjuring Culture: Biblical Formations of Black America*. Religion in America. New York and Oxford: Oxford University Press, 1994.

Spiritual Narratives. Schomburg Library of Nineteenth-Century Black Women Writers. New York: Oxford University Press, 1988.

Stewart, Maria W. "Productions of Mrs. Maria W. Stewart, Presented to the First African Baptist Church and Society in the City of Boston." In *Spiritual Narratives*, 1–84. New York: Oxford University Press, 1988.

Thurman, Howard. *Jesus and the Disinherited*. Richmond, IN: Friends United, 1981.

Tooley, Mark. "Niebuhr and Obama." *American Spectator*, January 20, 2009, http://spectator.org/archives/2009/01/20/niebuhr-and-obama.

Walker, David. *David Walker's Appeal to the Coloured Citizens of the World*. Edited by Peter P. Hinks. University Park: Pennsylvania State University Press, 2000.

Weems, Renita J. "Reading Her Way through the Struggle: African American Women and the Bible." In *Stony the Road We Trod: African American Biblical Interpretation*, edited by Cain Hope Felder, 55–77. Minneapolis: Fortress, 1991.

Weisenfeld, Judith, and Richard Newman, eds. *This Far by Faith: Readings in African-American Women's Religious Biography*. New York: Routledge, 1996.

Weisman, Jonathan. "Obama to Deliver Values Speech at St. Louis Church Conference." *Washington Post*, July 5, 2008, http://voices.washingtonpost.com/44/2008/07/obama-to-deliver-values-speech.html.

Welter, Barbara. "The Cult of True Womanhood: 1820–1860." In *Dimity Convictions: The American Woman in the Nineteenth Century*, 21–41. Athens: Ohio University Press, 1976.

———. "The Feminization of American Religion: 1800–1860." In *Dimity Convictions: The American Woman in the Nineteenth Century*, 83–102. Athens: Ohio University Press, 1976.

"Were You There?" In *Songs of Zion*, edited by J. Jefferson Cleveland and Verolga Nix, 126. Nashville: Abingdon, 1981.

West, Cornel. *Prophesy Deliverance! An Afro-American Revolutionary Christianity*. 1st ed. Philadelphia: Westminster, 1982.

Williams, Demetrius K. *An End to This Strife: The Politics of Gender in African American Churches*. Minneapolis: Fortress, 2004.

Wiltse, Charles Maurice. Introduction to *David Walker's Appeal, in Four Articles, Together with a Preamble, to the Coloured Citizens of the World, but in Particular, and Very Expressly, to Those of the United States of America*, by David Walker, edited by Charles Maurice Wiltse. New York: Hill and Wang, 1965.

Wimbush, Vincent L. "Reading Darkness, Reading Scriptures." Paper presented at the African Americans and the Bible Conference, Union Theological Seminary, New York City, April 8, 1999.

———. *Theorizing Scriptures: New Critical Orientations to a Cultural Phenomenon*. Signifying (on) Scriptures. New Brunswick, NJ: Rutgers University Press, 2008.

Wimbush, Vincent L., and Rosamond C. Rodman. *African Americans and the Bible: Sacred Texts and Social Textures*. New York: Continuum, 2000.

Index

Subject Index

"Address to the Negroes in the State of New York" (Hammon), 170

Africa. *See* colonization movement; Ethiopianism; Ethiopian prophecy

African American hermeneutics: and authorial intent as divine intent, 29, 32; and Bible as tool of liberation, 21–22, 29–32; and centrality of Bible to African Americans, 36–38, 38n88, 107n52; decoding of, 176; distinctiveness of, 180–81; harmonization strategy in, 31–32, 32n73, 103–5, 110; intellect of, 45, 45nn16–17, 87, 92; and interpersonal interpretation, 35–36; and metaphor of tongues, 26–27; mirror metaphor for, 31, 36; scholars on, 6–7n12, 7–8, 24, 35–36, 59n72; of Stewart, 19–22, 26, 37, 39–42, 42n1, 91–110, 129–30, 176–79. *See also specific theologians and scholars by name*

African Americans: agency of, 64n99; alleged inferiority of, 45n16, 80n173, 86–87, 86–87n211, 92, 95, 150; and Bible, 32, 36–38, 38n88, 91–94, 107n52, 168, 177; businesses of, 77, 77nn163–64; churches of, 32, 53n47, 63n94, 126, 135, 136, 177; and colonization movement, 156–57; compared with Israelites, 49n34, 56, 56–57n58, 59n73; as created in image of God, 45, 45nn15–18, 95; disposition of, 77; double-consciousness of, 24–26, 24n53; as "dust of the earth," 54, 54n49; economic empowerment for, 77, 77nn163–64; education and literacy of, 55n52, 70, 70n128, 72, 72nn138–39, 76, 76n160, 87n212, 88, 88n216, 92, 93n6, 139–40, 157; exploitation of, by whites, 67, 67nn115–16, 75n154, 76–84, 76n161, 77n162, 79n170, 101–2, 140–41, 176; God's covenant with, 40, 44n9, 49n34, 54n49, 63n93,

74, 74nn150–51, 140, 170, 174, 178; ignorance of, 42, 42n2, 48, 48n27, 54, 56, 56n56, 68, 73, 73n142, 76, 76n161, 87, 87n213; and jeremiad, 165–71, 174; lack of inheritance rights for, 121; and Masonic movement, 155n6, 156; need for love and unity among, 76, 76n161, 177; as "People of the Promise," 19; perseverance by, 68, 68n117, 78, 78n168, 88; qualifications of leadership of, 58–59, 58nn68–69; responsibility of, for their plight, 61n82, 64n99, 139, 176–77, 177; sins of, 68, 68n120, 69n121, 73; and spirit of independence, 78, 78n165, 84; spirituals of, 36, 37, 81n179, 153, 168, 177; and "talented tenth," 55n52; talents of, 44, 44n12, 49–54, 67–68, 77, 139, 169; uplift for and reformation of, 40, 65n103, 72–79, 72n140, 73n142, 75nn154–55, 87–88, 87n214, 139–40, 177; useful knowledge for, 55, 55n52, 72; wisdom for, 65, 65n101, 73, 73n144; wretched conditions of, 56, 56n58, 61n82, 75, 75n154, 87, 87n214, 176–77. *See also* African American women; civil rights movement; race and racism; slavery and slavocracy; slaves

African American women: and abolitionism, 130–32; as Baptists, 65n103; and Cult of True Womanhood, 111, 115–19, 130; and culture of dissemblance, 130, 130n55; decoding of autobiographies by, 175–76; and "dialectic of identity," 25; and "dialogic of differences," 25; domestic labor of, 76–77, 76n161, 77n162, 115–17; employment of, 138–39; preaching by, 9–12, 113–14, 118n25, 119, 126, 128, 132–38; in public sphere generally, 131; and respectability, 65n103; and school building, 139–40; sexual exploitation of, 76–77, 77n162, 81,

81nn177−78, 117−18, 172; and spirit
of independence, 78, 78n166; stereo-
types of and prejudice against, 118,
119, 138−39; and tongues metaphor,
24−27; writings by, in nineteenth
century, 9, 121, 136, 175−76. *See also*
gender *and specific women by name*
African Methodist Episcopal (AME)
Church, 53n47, 126, 135
African Methodist Episcopal (AME)
Zion Church, 136
Allen, Richard, 135
AME Church, 53n47, 126, 135
American Colonization Society, 156
American people: acknowledgment
of other nations by, 82; admirable
qualities of, 67, 67n110, 67nn112−14,
75n154, 75n156, 76n157, 78−79,
78n165; and American Exceptionalism, 163n35; and American Revolution, 79, 79n172, 107, 164−65, 173,
174; compared with slaveholding
Egypt, 83, 83n188, 87n211, 153, 174;
demise of United States, 85−86,
86n205; exploitation of African
Americans by, 67, 67nn115−16,
75n154, 76−84, 76n161, 77n162,
79n170, 101−2, 140−41, 176; and
fear of slave revolts, 82−83n184, 169;
God's judgment against, 160−61,
163−64, 168, 171, 173−74, 177; as
hypocrites, 89−90, 89−90n225,
90n226; identification of, with Israel,
153, 174; prodigality of, 163, 163n35;
racial unity of, 67n114, 76n157;
sexual exploitation of African American women by white men, 76−77,
77n162, 81, 81nn177−78, 117−18,
172; and spirit of independence,
78, 78n165; Stewart's accusations
against, 80−87, 80−81n176, 81n177,
81−82n180, 82n183, 99−103, 108,
109−10, 173−74, 173n62; Stewart's
withholding of blame against, 68n120;

virtues of white women, 75−76,
75n156. *See also* slavery and slavocracy
American Revolution, 79, 79n172, 107,
164−65, 173, 174
AME Zion Church, 136
Antichrist, 81n176
apocalypse, 70n132, 70−71n133, 101, 168.
See also jeremiad; Judgment Day
*Appeal to the Coloured Citizens of the
World* (Walker). See David Walker's
*Appeal to the Coloured Citizens of the
World* (Walker)
"Ar'n't I a Woman?" (Truth), 123, 126

Bakhtin, M. M., 24, 26, 96−97, 180
Balaam, 148n134
Balak, 148n134
Balmer, Randall, 13n28
Baptist churches, 65n103, 112n2
Bearden, Romare, 155
Bebbington, D. W., 13n28
Bible: centrality of, to African Americans, 32, 36−38, 38n88, 107n52,
168, 177; as complex cultural and
historical force, 20−22; evangelical
approach to, 13−14, 13n28, 41, 59n72,
103−8, 110, 178−79; feminist and
womanist interpretations of, 20−21,
30; Gates on, as "white text," 24;
and harmonization strategy, 31−32,
32n73, 103−5, 110; higher biblical
criticism, 103; historical-critical
method on, 28−29, 31−32, 34, 35,
181; interpersonal interpretation
of, 35−36; Obama's use of, 179−80,
179−80n5; and Pentecostal women's
testimonies, 14−18; richness in
Stewart's use of, 99−103; as Rosetta
stone, 37−38; as script, 14−20,
18n42; on speaking in tongues,
24−27, 96; and spirit of independence, 106−10; Stewart's use of,
4−7, 14, 16−20, 26, 37, 39−42, 42n1,
91−110, 129−30, 176−79; and "trope

Bible (*continued*)
of the talking book," 93n6; versions of, 100n28, 107n52; webs of meaning in Stewart's use of, 94–99; as Word, 94. *See also* African American hermeneutics; hermeneutics; prophets; *specific persons in the Bible by name; and entries in index of biblical sources*

black churches, 32, 53n47, 63n94, 126, 135, 136, 177

Black Nationalism, 3, 3n5, 5n9, 48n29, 67n116, 76n159, 79n171, 139, 155

blacks. *See* race and racism *and entries beginning with* African American

black uplift and self-determination, 40, 65n103, 72, 72n140, 75–79, 75nn154–55, 87–88, 87n214, 139–40, 177

Blight, David W., 164–65

blindness, 61–62, 61n85, 62n87, 87n213

Blount, Brian, 6–7n12, 33–36

Blyden, Edward Wilmot, 155–57

Bovon, François, 7n13

Brand Plucked from the Fire, A (Foote), 136

Brekus, Catherine A., 113n9, 118n25

Britain. *See* England

Broughton, Virginia W., 2n3, 9

Brown, Rev. Antoinette L., 137

Brown, Elsa Barkley, 118, 118n22

Bultmann, Rudolph, 32, 34

Bush, George W., 98–99n24

Byron, Gay, 29n62

Cain's mark, 45n13, 172

Callahan, Allen Dwight, 6n12, 35–36, 155–56

call-and-response, 32

Celia (slave), 117

charity, 82, 82n183

children: discipline of, 70, 70nn130–31; education of, 70, 70n128, 72, 72nn138–39, 76, 76n160, 139–40;

parents' responsibilities for, 51, 51n41, 51–52n42, 55, 55n53, 69–72, 69n126, 70n127, 70nn130–31; as slaves, 84n190; virtue formation in, 70

Christie, Agatha, 30

churches. *See* black churches *and specific church denominations by name*

civil rights movement, 165–68. *See also* King, Martin Luther, Jr.

Clement, 137n81

colonization movement, 156–57

communion, 142–43, 143n110

Cone, James, 36, 59n72

Constitution, U.S., 45–46, 46n19, 95, 163

conversion. *See* salvation

Copher, Charles, 35

corporal punishment of children, 70nn130–31

Cott, Nancy F., 112n3

covenant: between blacks and God, 40, 44n9, 49n34, 54n49, 63n93, 74, 74nn150–51, 140, 170, 174, 178; with Christ, 143–44; between Israel and God, 40, 44n9, 54n49, 69n125, 170–71; and jeremiad, 164

crucifixion of Jesus, 36, 45n18, 95n14, 99n24

Crummell, Alexander, 155, 156, 156n10

Cult of True Womanhood: and African American women, 111, 115–19, 130; and blame of women for society's problems, 64n99, 178; and Ethiopian prophecy, 154–55n5, 156n11; and traditional gender roles, 51n39, 53n48, 131, 138

culture of dissemblance, 130, 130n55

David, 74nn150–51

David Walker's Appeal to the Coloured Citizens of the World (Walker), 2–3, 38, 47n24, 49n34, 133, 149–50, 150n139, 153–54

Davis, Stacy, 19n43

death: equality based on shared
mortality, 49n33; no need to fear,
78, 78n169, 84, 84nn193–94, 122;
sleeping as euphemism for, 85n201;
of Walker, 47, 47n24, 68n120, 85,
86n205, 107, 119, 120n28, 133, 142. *See
also* martyrdom
Deborah, 49–50n35, 59nn73–74,
60n75, 97, 130, 134, 137
Declaration of Independence, 43n8,
46n19, 95n15, 96, 108, 150, 163, 167, 171
De Groot, Christiana, 11n23
Delaney, Martin, 155, 156
devil. *See* Satan
"dialectic of identity," 25
"dialogic of differences," 25
"Dialogue between Christ, a Youth,
and the Devil, A," 57–58
discipline of children, 70, 70nn130–31
dissemblance, culture of, 130, 130n55
double-consciousness of African
Americans, 24–26, 24n53
Douglass, Frederick, 2, 72n141, 92, 165,
168, 170, 172–73
dry bones, 62–63, 63n94, 64n96
Du Bois, W. E. B., 24, 24n53, 26, 55n52,
156n10

economic empowerment for African
Americans, 77, 77nn163–64
education: of African Americans,
55n52, 70, 70n128, 72, 72nn138–39,
76, 76n160, 87n212, 88, 88n216, 92,
93n6, 139–40, 157; Americans' valuing of, 76n157; and equality, 87n212;
of Stewart, 43, 72n139, 106, 128
Elaw, Zilpha, 113, 118n25
Elisabeth (mother of John the Baptist),
148n133
Elkins, Stanley M., 92n5
Elrod, Eileen Razzaria, 11n23
Emancipation Proclamation, 166
England, 79, 79n172, 158n22, 159n25,
163, 173, 174

Enlightenment, the, 45n16, 92
equality: and agency of African Americans, 64, 64n99, 121–22; based on
shared humanity and mortality,
49n33; Bible on, 32, 32n72, 146;
biblical support for female, 113,
135–37, 135n72; Declaration of
Independence on, 46n19, 95n15,
96, 167; and evangelical salvation
experience, 113–14; harmonization
strategy used in African American
hermeneutics, 32, 32n73; and Judgment Day, 178; and literacy, 87n212;
and respectability, 65n103; Stewart's
crusade for, 55n53, 57n62, 63n94, 78,
78n169, 79, 79n171, 87–89, 88n215,
121–22, 178; Stewart's "Religion and
the Pure Principles of Morality" on,
43–46, 49, 78, 78n169, 95; vision of
racial inclusiveness, 66, 66nn107–8
Equiano, Olaudah, 38n89
eschatology, 41, 52n44
eschaton (end time), 64n95
Esther, Queen, 130, 134, 137
Ethiopianism, 48n26, 56–57n58, 65,
65–66n105, 73nn141–42, 154–63,
174
Ethiopian prophecy: biblical reference to, 14, 14n31, 40, 45n13, 49n34,
98, 98n23, 133, 140, 154–56, 154n4,
157n16, 158, 159n23, 178; Callahan on,
155–56; and colonization movement,
156–57; and Cult of True Womanhood, 154–55n5, 156n11; Hall on, 155,
156; and poem "The Negro's Complaint," 158–61, 163; on rise of Africa
and decline of the West, 161–63, 171;
and "romantic racialism," 154–55,
154–55n5, 156n11; Stewart on, 14,
45, 45n13, 49n34, 98, 133, 140, 154,
157–63, 157nn16–17, 158nn18–19,
178; Walker on, 155–56, 155n6, 161
European Americans. *See* American
people

independence: and American Revolution, 79, 79n172, 107, 174; Declaration of Independence, 43n8, 46n19, 95n15, 96, 108, 150, 167; as God-given gift, 40, 43, 43n8, 46n19, 107–8; Stewart on spirit of, 40, 43, 43n8, 46n19, 78n165, 106–10, 114; term not found in King James Version of Bible, 43n8, 107n52

Irons, Charles, 19n43

Israel: compared with African Americans, 49n34, 56, 56–57n58, 59n73; covenantal relationship between God and, 40, 44n9, 54n49, 69n125, 170–71; as "dust of the earth," 54n49; and Exodus story, 30, 153–54; and Jeremiah, 56, 57n59, 164; "mothers and daughters of Israel," 49n34, 59n73, 170–71; repentance by Israelites, 68–69n121; sacrifices by Israelites, 90n226, 104n36; slavery of Israelites in Egypt, 83n186, 83n188, 87n211, 153–54, 174; white Americans' identification with, 153, 174; wretched condition of, 56, 56n56, 56n58. See also prophets and specific persons of Bible by name

Jackson, Rebecca, 113
Jacobs, Harriet A., 118n24
jazz, 22–23, 37
Jea, John, 93n6
Jefferson, Thomas: Declaration of Independence, 46n19, 95n15, 150, 165; Notes on the State of Virginia, 86–87n211, 87n212, 150, 161; on race, 45n16, 86–87n211, 92, 150–51, 161; Walker on, 87n211, 150–51, 161

jeremiad, 57n59, 163–71, 174
Jeremiah, 56, 57n59, 132–33, 148n134, 159n23, 164, 171

Jesus Christ: arrest of, 84n189, 85n195; and the disinherited and the underprivileged, 37; in Garden of Gethsemane, 129, 129n52, 143, 143nn111–12; and John the Baptist, 54n50; kingdom of, 66, 66n106; as Lamb of God, 81, 81–82n180, 102–3n34, 169; and Lord's Prayer, 129; meekness of, 65, 65n104, 162; parables of, 7, 44n12, 55n54, 71nn135–36, 84n191, 99–103, 163n35, 171; on prayer and persistence in prayer, 78n168; resurrection of, 134, 135–36, 136nn75–76, 137; righteousness of, 103, 105, 105n43; on scribes and Pharisees, 173; Simeon's prophecy on, 60–61n81; sufferings and crucifixion of, 36, 45n18, 95n14, 99n24, 142–43; as warrior, 168, 169; and wrath of the Lamb, 81, 81–82n180

Johnson, Sylvester A., 19n43
John the Baptist, 54n50, 148n133
Jonas, 72n137
Joshua, 169, 169n45
Judgment Day, 41, 49n32, 51–52, 51n41, 70n132, 70–71n133, 72, 72n137, 81n179, 82n182, 90, 90n227, 178
Juster, Susan, 112n2
justice: of God, 3, 41–42, 88n217, 101–2; and peace, 61, 61n84; Stewart's crusade for, 55n53, 57n62, 63n94, 78, 78n169, 79, 79n171, 87–89, 88n215, 121–22, 178; Stewart's demand of rights for African Americans, 84, 101, 121. See also Judgment Day

Kant, Immanuel, 92
Keckley, Elizabeth, 118n24
King, Martin Luther, Jr., 38, 46n21, 161, 165–68, 180n5
kingdom of God, 58–59, 58–59n71, 66n106

Lamb of God, 81, 81–82n180, 102–3n34, 169
Lash, Nicholas, 18n42
Lazarus and the rich man parable, 7,

84n191, 99–103, 99–100n26, 100n28, 104n37, 171
Leah, 51n42
"Lecture Delivered at the Franklin Hall" (Stewart), 157, 157n17, 162
Lee, Jarena: and AME Church, 126, 135; autobiography by, 2n3, 9, 11n23, 121n34, 126, 127; and biblical support for female equality, 135–36, 135n72; children of, 118n25, 135n72; illustration of, 126, 127, 129, 130; opposition to, 126, 128; ordination refused to, 135; preaching by, 9n19, 10, 35, 113, 118n25, 119, 121n34, 126, 128, 135–36; on resurrection, 135–36, 136n75; as widow, 136, 145
Lee, Rev. Luther, 137
liberation: Bible as tool of, 21–22, 29–32, 168–69; and Exodus story, 30, 153–54. See also independence; liberty
Liberator, 85n200, 120, 158n21
liberty: Bible's use of term, 107, 107n53; Declaration of Independence on, 46n19, 95n15, 96, 167; Stewart's "Religion and the Pure Principles of Morality" on, 43–46, 53–54, 53n47, 84, 84n192, 95. See also independence
Lincoln, Abraham, 166
literacy. See education
Livermore, Harriet, 113
Lord's Prayer, 129
Loving v. Virginia, 84n190
Luther, Martin, 13, 13n28

martyrdom: Stewart on risk of, 46–47, 46–47n22, 50n37, 106–7, 114, 120, 128, 133, 142; and Walker, 47, 107, 120n28, 133, 150, 171. See also death
Mary Magdalene, 10, 10n20, 134, 135–36, 135n74, 136n76, 137
Masonic movement for blacks, 155n6, 156
Mather, Cotton, 155

McKay, Nellie Y., 94
Meditations from the Pen of Mrs. Maria W. Stewart (Stewart), 2, 48n28, 102–5, 121
Melville, Herman, 44n10
Meshach, 47n24, 104n36
metaphors: meaning of, 99; of mirror for hermeneutics, 31, 36; noncomplementary use of literary allusions, 98–99n24; of scripture as script, 17–20; of speaking in tongues, 24–27, 96
Methodism and Methodist Church, 53n47, 135
Millerite movement, 113n5
Million Man March, 38n88
mirror metaphor for hermeneutics, 31, 36
miscegenation, 84, 84n190
modernity, 32–33, 33n75
Moody, Jocelyn, 5n10, 7n13, 175
Mordecai, 68n121
Morehouse, Henry, 55n52
Morrison, Toni, 37
Morton, Sarah Wentworth, 44n10
Moses, 83n187, 100n26
Moses, William J., 161
mothers. See parents
music, 36, 37, 97. See also jazz

Narrative of Sojourner Truth (Truth), 123, 124
Nebuchadnezzar, 47n24, 104n36
"Negro's Complaint, The," 158–61, 158n21, 163
"No Hidin' Place," 81n179, 177
Noll, Mark A., 13n28, 19n43
Notes on the State of Virginia (Jefferson), 86–87n211, 87n212, 150, 161

Obama, Barack Hussein, 179–80, 179–80n5
obedience, 74, 74n151, 107, 168n43
oral tradition, 32, 94

Paine, Thomas, 79n172
Painter, Nell, 122–24, 123–24n44, 126
Pan-Africanism, 155
parables: of Good Samaritan, 55n54; of
    Lazarus and the rich man, 7, 84n191,
    99–103, 99–100n26, 100n28, 104n37,
    171; of prodigal son, 71nn135–36,
    163n35; of talents, 44n12
parents, 51, 51n41, 51–52n42, 55, 55n53,
    69–72, 69n126, 70n127, 70nn130–31
Paul, 135–36, 135nn72–73, 136n76,
    145–47, 178. See also specific epistles
    in index of biblical sources
Paul, Rev. Thomas, 13n27
peace, 61, 61n84
Pentecostal movement, 14–18, 15n33,
    58n65
Peter, 48n28, 49n31, 85n195, 136n76
Phillips, Ulrich Bonnell, 92n5
Phoebe, 137
piety, 57–61, 57n63
Pliny the Younger, 137
"politics of respectability," 65n103
prayer, 62, 62n90, 78n168, 88, 88n217
preaching: arguments in favor of
    women preachers, 132–38, 137n81,
    141–49; biblical prohibitions against
    women's public speaking or teaching,
    16, 16n36; by black women, 9–12,
    113–14, 118n25, 119, 126, 128, 132–38;
    compared with public speaking,
    9–12, 57n62, 114; definition of,
    10–11; by evangelical women preach-
    ers, 13–14, 113–14, 113n9, 118n25, 119;
    by Mary Magdalene, 10, 10n20, 134,
    135–36, 135n74; Ricoeur on, 10–11;
    Stewart on calling to, 141–49
prodigal son parable, 71nn135–36,
    163n35
Productions of Mrs. Maria W. Stewart
    (Stewart), 1, 2
prophets: God's anointing of, 148n134;
    of Hebrew Bible, 56, 56n56, 57n59,
    63n94, 132–33, 164; Simeon as,

60–61n81; Stewart's role as, 47–48,
    48n25, 54, 54n50, 60–61, 61n81, 69,
    69n123, 86, 86n206, 178. See also
    specific prophets by name
Prosser, Gabriel, 82n184
Puritans, 112n2, 164, 174

Quarles, Benjamin, 1n1

Raboteau, Albert, 93n6, 153
race and racism: alleged inferiority of
    African Americans, 45n16, 80n173,
    86–87, 86–87n211, 92, 95, 150; bibli-
    cal defense of, 34; blackness as mark
    of God's disfavor, 172; categories
    of race based on skin color, 33n74;
    and evolution of humans, 33n74;
    and gender, 22–23, 25; and Human
    Genome Project, 33n74; Jefferson
    on, 45n16, 86–87n211, 92, 150–51,
    161; as metalanguage, 23; "romantic
    racialism," 154–55, 154–55n5, 156n11;
    roots of racism, 33nn74–75; Stewart
    on, 46, 46n20; Victorian view of,
    116; vision of racial inclusiveness, 66,
    66nn107–8. See also Black National-
    ism; civil rights movement; Ethio-
    pian prophecy; slavery and slavoc-
    racy; slaves; and entries beginning
    with African American
rape. See sexual exploitation of African
    American women
rap music, 37
"Religion and the Pure Principles of
    Morality" (Stewart): on accusations
    against American people, 80–87,
    80–81n176, 81n177, 81–82n180,
    82n183, 99–103, 173–74; on admi-
    rable qualities of American people,
    67, 67n110, 67nn112–14, 75n154,
    75n156, 76n157, 78, 78–79, 78n165;
    apologia by Stewart in, for her
    lack of ability, 43, 43nn4–5, 47, 48,
    48n28, 132–33; biographical infor-

mation on Stewart in, 43, 43n6, 106, 108–9; on blacks' protesting unfair treatment, 52, 52n45; on blacks' use of their talents, 44, 44n12, 49–54, 77, 169; on black uplift and reformation, 72–79, 72n140, 75nn154–55, 87–88, 87n214; call for black unity and self-sufficiency in, 48, 48n29; date of, 42, 133; "daughters of Africa" addressed by Stewart in, 49–54, 49n34, 52n46, 140, 170; demand of rights for African Americans in, 84, 101, 121; on economic empowerment for African Americans, 77, 77nn163–64; on Ethiopian prophecy, 45, 45n13, 49n34, 157, 157n16, 162; on exploitation of African Americans by whites, 67, 67nn115–16, 75n154, 76–84, 76n161, 77n162, 79n170, 101–2, 140–41; on God's protection, 47, 47n24, 120; hymn at end of, 61n83, 89–90, 89–90n225, 90n226; on ignorance of African Americans, 42, 42n2, 48, 48n27, 54, 56, 56n56, 68, 73, 73n142, 76, 76n161; on liberty and equality, 43–46, 46n19, 49, 49n33, 53–54, 53n47, 55n53, 78, 78n169, 84, 84n192, 95; on martyrdom, 46–47, 46–47n22, 106–7, 120, 128, 133; opposition to violence in, 44, 44n11, 83–85, 84n189, 85nn195–97, 101, 169–70; on parents' responsibilities, 51, 51n41, 51–52n42, 55, 55n53, 69–72, 69n126, 70n127, 70nn130–31; on piety and purity of religion, 57–61, 57n63; prayer in, 61–66, 61n83; on qualifications of spiritually minded people, 58–59; on racism, 46, 46n20; on reformation of African Americans, 73–79, 73n142; on repentance for sins, 62, 62n91, 68–69, 68–69n121; on salvation, 59n72, 62, 62n92, 63–64n95, 66, 66nn108–9, 71, 71n136, 74n151; on

sins of omission, 55, 55–56n54; on spirit of independence, 40, 43, 43n8, 46n19, 78, 78n165, 84, 106–10; on Stewart's faith in Christ and dedication to glory of God, 57, 57nn61–62, 66, 66n108, 88–89, 89n223; Stewart's role as prophet in, 47–48, 48n25, 54, 54n50, 60–61, 61n81, 69, 69n123, 86, 86n206; text and commentary on, 42–89; theme statement of, 47, 57; on traditional gender roles, 40, 51, 51n39, 52–55, 52n44, 52–53n46, 53nn47–48, 54n51, 59–60, 59n74, 60n75, 75–76, 75n156, 76n158; on Walker as martyr, 47, 107, 120n28, 133, 150; on wretched conditions of African Americans, 56, 56n58, 61n82, 75, 75n154, 87, 87n214
repentance, 62, 62n91, 68–69, 68–69n121
republican rhetoric: of American Revolution, 79, 79n172, 107, 164–65, 173, 174; in Declaration of Independence, 43n8, 46n19, 95n15, 96, 108, 150, 165, 167, 171; and jeremiad, 164–65. See also Constitution, U.S.; equality; independence; liberty
respectability, 65n103
Rexford, Ann, 119
Richardson, Marilyn, 2n3, 3n6, 6, 13n27, 150n139, 151n143, 158n21
Ricoeur, Paul, 10–11
Roberts, Abigail, 119
Robinson, Marius, 123
"romantic racialism," 154–55, 154–55n5, 156n11
Romero, Lora, 3n5
Roots (Haley), 73n141
Rosetta stone, 37–38

Sabbath, 62, 62n89
saints, 65n100, 80–81n176
salvation: and evangelicalism, 112, 113–14; of Saul/Paul, 146; Stewart's

West, Cornel, 33n75
Wheatley, Phillis, 87n212
whites. *See* American people; gender;
  slavery and slavocracy
Williams, Demetrius K., 6–7n12
Wiltse, Charles M., 2n3, 3n6, 6, 13n27,
  150n139

Wimbush, Vincent, 6n12, 7–8, 26–27,
  35–36, 180
womanist viewpoint, 23, 30
women. *See* African American women;
  gender

Zacharias, 148n133